Leadership in Asia

Books by Robert T. Oliver

On Asia

Leadership in Twentieth-Century Asia
Communication and Culture in Ancient India and China
Syngman Rhee: The Man behind the Myth
Syngman Rhee and American Involvement in Korea, 1942–1960: A
  Personal Narrative
Korea: Forgotten Nation
Why War Came in Korea
The Truth about Korea
Verdict in Korea

On Leadership and Speech Communication

The Influence of Rhetoric in the Shaping of Great Britain
Public Speaking in the Reshaping of Great Britain
History of Public Speaking in America
The History of Public Speaking in Pennsylvania (with DeWitt Holland)
Four Who Spoke Out: Burke, Fox, Sheridan, and Pitt
The Psychology of Persuasive Speech
Culture and Communication
The Healthy Mind in Communion and Communication (with Dominick
  Barbara)
Becoming An Informed Citizen
Effective Speech (with Rupert Cortright)
Communicative Speaking and Listening (with P. D. Holtzman and H. P.
  Zelko)
Effective Speech for Democratic Living
Making Your Ideas Effective
Training for Effective Speech

Leadership in Asia

PERSUASIVE COMMUNICATION IN THE MAKING OF NATIONS, 1850–1950

Robert T. Oliver

DELAWARE

NEWARK: University of Delaware Press
LONDON AND TORONTO: Associated University Presses

Associated University Presses
440 Forsgate Drive
Cranbury, NJ 08512

Associated University Presses
25 Sicilian Avenue
London WC1A 2QH, England

Associated University Presses
P.O. Box 488, Port Credit
Mississauga, Ontario
Canada L5G 4M2

The paper used in this publication meets the requirements
of the American National Standard for Permanence of Paper
for Printed Library materials Z39.48-1984.

Library of Congress Cataloging-in-Publication Data

Oliver, Robert Tarbell, 1909–
    Leadership in Asia.

    Bibliography: p.
    Includes index.
    1. Asia—Politics and government.   2. Political
leadership—Asia—History   3. Communication in
politics—Asia—History.   I. Title.
DS34.045   1989   950′.4   88-40218
ISBN 0-87413-353-X

PRINTED IN THE UNITED STATES OF AMERICA

For Margaret

. . .

whose influence is immeasurable

"One cannot know people without knowing their words."
                                        —Confucius, *The Analects*

"Action is easy; understanding is difficult."

                            —Sun Yat-sen, *Memoirs of a Revolutionist*

"Freedom of speech is the most important index to the extent of the establishment of civilization."

                            —Fukuzawa Yukichi,
                                One Hundred Essays of Fukuzawa

"Two enemies must be guarded against: first, the people who try to destroy the nation; and second, those who sit passively by, being without any hope or sense of responsibility."

                        —Syngman Rhee, *The Spirit of Independence*

Contents

Preface

What distinguishes this book from many other histories of modern Asia is its emphasis upon dynamism. My concern is not only with what happened but especially and most particularly with why and how changes were brought about. Specifically, the mechanism of change that is dealt with is the persuasive communication of leaders who envisioned modern nationalism and induced their peoples to accept it as their goal.

It is the theme of this book that such leaders are makers of history—as surely and more effectively than militarists or traditionalists. What they sought to achieve for their respective peoples was modernity and nationalism. In order to accomplish this purpose they had first of all to bring about a fundamental change in the tradition-bound sentiments of their respective peoples. They had to conceive and then to induce support for new social and political structures. The widespread audiences to which they addressed their persuasion were for the most part passively acceptive of their established circumstances. They were largely illiterate and not widely informed. They had much with which to be dissatisfied but had to be aroused and guided to seek a solution in national independence.

Like all histories, this account is selective, reflecting the author's chosen perspective. The emphasis is upon individual leadership and upon the method of persuasive communication. In order to make manifest the role of persuasive leadership, however, it is necessary to explain the circumstances from which it arises, the barriers and impediments that had to be surmounted, the problems that had to be dealt with, and the goals that had to be clarified. Differing from social, military, or economic histories, and more than in rhetorical histories, this book aims to clarify the role of dynamic discourse amid processes of wide ranging societal changes.

Realistic development of this theme requires a framework of historical developments, so that readers will understand the problems that had to be solved and the variety as well as the limitation of choices that were available.

The starting point is the mid-nineteenth century, with Commodore Perry's advent in Japan; with the initial stirrings of modernism in China; with the establishment of the Indian National Congress party; and with

9

the changing patterns of colonialism in Asia. The terminal point is the attainment of modern nationhood, insofar as that goal has been attained.

Definitive as this theme is, it nevertheless leads into complexities. In every country the problems were different. Beginnings are often difficult to determine, and so are endings. For some countries, notably in India and Pakistan, it seems suitable to conclude the account with the inauguration of the first independent government. In others, such as Indonesia and the Philippines, the establishment of national unity and identity have no such precise climax. In Japan the transformation was not from colonialism to freedom but a no-less-dramatic shift from traditional to innovative sociopolitical patterns. In China the modernization process is currently turning toward some degree of private enterprise. Southeast Asia represents a considerable variety, ranging from the prosperity and stability of Singapore to the inconclusive struggle still unfolding in Cambodia. In Korea the historically homogeneous nation remains split in two, with each part still distraught by the tensions of the hostile division.

There is room for ample disagreement as to appropriate ending points in the modernizing and nationalizing processes in these fifteen Asian countries. No history, of course, ends. But the theme of this book is how independence was attained, not what happened afterward. The attainment of independence and the acceptance of modernism were movements warmed and illuminated by exuberant hopefulness. The urging by leaders that the people take their destiny into their own hands was marked by promise and by hope. But once the goal was attained there has been a significant difference in conditions, in problems, and in sentiments. Exuberant expectations had to be reassessed in terms of more somber realities. Leaders who stressed freedom, human rights, and prospects for prosperity were succeeded in the new set of circumstances by others (or by themselves in their new roles) who were less free to make promises and were more constrained to impose curbs and restrictions as they confronted the problems of governing.

Necessarily, in the writing of this book I have drawn extensively upon the research of specialists. Notes and references indicate many, but by no means all, of my indebtedness to them. General historians, too, have been helpful, for the terrain of modern Asian history has been often explored.

Nevertheless, this history differs from others because its focus—and therefore its general interpretation—is different. No book merits attention unless it offers something that is both new and significant. The function of this book is to survey the rhetorical influences and communicative effectiveness of leaders who guided the emerging growth of fifteen Asian nations. What is reported is the energizing and directive influence of personal leadership as it is exercised through the various methods of persuasive communication.

To the best of my knowledge, this is a new mode of interpreting modern Asian history. By its very nature, it cannot be rigorously definitive. Influences of many kinds flow together from many sources, in many ways. Persuasive discourse is but one strand among many. It is worth looking at by itself but it does not stand alone. It has to be viewed as one factor among others. To examine individual speakers or particular speeches by themselves, dissevered from their context, would be futile.

For any nation, in any part of the world, the exploration of its dynamism, of its driving and directive force, is at best difficult and is necessarily partially indeterminate. The long history of Asia, however, presents this problem in a special guize. From at least the time of Confucius and of Gautama Buddha there has been emphasis upon the responsibility of individuals in establishing and maintaining the healthfulness of society. But until Asians began, in the nineteenth century, to entertain ideas of individuality, of equality, of initiative, and of innovation, there was little opportunity and little reason for leaders to seek to exert country-wide influence through persuasive appeals to public opinion as a viable means of renovating the state.

My own effort to understand the nature of this dynamism has been less academic than practical. As a participant in modern Korean affairs, and as a counselor to Dr. Syngman Rhee from 1942 to 1960, while he was striving to accomplish the independence of Korea and then to solve the problem of governing the southern half of that peninsular nation, I had to deal with the dynamic forces that in part directed and in part impeded these processes. While attending international conferences as an adviser to Korean delegations, my duties included analysis of the interactions among contentious forces. Efforts to interpret the dynamism of such processes were vital parts of my daily experience. During the course of some two decades my concern had to be the interactions of the various Asian states and of their relations with the Western world.

Personal experience has been clarified and enlarged by the judgments of associates. My appreciation is gratefully extended to many individuals who have encouraged and assisted in my endeavors. Primary among them are Dr. Syngman Rhee and his wife Francesca, Prime Minister Young Tae Pyun, Ambassador Ben C. Limb, and Minister (afterward Ambassador) Pyo-Wook Han. Over a long span of years my views of Northeast Asia have been helpfully influenced by Dr. Chong-Sik Lee of the University of Pennsylvania and Dr. Dae-Sook Suh of the University of Hawaii. To all of these I owe a debt that is immeasurable for shaping my basic understanding.

In the more immediate work of writing this book, primary grateful acknowledgement must be made to Dean Sumi Makey of the Open Grants section of the East-West Center in Honolulu for my appointment as a

Fellow, which provided not only substantial support but also office facilities, secretarial help, and access to the rich resources of library materials. During my six months at the Center, the faculty, staff, and extensive student group from all parts of Asia generously shared their knowledge and insights. Ambassador Yang Lee, Dr. Lee-Jay Cho, Dr. Hugh Kang, and Dr. and Mrs. Young-Ho Choe were good comrades and helpful guides.

Special mention is reserved for those who generously read and helpfully commented on specific chapters in their early drafts. Notable among them are Mr. Michael Macmillan, Mr. Mallikarjuna Aradhya, Ms. Saba Gul Khernak, Mr. Weidong Li, Dr. Danelo Canette, Dr. Akira Miyahara, Dr. Roichi Okabe, and Dr. Ding-ren Tsao.

Personal appreciation is extended to Mrs. Colleen Maielua for her always gracious, patient, and skillful typing and retyping of the manuscript and for her valued help in alphabetizing the reading list. In the final stages of the book-writing process, I am greatly indebted to Ms. Carolyn Wenger, for her dedicated, enlightened, gracious, and skilled copy editing.

The basic character of the book, of course, is my own—with all its judgments, all its limitations, its selected substance, and its interpretations. Since this book devolves from many years of immersion in some of the international political problems of the area, it inevitably reflects a tone of personal involvement. My hope is that it may help readers, too, to become involved. For the affairs of Asia are no longer remote. They have become inevitably a part of our own lives, wherever and however we live.

On the Usage and Spelling of Names

The transliteration of names from Asian languages to English is far from uniform. My practice is to adhere to generally established practices, sometimes at the cost of consistency.

The spelling of proper names is a matter of personal preference. For example, Korea's Yi Seungman changed his name to Syngman Rhee. In Korea both of these spellings and pronunciations are freely used.

In general practice, surnames precede the first name or names except when a title is used. Thus Okuma Shigenobu becomes Marquis Shigenobu Okuma. But this, too, is a matter of personal preference. Syngman Rhee is also cited as Dr. or President Syngman Rhee, and Sun Yat-sen, as President Sun Yat-sen. The hyphenation of first and second names is also a matter of personal choice, whether by the individual or those writing about him. Thus Kimm Kiusic may also be rendered as Kimm Kiu-sic, and K'ang You-wei, as K'ang You wei. The use of the apostrophe to guide pronunciation also varies, so that Yuan Shih-k'ai is also rendered as Yuan Shih-kai.

South of the Himalayas there are still other problems. Indonesian individuals generally had only one name. But as leaders came into frequent contact with the West, they either adopted or were accorded first names. Thus Sukarno (also frequently spelled Sokarno or Soekarno) came to be identified as Mohammed Achmed Sukarno. Jinnah became known as Mohammed Ali Jinnah.

A further complicating factor is that some individuals had different names in succession, so that Sun Wen became Sun Yat-sen, and Nguyen That Thanh became Nguyen Ai Quoc and afterward Ho Chi Minh (or Ho Chi-Minh).

I have used both the spellings and the names best known in the West.

13

Leadership in Asia

Introduction
Leadership and Communication in the Asian Mode

How it happened that new nations sprang into being in Asia during the century between 1850–1950 is a question important not only to Asians but to all the world. It is a story not only of courage but of skill. It is a study in leadership, in mass communication, and in cross-cultural persuasion that is unique in its dimensions. The circumstances in every part of Asia were different from those in all the others. The leaders who guided the course of events were different from one another in personality, in their aims, and in their methods. The period of transformation into modernity is a vast laboratory offering multiple contrasting methods for dealing with a single problem: how to reshape old patterns into a modern nation.

The emergence of modern Asia in the twentieth century is as important historically as was the exploration of the New World in the sixteenth. Both of these great mass movements had far-reaching effects not only in their own regions but upon all the peoples and nations of the world. The coming into independent nationhood, or the reshaping of old nations, that directly involved half the world's population was accomplished in a brief span of time—mostly within a single generation. It could not have been done without extraordinary leadership. And the method upon which the leadership depended was, fundamentally, persuasive communication.

Of course there were other factors also—including the exhaustion of the great powers after two world wars. Equally important, major improvements in the means of communication and transportation, by reducing spatial and temporal distances, made it difficult to maintain differential standards of morality and national behavior in different parts of the world. Perhaps the decline of imperialism and the virtual erasure of colonialism were inevitabilities. Even so, there was need for speakers to define goals and to translate discontent into unity of action. Most notably, the emergence of new nations and of new kinds of government in Asia was accomplished largely not by arms but by negotiation and persuasion. The process was different in different countries, but this was the general pattern. It was revolution of a strikingly new kind.

The transformation commenced with the Meiji Reformation in Japan, the overthrow of the Ching, or Manchu, dynasty in China, the founding of the Congress party in India, and the proclamation by Aguinaldo of the Republic of the Philippines. A generation later, in the wake of the two world wars, the Western colonizing powers yielded to the demands for independence that spread across the hemisphere, from Korea southward to the Philippines, and from Indonesia westward to India and Pakistan. The processes of transition took many forms, and so did the nature of the independent governments that were established. Nevertheless, one by one the remarkable progression of nation building was accomplished.

Asian leadership proved its worth in these accomplishments. Notably, in country after country, the result was largely owing to the magnetic persuasiveness of individual leaders who won their way more by the force of their personalities than by military superiority.

What these leaders had to do was to direct their communication to two distinctly different audiences—the one, their own people, who had to be unified and aroused; the other, the foreign rulers (or, in Japan and China, the domestic traditional aristocracy) whose dominion they overturned. This meant that they had to deliver different kinds of messages, in different styles, to two audiences, one at home, the other abroad, under the confusing circumstance that each audience also received what was meant only for the other.

A fundamental complicating factor was the vast extent of cultural difference between the East and the West, which made it difficult for one side to understand the other. When Oriental leaders addressed their remarks to the West in terms the West understood, their own people tended to be confused or dismayed. And when they addressed their own people in the context of their own cultural norms, the peoples in the West tended to be at least puzzled, when not actually outraged.

The leaders who guided the emergence of Asia into modernism and independence were required to use both the Western and the Eastern motivational patterns, with appropriate shifts from one to the other. As a group, they represented an unusual degree of cosmopolitanism and sophistication. Most of them had been educated not only in their own cultures but also in Western universities. Their personalities were marginal, belonging not wholly to either their old or their new cultural traditions, yet sufficiently imbued with both heritages to enable them to understand and, generally, to surmount the barriers that separated them.

As individuals, they differed greatly from one another. There also were essential differences in the circumstances with which they had to deal. In Japan and in China, the new nations emerged primarily from within deeply embedded Asian traditions. This was a problem also in all the other Asian societies, but it was complicated further in most of them by the need to escape from foreign bondage. From the Western perspective, understanding of Asian nationalism, Asian leadership, and Asian communication had to comprise the comprehension of, and an empathic feeling for, the value systems of an extremely large population shaped by cultural traditions that developed in isolation from the West.

The reaching out across this gulf, from both sides, was complicated by a mixture of attraction and repulsion. During the twentieth century Asians have urgently wanted to become more like Westerners, while simultaneously maintaining loyalty to their own past and deeply resenting not only Western dominance and intrusions but also patronizing Western claims of ethical superiority. Westerners, meanwhile, have generally regarded Eastern religions as heathenism and superstition, and have been smugly pleased with their own technological superiority; but they have also been attracted to the quietism and stabilizing ritualism of the East. Neither hemisphere has wanted either to renounce or to accept the other. Such a confusion of feelings has still further complicated the difficulties of communication between them. These difficulties I have explored through my own experiences, and I have discussed them in a series of lectures. A few excerpts will be illustrative of problems that matter most.

A lecture given at the University of Denver, published in *Vital Speeches of the Day,* 13 September 1963, describes what is perhaps the most basic barrier to cross-cultural communication:

> It happens that some time ago I engaged over a span of months in a running discourse—you might even call it an argument—with a professor who was on our campus as a visitor from his native land of India. The subject of our discussion was the nature of certain qualities of the oriental value system with which our own democratic heritage could most readily interlock. For months he kept insisting to me that I had the ideas almost but never quite right. Then I had occasion to ghost-write a speech for a distinguished oriental statesman on this very theme; and in a short time it appeared in print. A day or so afterwards the Indian Professor burst in to see me with the published speech in hand and said, "I want you to read this. Here is a statement by one of my fellow Orientals that says exactly what I have been trying to tell you and says it so clearly that I don't think you can miss the point."

The point is clear. When we try to address one another across cultural gaps, we encounter two serious kinds of difficulties. The first is that we may not and probably usually do not fully understand one another's point of view. And the second is that even when we do, we speak to one another essentially as strangers, as foreigners, as spokesmen for and from differing and even competing ways of life.

For further illustration of the problems, another quotation is relevant—this from an unpublished lecture I gave at Memphis State University on 8 December 1964.

> We often say that "travel is broadening," and of course it is, or should be, or may be. But in my observation, for a great many people travel is actually narrowing. The further they get away from Dubuque, Iowa, the better Dubuque looks to them.
>
> A prime example is the group of people who used to be known as "Old China Hands." They had lived in China for twenty or thirty years or more, and, consequently, what they wrote for our journals and what they advised our Department of State was presumed to be pretty close to gospel truth. The trouble is that in general they possessed what I may call "plantation minds." They lived in China but carefully avoided ever becoming a part of it. They built separate occidental communities, erected high fences around their dwellings (and their minds), put up signs saying "No dogs or Chinese allowed," and asserted loudly that they and they alone knew how to deal with the simple-minded Chinese, who make wonderful servants and are very docile and peaceful, as long as they are kept in their places.
>
> Much of our discourse is aimed less to define meanings than to create or magnify or minimize attitudes. And attitudes are not fact-items as they exist in the external world but are personal and social preferences. They assume forms and serve functions prescribed by a society's culture. But the languages in differing cultural systems are both more and less than words. Vocabularies and grammars differ—but so do gestures, and postures, and modes of communicative behavior.
>
> This language of behavior takes on even greater significance when it is forced to bear the principal burden of communication because the visitor is among people whose verbal language he cannot use. If the gestures and postures and acts which are misunderstood could be supplemented with a ready flow of verbal interchanges, mistakes would be interpreted as being merely mistakes. What was genuinely intended could be stated in words, and anger or bewilderment would be either avoided or flushed away in a burst of understanding laughter. It is when verbal communication is greatly restricted or altogether prevented that behavioral communication takes on transcendent importance.

In communicative exchanges between people of the East and the West, the attitudes that govern understanding are shaped in part by obvious differences that separate the two hemispheres. Among these are such physical factors as skin color, shape and color of eyes, color and texture of hair, and differences in dress, in posture, in cosmetic adornment, and in ways of walking, standing, and sitting. Differences in religion have greater significance, for it is as difficult for most Asians to understand fully the Judeo-Christian religions as it is for most Westerners to view Hinduism, Buddhism, and Islam as being other than harmful superstitions.

Not more than a mere generation ago, at least in Western liberal circles, part of becoming educated included development of the view that everyone was to be regarded as an individual in his own right, without consideration of his race, religion, or social status. In the words of the Scottish poet Bobby Burns, "A man's a man, for a' that." We were taught not to think of a person as a Catholic, or a black, or a laborer, but purely and simply as a person—good or bad, companionable or not, pleasant or disagreeable. We were induced to believe that it is basically wrong to think of an individual as being blind, or crippled, or uneducated. What mattered, and the only thing that mattered, was *persona*.

Then cultural anthropology implanted a new idea, that it matters a great deal whether a person is a Jew, or a Hindu, or a sharecropper. Cultural anthropology taught us all that the cultural context within which an individual grew up, and in which he or she lives actually makes a world of difference. Social manners and attitudes, we came to understand, are inbred—not innate. In one sense, all people are basically alike and must be dealt with as fellow human beings, regardless of their many dissimilarities. Concurrently, every individual is unique and must accordingly be dealt with in terms of his or her special character. Both these views remain true, and each of them is deeply meaningful. But there also is the fact that every individual is a member of some special kinds of groups—and must be dealt with in terms of the values and sensibilities of those groups. A Jew, for example, is not merely a person but is also a Jewish person. A blind individual is not merely a person but a person who is blind. It is not only unkind but also unwise to insist that everyone else is like oneself. What is far truer is that every individual is *acculturated,* a cultural complex, with ideas, feelings, attitudes, customs, preferences, prejudices, needs, and desires that have been inculcated within the personality and become a vital part of the individual.

More broadly, it is also evident that societies, no less than individuals, have their own special character, ideals, modes of behavior, convictions, and activities. Korean society can not and must not be assessed in terms of how much it resembles or varies from American society. Japan is different, China is different, Indonesia is different, India is different; and their societies, their social and political behavior and their value systems, must be dealt with in their terms, rather than in ours.

What matters in crossing national and cultural boundaries is that communication is effective when it is *with* diverse peoples, rather than *to* them. We must try to see with their eyes, feel with their feelings, judge them in accord with their standards, if we truly are to enter into communion and communication with them. Every new nation that emerged in Asia has had its own problems, its own methods, and its own characteristics.

While the diverse countries of the world have been brought so closely into relationship as to constitute, in one sense, a "global village," the peoples of the world have simultaneously been confronted with a new need to consider not only similarities but also differences. This is a problem that is particularly difficult. We are strongly inclined to believe that elements of our own culture are akin to nature itself—that they are the way individuals basically are, and how they are supposed to behave. Alien cultures that deny or flout or lack such realities seem to be misguided, or incompletely developed, or just fundamentally wrong. This is how civilized people regard cannibalism. This is how an orthodox Hindu vegetarian regards the eating of animal carcasses. This is how the adherents of any enlightened religion (and to its own devotees any religion is enlightened) regard the heathen who cling ignorantly to their own superstitions.[1]

The questions we all must deal with have been well posed by William S. Howell. "Are we capable of *appreciating* values that differ from ours? Can we love people who violate our treasured standards? Is it possible for us to bestow genuine respect and affection upon persons who believe that what we know to be wrong is right? When we offer to 'lay aside' our convictions, are we sincere, or are we really saying, 'let's pretend'?"[2]

To what degree is it possible to communicate truly and completely across cultural barriers? By what means can the best results be attained? These are basic issues that must be identified and dealt with. They were urgent problems not only for the colonizing powers but also for the leaders of the Asian independence movements.

These leaders did not become spokesmen for their people by birthright or by some automatic method of selection. They had to win their positions. More than this, most of them had to shape the circumstances that made their leadership possible. Many of them had to create the feeling of nationalism before they could appeal to it as a reason for demanding independence. The special kind of cultural identity that is circumscribed by a nation's boundaries has to be developed—has to be carved out from the more inclusive culture of the region. Individuals have to be taught to organize their thinking, their feeling, and their behavior in a special way, as members of a society who are indissolubly bound together. Patriotism has to be nurtured. A sense of citizenship must be invoked to create a community of individuals who feel themselves to be distinct from all others. They must learn to communicate these feelings among themselves by means of special laws and customs, and to regard members of other sovereignties as outsiders. Where independence does not exist, it does not spring spontaneously into being.

Someone (or perhaps several assertive individuals) speaks to the group and in the course of time wins sufficient acceptance to also speak for it. Public opinion is formed and becomes a force that leaders are able to utilize. As this happens the leader becomes more than an individual whose messages are listened to. He is also a spokesman who repeats back to the people what they want or at least expect him to say. He becomes a mouthpiece for the common will. This is how the German philosopher Hegel described leadership in his *Philosophy of Right*, when he wrote that "the great man of the age is one who can put into words the will of his age, and tell its age what its will is, and accomplish it. What he does is the heart and essence of his age; he actualizes his age."[3]

The English historian, E. H. Carr, best known for his history of Russia, when surveying the vast global changes of recent decades in his book *What Is History?*, concluded that "the most significant of these changes have probably been those brought about by the development and use of modern methods of persuasion and indoctrination."[4] Instant communication and rapid transportation have brought knowledge of global affairs to people everywhere. But knowledge alone has not transformed affairs. There is also the factor of indoctrination or interpretation. Attitudes and feelings are what matter most, and these have to be reshaped. The emergence of new nations that transformed dramatically the nature of Asian society could occur only as individuals changed their ways of conceiving of themselves and their communal relations.

How people think about themselves and their group is only in part individual choice. Fundamentally, it is cultural. Deliberate mind control in some forms and to some extent is a natural tendency in any group, whether it be a family, a clan, or a nation. Group loyalty and peer pressure are powerful inducements. Formal education in all countries tends to uphold the values and extol the virtues of the government by which the schools are maintained. In different nations there are widely varying degrees and methods of censorship and other impediments to free speech, with the aims of enhancing patriotism and of enforcing unity and subordination. Leaders who sought to guide their followers from one established and enforced set of loyalties to a new ideal of national independence had somehow to deal with such barriers to change.

A central way of estimating the effects of communication is to note differences of skill in its utilization. Freedom to communicate is of little worth to people who do not know how to do it. Illiteracy, for example, is as potent a barrier to knowledge as is censorship. Traditions of unquestioning obedience, customs of subordination, and passive acceptance of things as they are—as they always have been—are problems confronting leaders who espouse revolutionary change. Traditions that renounce individualism and that decry assertiveness make change especially difficult. The inability to read perceptively, to speak well, to listen acutely, or to write are fully as restrictive as are prohibitions against free speech and public assembly. "You can't do it" has two very different meanings, though both have the same result. The sentence may mean "You are not allowed to do it," or it may mean "You lack the ability or the will to do it." In varying degrees across the breadth of Asia, these were all problems with which the leaders advocating independence had to deal.

Most explicitly, these Asian leaders had to master rhetorical forms and methods that were different from those in their own cultures. This means that they had to relearn, to reshape, their modes of thinking. They not only had to learn to think different kinds of thoughts than they, and their own people, were accustomed to; they had also to learn to think in different ways. Standards of value that Asian cultures applied in reaching decisions were not acceptable to the Western audiences that the leaders sought to influence. Some of what was appealing to Orientals was actually antithetical to Occidentals.[5] In short, the rhetorics of the East and of the West were so different that their conjunction often led not to better understanding but to misunderstanding, confusion, and enhancement of animosities.

A primary necessity for Asian leaders who sought to persuade Western peoples and governments was to perceive the rhetorical differences that had to be dealt with, and then to learn to use the kind of rhetoric that would make sense to those whom they undertook to influence. Of course the obverse was also true. Westerners dealing with the East had equal need to be aware of the differences that had to be bridged, and to learn how to bridge them. But since the West had the power, the wealth, and the technology that the East wanted, urgency in acquiring the requisite communicative understanding bore more sharply and more immediately upon leaders of the East.

A Pakistani scholar, seeking to interpret Ali Jinnah, the founder of his nation, wrote:

> Heroes, it may seem platitudinous to remark, would be no heroes if they were not to become the fount of inspiration for their peoples. Anyone concerned with goading his nation to work for lofty ideals, pursue worthy goals, and do great deeds, could hardly resist the temptation to use symbolism based on the achievements of its great cohesion, in order to revive national spirit, and, above all, to strengthen the nation's moral fiber.[6]

In short, a leader who brings about fundamental changes has to be able to portray the future in terms of the past. He has to utilize traditional values as instruments with which to construct new concepts and new loyalties. He has to teach his people that what they have always believed provides the incentive for reaching up and beyond past practices toward new goals and new methods. The ability to accomplish such a feat is what makes these leaders heroic. It is what makes their leadership invaluable.

Sidney Hook, an American social critic, helps to identify these heroes:

> The *eventful* man in history is any man whose action influenced subsequent developments along a quite different course than would have been followed if these actions had not been taken. The *event-making* man is an eventful man whose actions are the consequence of outstanding capacities of intelligence, will, and character rather than accidents of position . . . a hero is great not merely in virtue of what he does but in virtue of what he is.[7]

Professor Hook added that the event-making man not only appears at "forking points of history," when significant decisions have to be made, but more than this he helps to create "a fork in the historical road." Moreover, he "increases the odds of success for the alternative he chooses by virtue of the extraordinary qualities he brings to bear to realize it."[8]

The chapters that follow trace the careers of remarkable men as they dealt with the particular circumstances that had to be molded and reshaped in order for them to lead their peoples out of ancient ways into modernity, and out of subjection into independence. It is an inspiring story of courage and of skill. It is an account of leaders who did not merely watch history but who made it. And it is a comparative study of the variable persuasive methods which they found to be effective. Hence it is not only a review of the past but also suggestive of how to deal with present problems in ways that point toward a better future.

1

Meiji Japan: A Transformation Planned and Guided

During the latter half of the nineteenth century, the rigid hierarchal societal forms of ancient Japan were shattered by what is known as the Meiji Reformation. Within a generation the nation was essentially modernized. This revolutionary transformation did not occur automatically. It was planned and guided by able men who had a vision of a new way and who also had skill in winning support by persuasion in order to bring it about.

In order to understand the significance of the persuasive leadership that guided the changes in government, and that inspired and developed the popular support for basic changes in social attitudes and relationships, it is necessary to view the circumstances from a broad perspective. This chapter will undertake to show what Japan was, what it became, and how the innovations were introduced and championed by men who adopted the new (and for Japan the startling) methods of appeal to public opinion.

The Japanese people traditionally are sturdy, firm-minded, and hard working. For many centuries they also were poor, exploited, and tightly controlled under an aristocratic system that demanded obedience and enforced stability. The new leaders not only made their nation efficiently productive and militarily strong but also implanted progressive ideas of individual and civic rights. Theirs is an epic story of government by persuasion.

Historians have argued and will argue about how Japan so quickly forced its way into modernity.[1] Was the traditional pattern broken from outside after Commodore Matthew Perry sailed into Uraga Bay in July 1853, to urge an end to Japan's isolation, while assuring the emperor that the United States had nothing but friendly intentions? Or were there existing domestic impulses to change? Within the next five years a series of "unequal treaties" was imposed upon Japan, giving Western nations rights of trade under protection of their own laws.[2] Ready or not, Japanese society was opened to strong influence from the technologically and militarily superior powers of the West. There were, however, internal pressures for change that were domestically inspired and that were peculiarly Japanese in character.[3]

Challenge to Traditionalism

There were also significant internal pressures that developed from new Western ideas that were distinctly un-Japanese in character. Important among them was something very alien to the traditional culture—the development and use of discussion and public speaking as essential instruments of government. How this came about is the theme of this chapter.

Like the Chinese and the Koreans, the Japanese confidently regarded themselves as the custodians of civilization, viewing the world outside as inhabited by barbarians. In addition, the Japanese were convinced that they were a chosen people, directly descended from the divine Amaterasu. As one of their writers put it, "Our country, as a special mark of favor from the heavenly gods, was begotten by them, and there is so immense a difference between Japan and all other countries of the world as to defy comparison."[4] Such attitudes did not readily yield to pressures—whether internal or from the "barbarians" who came knocking at the gates.

The society of Japan was unusually static and rigid. The governing philosophy was Confucianism—differing, however, from that of China and Korea, where upward mobility was possible through Confucian examinations that allowed commoners to attain government positions. In Japan the four classes (warriors, farmers, artisans, and merchants) were self-contained. Individuals might better their lot by rising within their own class but could not proceed from one class to another. The government was in some respects feudal, but still very different from the feudalism of Europe. The emperor was a religious symbol of national unity, empty of power. Rule was by a hereditary shogun, headquartered in Kyoto. The country was divided into some two hundred fifty domains, greatly unequal in size and wealth, each headed by a hereditary *daimyo*. The daimyos collected taxes for themselves and the shogun and maintained internal order with their warriors, the samurai corps. In order to prevent revolution or internal warfare among the domains, every daimyo was required to maintain a second residence in Kyoto, and there he had to leave his family and principal retainers as virtual hostages. The daimyos also had to come to Kyoto every second year, along with a procession of their chief officials, to render homage and to make reports to the shogun. The system maintained peace, for the daimyos had neither opportunity nor funds with which to wage war against their neighbors. It was also too static to allow for initiative or for change. With no incentive for progress and with only fixed duties that stultified rather than stimulated their minds, officials naturally became languid if not lethargic. As Peter Duus found, "By 1800 complaints that the highest leaders of the land were weak, ignorant, stupid, ostentatious, self-indulgent, extravagant and arrogant were common among samurai writers and thinkers."[5] As firmly established as the traditional social and political systems seemed to be, they were nevertheless beset by severe dissatisfaction.[6] This was a dynamic power new leaders found a way to unleash.

The general assumption of Japanese superiority was also beginning to be questioned by a few scholars who studied European languages and writings at the Dutch and Chinese trading posts that were permitted in Nagasaki. This questioning naturally aroused a defensive reaction. Japanese intellectuals were aware of the English and French wars against China and of the aggressive intrusions by these foreigners into both Chinese territory and the Chinese way of life. When Perry came in 1853 with offers to commence trade, the general reaction was negative. "To exchange our valuable articles like gold, silver, copper and iron for useless foreign goods like woolens and satins is to incur great loss while acquiring not the slightest benefit."[7] As early as 1825, Aizawa Seishisai, the author of the most influential work on politics, *Shinron,* had warned that "when those barbarians plan to subdue a country not their own, they start by opening commerce and watch for a sign of weakness. If an opportunity is presented, they will preach their alien religion to captivate the people's hearts."[8] Because of such sentiments, the first impulse after Perry's arrival was to fight rather than negotiate. Tokugawa Nariaki, one of the most powerful daimyos, argued in a memorial: "If we put our trust in war the whole country's morale will be increased and even if we sustain an initial defeat we will in the end expel the foreigner; while if we put our trust in peace, even though things may seem tranquil for a time, the morale of the country will be greatly lowered and we will come in the end to complete collapse."[9] As late as 1879, long after the die was cast for Westernization, Yamagata Aritomo was still arguing: "Every day we wait, the evil poison will spread more and more over the provinces, penetrate into the minds of the young, and inevitably produce unfathomable evils." These arguments, however, did not prevail. They could not, once they became subject to discussion and debate.

The better way, the leadership concluded, was to learn as rapidly as possible from the West in order to become able to deal with it on a basis of equal strength. In the words of Sakuma Shōzan, "Why did an upright and righteous great country like China lose to an insolent, unjust, and comtemptible country like England? It is because China's rulers prided themselves on their superiority, regarded the outside world with contempt, and paid no heed to the progress of machinery in foreign countries."[10]

The view that prevailed was that Japan's government and its society must be changed promptly and substantially. The independence of the domains was abolished, bringing their administration directly under the shogunate, in acceptance of the argument presented by Kido Kōin: "A single rod, even though a stout one, may be broken by a small child, but if ten rods, though all weak, are made into a bundle, they cannot be broken even by a strong man."[11]

The bureaucracy of the shogunate, called the *bakufu,* was wholly unable to deal with the new political arrangement, with the influx of foreign goods and ideas, and with the roiling dissatisfactions of the displaced daimyos and samurai. In 1858 Hotta Masayoshi, head of the bakufu, decided to accept the treaty tendered by Townsend Harris, the first American consul to Japan. Hotta sought to reduce his own responsibility for so drastic and unprecedented an action by presenting the treaty to Emperor Komei for ratification. To Hotta's surprise and mortification, the emperor assumed the political authority to reject the treaty and also recommended a new heir to the shogunate. Hotta was forced to resign, to be replaced by a strong personality, Ii Naosuke, who took office as the Great Elder, a position created only in times of crisis. Ii signed the Harris treaty and others with the British, French, Russians, and Dutch. The end of isolationism was accomplished, and this also led to the end of the shogunate.

Nationwide fears and resentment were expressed in a popular slogan, "Revere the emperor and expel the barbarians." Disorders continued until, in 1868, a palace revolt was led by a new class among the intellectual elites, some of its members from the commoner class, "whose success depended in part on symbol manipulation —the business of journalists, teachers, statesmen, and lawyers."[12] Under the leadership of this elite group, the capital was removed from Kyoto to Edo, renamed Tokyo; the shogunate was ended; nominal authority was given to the emperor; and actual decision making was lodged in a council of state. A "Charter Oath" was signed by the new officials, committing the government to abandon "absurd customs of olden times," to enforce "the principles of international justice," to encourage "seeking knowledge from all over the world," and to establish a national assembly for the discussion of national policies that would represent "all classes high and low."[13]

When the new young emperor Meiji signed the bill that abolished the domains and replaced them with prefectures, a furor of debate broke out all over Japan; on one side were the officials whose traditional positions were undermined; on the other were the rising young intellectuals who advocated decisive change. As Duus points out, "It was only after much turmoil and debate that the choice became clear: either Japan had to become a highly centralized bureaucratic regime indifferent to the interests of the old ruling class or it would remain no stronger than it had been when Perry first sailed into Uraga Bay."[14]

In a sense the transformation of Japan was only part of a worldwide outburst of revisionism, resulting largely from the industrial revolution and from the intellectual revolution that accompanied it. Europe was swept by the regime-altering revolutions started in 1848; the Taiping rebellion in China, in 1850, unsettled the imperial regime sufficiently to introduce a wholly new spirit (slow, however, in its development) of welcoming innovations; the Sepoy Rebellion of 1857–59 in India led to a tightening of English control; in the United States a civil war led to abolition of slavery. All of these were major events. Nevertheless, it was the Meiji Reformation that had the greatest effect throughout the vast expanse of Asia. As Jansen points out, "The successes of the Japanese leaders had an effect on neighboring Asian societies as stimulating as was that of revolutionary France on Europe. Sun Yat-sen, K'ang Yu-wei, Kim Ok-kyun, Emilio Aguinaldo, Subhas Chandra Bose, and many others dreamed of creating in their own countries something of the drive and unity that had first established in Japan the equality of Asian with European strength and ability."[15]

Among the many who contributed to the renovation of Japan, special attention is merited for Ōkubo Toshimichi, who has been called "the architect of modern Japan";[16] Marquis Shigenobu Ōkuma, "Autocrat of the Council Table";[17] and Fukuzawa Yukichi, "the intellectual pioneer of the Restoration era."[18] These three were the major shaping influences in that time of "confusion and conflict which permitted greater freedom of debate on government policies on all levels of society."[19] For the first two of this trio, politics was their arena, and their aim was primarily to enable Japan "to attain an equal footing with the other powers."[20] Fukuzawa, not a politician but an educator, guided "the adoption of Western values and institutions and the fundamental transformation of Japanese culture."[21] Since the politicians occupied the center stage, they will be discussed first, even though their influence reflected Fukuzawa's teachings.

Ōkubo Toshimichi: Architect of Modern Japan

Ōkubo Toshimichi's predominance has been so generally recognized that Marius Jansen very simply identified him as "the Meiji leader."[22] His essential qualities were clarity of mind about his objectives, and strength of will in pursuing them.[23] Scholars who sought to depict central tendencies in Japanese history concluded that "Ōkubo's consuming passion was internal order and systematic progress. . . . As the personification of those virtues which were to distinguish the Meiji bureaucrat, Ōkubo had long-range vision, unshakable tenacity, and a remarkable gift for spotting young men of talent who could help realize his plans."[24] So effective was he that Sansom calls him "the most influential member of the Meiji government."[25] Kenneth Pyle in his discussion of the development of

Japan's foreign policy, cites Ōkubo's central influence, concluding that "his arguments carried the day and set the basic course of government policy for the next two decades."[26] The primacy of Ōkubo's leadership is well attested.

Ōkubo was born on 26 September 1830, an only son in a family of seven children, on the southernmost Japanese island, Kyushu, apart from Kyoto, the capital.[27] The family was of ancient lineage but poor. Toshimichi's father, Jūemon, was in the bottom rank of the minor samurai, serving as a member of the bodyguard of his daimyo, and the family lived on his small salary. Nevertheless, Jūemon was a scholar who valued learning, an indulgent parent, and such a believer in equality that he mingled freely with men of all classes, from the higher-ranking samurai to the farmers and artisans. He also had superior ability, which resulted in his elevation to a minor official position with a consequent improvement in the family's living conditions. Perhaps most significantly of all, he was also possessed of a fiercely independent spirit, which led him to participate in a palace revolt against the domain chief, in 1849, when his son Toshimichi was nineteen years old. The revolt was quickly subdued and thirteen of its leaders were ordered to commit hara-kiri. Jūemon, more fortunate, was among the nine who were exiled on a small nearby island.

Throughout his childhood Ōkubo was influenced by his maternal grandfather, Minayoshi Hōtoku, a scholarly and prestigious physician who was one of the first intellectuals to gain a knowledge of Western technology. Dr. Minayoshi studied Dutch books, became interested in marine architecture and navigation, and constructed the first Western-style ship built in Japan, which was used in the Ryukyu trade. Like his son-in-law, Minayoshi became embroiled in political intrigues, but he escaped with only a censure.

The town of Kagoshima, in which the family lived, possessed two unusually good schools, which Toshimichi attended, learning the military skills demanded of samurai, although his physical frailty limited his accomplishments in jujuitsu and the use of weapons. His intellectual interests were both broad and intense, and he read voraciously the books that were available. He also participated in the school debates, in which he excelled.[28] He became an ardent disciple of Zen Buddhism and of the Wang Yang-ming school of Confucianism, both of which stressed introspection, self-study, self-control, and the authority of conscience—teachings well in accord with the character of his father and grandfather. His success in scholarship won for him, at the age of sixteen, the position as aide to the domain archivist, which gave him access to a wide range of knowledge.

In 1849 the exile of his father and his own minor part in the revolt led to his loss of the position as aide, and he was imprisoned for six months. For the next four years, until his father was permitted to return home, the family lived in dire poverty, and responsibility for its support rested wholly upon Toshimichi. According to his biographer, "he was to emerge from his trying experiences as a cold and reserved individual."[29]

In 1851 a new daimyo, Nariakira, became head of the Satsuma domain and commenced a series of such reforms as Ōkubo's father had sought. When Commodore Perry demanded the opening of Japan, Nariakira advised the shogun to accept the proffered treaty in order to buy time while Japan strengthened itself sufficiently to expel the barbarians. Nariakira set an example by building the military forces of his domain and by improving the bureaucracy through appointment of able young men. He recognized Ōkubo's abilities and promoted him rapidly through the lower ranks of the government. Ōkubo fully shared Nariakira's urgent desire to modernize Japan as a means of attaining equality of power with Western nations. Then, in 1858, Nariakira died, and under his successor a conservative reaction swept away the reforms. Ōkubo was dismissed from office and was once more poor; his future prospects were darkened. In the opinion of his biographer, this experience had a profound influence in the formation of his personality:

> It is a truism that hardships can make an individual either sympathetic and compassionate or cold and indifferent toward others. . . . Within Ōkubo a core of coldness developed, and an obsessive desire to forge ahead in life regardless of difficulties . . . and by the time he was twenty-eight he had been transformed into a serious, determined, calculating enemy of traditionalism, a reformer, psychologically prepared to achieve his objective by any means that would assure success.[30]

Ōkubo's first impulse after Nariakira's death was to organize a revolt against the bakufu leaders in Kyoto. After several months of success in organizing support for such a dangerous mission, Ōkubo became convinced that his resources were inadequate and the attempt would fail unless it was delayed until wider participation was assured. When he told his followers of his decision, they threatened to proceed without him.

> The meeting was obviously beginning to get out of hand when Ōkubo demanded attention. Speaking quietly and deliberately, he told the gathering that he expected them to do as they were told. If, he warned, any of them insisted upon acting contrary to his order, they must do so after first cutting him down. He argued that the scheme to reform the Bakufu was contrived by him, and hence there was no one more anxious to act than he, but . . . he insisted that it was not the proper season to act. He placated his aroused followers by reiterating the promise of eventual action.[31]

During the succeeding months Ōkubo proved to be cold, calculating, and guileful. He enraged his followers by winning the confidence of Nariakira's successor, Hisamitsu, the conservative against whom Ōkubo had rebelled. Hisamitsu recognized Ōkubo's abilities and in a period of two years advanced him rapidly to the position of adviser, the highest rank yet to be held in Japan by a samurai of the lower order. Immediately Ōkubo set about intriguing for the reforms he deemed necessary. To the domain leadership he urged, "The need of the moment is to consider popular sentiment and bring into government leadership a person who is favorable to the people."[32] Overcoming the objections of his chief, Ōkubo systematically introduced reforms into Satsuma's administration and military forces, so that when the Meiji Restoration took place in 1868 Satsuma was able to play the leading role. Summing up this period in Ōkubo's life, his biographer likened him to Henry Clay, "compromising, yielding, flexible . . . a leader who bent to situations if to do so would mean the eventual attainment of a particular goal."[33] The goal was reached on 3 January 1868 when the imperial troops forced the bakufu to withdraw from the Kyoto administrative headquarters and a new Meiji government was proclaimed. Ōkubo not only helped to bring it to pass but also profited from it. As his biographer concluded,

> The question of leadership and class alliances with reference to the Restoration has become a subject for heated debate among historians. . . . A study of Ōkubo Toshimichi should bring to light some of the interacting forces that have been mentioned. He is typical of many of his peers. He was for the most part sympathetic to the distressed samurai class, generally loyal to the imperial house, deeply anxious about his homeland under Tokugawa rule in the face of foreign pressures, without any consuming fondness for the feudal master in Edo, and filled with tremendous ambition for personal power. Who would isolate any one of these several characteristics and dogmatically say that this particular characteristic consistently impelled Ōkubo to work for the loyalist cause?[34]

The new government consisted of three parts: a provisional administration, a senior council, and a junior council. Ōkubo was appointed a junior councilor. Satsuma men predominated in the new regime, and Ōkubo was in a position of real power. As had been true in the domains, the actual governing was done largely by the middle bureaucrats, and Ōkubo was one of three who had crucial influence, along with his friends Saigo and Kido. In order to establish firm central control over the many prefectures that had replaced the multiple traditional domains, "Ōkubo and his colleagues were to adhere to a harsh and dictatorial policy."[35] With his unusual fixity of determination, "Ōkubo was to nurture the young Meiji government just as carefully as he had helped to plan and execute the detailed operations of the Restoration movement. Almost single-handedly, during the critical period from the spring of 1868 to 1871, he held the government together, coaxing and flattering jealous colleagues. . . . Because of his untiring efforts the Meiji government displayed sufficient unity to cope with the myriad problems, both internal and external, that beset it."[36]

Ōkubo was far from being democratic and had no trust in popular government. When an elective national assembly was proposed, Ōkubo prevented its establishment, arguing that "many unnecessary matters are raised in the course of a debate. It [the assembly] is not suited to our present national policy so the decision has been made to abolish it."[37] He insisted that the government pursue a steadfast policy of developing national wealth and strength, without being influenced by popular opinion, and to ensure this he stressed that policymaking should be secretive. The first real test of his power came in 1873, when many Japanese leaders were insisting upon a war to win dominance over Korea; Ōkubo opposed it, on the grounds that Japan was not yet strong enough and that such an expansionist move might bring against them the combined forces of England, China, and Russia.

The argumentative method and persuasive power of Ōkubo are well illustrated in the memorandum opposing the war that he presented to the council of state in early 1873:

The reasons why I am in no great haste to subscribe to the proposal come from much careful and earnest reflection on the problem. The gist of my arguments is as follows:

1. . . . His Majesty's reign is still young and the foundations of his reign are not yet firmly laid. . . . Due to their misunderstanding of the purport of public proclamations, or their misgivings about rising taxes, the ignorant, uninformed people of the remote areas have become easy victims of agitation and have started riots. A careful consideration of these facts constitutes the first argument against any hasty action regarding Korea.

2. Government expenditure today is already tremendous. . . . To start a war and to send tens of thousands of troops abroad would raise expenditures by the day to colossal figures. . . . This constitutes my second reason against any hasty action regarding Korea.

3. The government's present undertakings intended to enrich and strengthen the country must await many years for their fulfillment. . . . To launch a meaningless war now and waste the government's efforts and attention needlessly, increase annual expenditures to enormous figures, suffer the loss of countless lives, and add to the sufferings of the people so as to allow no time for other matters, will lead to the abandonment of the government's undertakings before their completion. . . .

This is the third reason against the hasty commencement of a Korean war.

In this same vein his argument continued, through parts 4, 5, 6, and 7, until he came to his conclusion:

Even if the campaign makes a favorable start, it is unlikely that the gains made will ever pay for the losses incurred. What will happen should the campaign drag on for months and years? Suppose total victory is gained, . . . we shall have to man garrisons to defend vital areas and to prevent their breach of the treaty terms. . . . If we permit the initiation of such a great venture, blithely and with no consideration for such an eventuality, we shall in all probability have cause for much regret in the future. . . . I consider such a venture entirely beyond comprehension, as it completely disregards the safety of our nation and ignores the interests of the people. It will be an incident occasioned by the whims of individuals without serious evaluation of eventualities or implications. These are the reasons why I cannot accept the arguments for the undertaking of this venture.[38]

The basic tenor of the memorandum was logical but also barbed. The urge to wage war against Korea was so deeply held and widespread that Ōkubo did not refrain from inserting sarcastic slurs upon those who opposed his views. Because feelings favoring war against Korea were so strong, Ōkubo's success in preventing it intensified the dislike of him felt by many high-ranking officials. This dislike further increased in the following year, when Ōkubo successfully advocated a war to seize Formosa, in direct violation of his arguments on the Korean issue. As his biographer wrote, "His enemies were numerous, and before long he was to become a victim of their hate."[39]

On 14 May 1878, Ōkubo rose early to hold a conversation with a visiting official concerning the future of Japan, in which he said that the progress made by Japan would have to be continued by other leaders. His words were prophetic. At eight that morning he left his residence by carriage to attend a meeting at the imperial palace. On the way several men attacked the carriage, dragged Ōkubo from it, and slashed him to death. The six assassins surrendered themselves to the police, were tried, and were executed. In the course of their trial they justified their deed "by charging that Ōkubo had 1) suppressed the rights of the people, 2) monopolized administrative affairs, 3) promulgated laws arbitrarily, 4) depleted the national treasury through expenditures upon unnecessary public works projects, 5) fomented disorders by weakening the authority of the patriotic samurai, and 6) prejudiced Japan's national rights through improper handling of foreign affairs."[40] Ōkubo's life lasted only forty-eight years, but during that time he shaped and put in place the forms and the programs that characterized the emergence of modern Japan.

A coldly calculating politician in public life, Ōkubo was a thoughtful and considerate parent, as is shown in a letter he wrote to his wife about their children in 1871: "The world today differs from that of the past as night does from day. . . . It is necessary as a child to apply oneself to writing, learning, and to the aquisition of the various arts. I have therefore purposely retained the services of a foreigner to educate them. They are both doing well, and their foreign teacher feels praise for them."[41] Despite his coldness he was filled with love—for his family, for his Satsuma clan, and for the nation that he did so much to forge through his power of persuasion—something new in the history of Japan.

Marquis Shigenobu Ōkuma: Autocrat of the Council Table

The founders of the Meiji government were a narrow group of conspirators who neither had broad popular support nor represented more than a small segment of the society. As has been noted, chief among those who directed the government was Ōkubo Toshimichi. Above him in rank, if not in authority, were members of the nobility. One of the nobles was Ōkuma Shigenobu, who was born on 16 February 1838 at Sata, on Kyushu, just sixty miles from the Dutch treaty-port of Nagasaki. and who built his political career through persuasion even more powerful than that of Ōkubo.

Ōkuma's family was wealthy, by standards of that time, and the boy's father was commander of a company of artillery. This post kept him in close touch with the Dutch, from whom he secured guns and learned about Western military tactics. His father died, however, when Shigenobu was only twelve, and he was raised thereafter by his mother, a woman of great ability with a pleasantly social personality. Shigenobu worried her because of his apparent dullness, as he lagged behind his fellows in the study of the Confucian classics. However, the death of his father apparently stimulated him, and shortly he rose to the head of his class. At the age of fifteen he enrolled in college, where he was indolent but canny and successful. In later life, he told how persuasion served his needs:

I was an idle fellow; I would not toil and moil like other chaps hugging their books day and night. I simply wanted to grasp the general meaning of a book. When I came across a book I thought worth reading, and particularly one of large size, I would not take the trouble to read it myself because it was a waste of my precious time. I knew my way. I would go round to those of my friends who were known to be diligent and possess a good reading knowledge, and tell them that I knew of an excellent book. I would talk of its merits in such a way that they could not resist the temptation of reading it. Sometimes I did the service of borrowing a copy from somebody or paying for it with my own money for those who could not either find any means to borrow or buy it. When I knew that they had finished the reading of the book I went to them and asked them to tell me the main points of its contents. Such parts as I thought important I would commit to memory. On the other hand I read with great care such works as were of smaller size and contained the general principles of a given subject and made myself thoroughly acquainted with their essentials. With such a method of acquiring knowledge I was able to beat my more hard-working friends in intellectual contests. I knew a friend who was a great reader. He read book after book from morning till night; but his knowledge, whatever the amount, was not of much practical use. Whenever I had some discussion with him on history or philosophy I was sure to beat him to the dust. He would never forgive me because he could not believe he was no match in intellectual controversy for so confounded a truant as Ōkuma.[42]

Despite his skill in avoiding studious labor, Ōkuma found college life intolerably dull and hated it. Freedom of inquiry was not allowed and classes consisted of the study of Chinese classics, to be learned by rote. Moreover, the underlying theme in all the teaching was the virtue of unquestioning obedience to superiors, which his personality could not accept. After two years in the college, Ōkuma was expelled. The reason was that he spent a long evening in a friend's room discussing philosophy and was so interested that he neglected to return to his own dormitory by closing time. Friends tried to force an entry for him and a melee broke out in which windows were smashed and arms broken. The year was 1855, two years after the arrival in Japan of Commodore Perry. Ōkuma's interests turned toward the West. What happened within his mind became, through his persuasive influence, the pattern for the new Japan.

Against the strong opposition of his relatives, who considered that education consisted solely of Confucian studies, but with the support of his mother, Ōkuma attended a medical college located outside of Saga, where he learned Dutch while studying both medicine and gunnery. The school library had only one Dutch-Japanese dictionary, divided into several volumes. Students were allowed to take single volumes to their rooms during the day but had to return them to the library at night. Industrious students sat late in the library, but this was not to Ōkuma's taste. Instead he again used persuasion to serve his needs. He would make lists of words he could not understand and persuade a fellow student to look them up for him. Obviously his powers of persuasion were already well developed. He was also developing ideas that he would persuade his countrymen to accept—ideas that vitally changed the nature of Japan.

Ōkuma spent five years in this Dutch college, acquiring broad knowledge though without depth in any particular area. During this time, his old ideas about Western civilizations were discarded one by one as he advanced in his studies. He had imagined, as all his contemporaries had imagined, that though the nations of the West were advanced in physical and mechanical science their moral culture was not much above the level of primitive life. But as he studied their history and institutions he came to realize that there was something in their civilization superior to the civilization of China and Japan. They knew, he said to himself, how to respect the rules of moral obligation, how to honour great men and great deeds, how to maintain peace and order in society, how to legislate, how to administer justice.[43]

Because of his knowledge of Dutch, he was appointed commissioner of trade at Nagasaki, to protect the interests of the lord of his domain. With his eagerly inquiring mind, he quickly learned about commerce and became interested in public affairs.

In 1860 the Tokugawa government sent a mission to the United States to exchange ratifications of the new treaty, and selected young students (including Fukuzawa Yukichi) were sent with it in order to learn what they could of American institutions. One of these students, named Koido, was an intimate friend of Ōkuma's, and he came back reporting that a knowledge of Dutch was useless—what was needed was English. Fukuzawa learned the same lesson, and he and Ōkuma, along with a group of other young men, promptly undertook to master the English language. Partly because he was busy with his duties, partly because of his tendency to laziness, Ōkuma did not progress far in his study of English until, five years later, he persuaded family friends to provide money for the opening of an English-language school in Nagasaki. While pursuing both his commercial duties and his study of English, Ōkuma became intensely interested in public affairs. He determined to guide them in new directions by new means.

> He became impatient, irritated, almost desperate. That he should be in such a mood was no wonder. It was patent to any discerning eye that Japan was at a cross-roads, that a great change was at hand, that the political system could not remain what it was. . . . But as things stood, a private person, whatever his abilities, could alone do almost nothing in a feudal society. It was therefore necessary to arouse the spirit of the whole fief, to form opinions, to stir up men's minds, and to throw the weight of a united Saga into the scale of the right cause.[44]

When the shogunate was replaced by the Meiji government in 1868, affairs in the new prefectures, which replaced the old domains, were in a state of disarray. Ōkuma was appointed to a board of commissioners in Saga to administer public business pending the arrival of a new governor.

His principal duties were to deal with foreign merchants in Nagasaki, concerning contracts and bills relative to trading arrangements. The departing governor had left the office in disorder, with papers scattered or missing. Ōkuma informed the foreign consuls that claims relating to commercial contracts must be presented to him within two months, and that only after that time would a decision be made about them. In resolving the disputes, Ōkuma "showed judgment, firmness, fair play. The foreigners, accustomed to delay, evasion and duplicity under the old system, were astounded to find a new method of doing business in a Japanese official."[45] Concurrently, Ōkuma was strict in dealing with abuses committed by foreigners. Under the "unequal treaty" provisions, foreigners were not subject to Japanese law. But when they transgressed against Japanese in Nagasaki, Ōkuma warned Japanese merchants to have no further dealings with them, and this boycott had the desired effect.

When the young emperor Meiji, then just sixteen years old, convened his first council of ministers on 6 April 1868, Ōkuma was among those summoned to Kyoto to take charge of the difficult problem of dealing with the foreign diplomats concerning the Japanese prohibition of Christianity. The spokesman for the foreigners was Sir Harry Parkes, the energetic and domineering British minister, who had lived in China from his youth and was accustomed to bullying Asians. Especially on this question of securing the right of missionaries to evangelize the Japanese, Parkes was arrogantly demanding. In a conference that began at 10:00 A.M. on 24 May 1868 and lasted without even a luncheon break until evening, Parkes at first protested that he would not negotiate with so inferior an official as Ōkuma, but when he was assured that Ōkuma had full powers to make a decision on this question, the discussion commenced. Quickly it grew heated as Parkes declared that in civilized countries freedom of religion was basic. Ōkuma replied that he was well aware of the religious wars of Christendom and that Japan would not abide entry into its society of a religion so antagonistic to its own. "Ōkuma stood by his guns. He would not be intimidated by the high language or frown of his adversary. The consciousness that he was in the right stood him in good stead. He yielded not an inch of ground."[46] He was then in his thirtieth year, and he established himself firmly in the minds of members of the foreign diplomatic corps and in officials of his own government as a man of steel will and high ability. In later life Ōkuma always looked back to this encounter as having laid the foundation for his political success.

In February 1869 Ōkuma was named vice-minister of foreign affairs, with, as was customary, full authority and responsibility for conduct of the ministry. A few months later he was also named to the even more important post of vice-minister of finance—vital because the Japanese government in its haste to modernize all aspects of society was virtually bankrupt. His home became the center for an informal political club where young men met to discuss how to overcome conservative opposition to new ideas. Elder officials naturally feared that innovations might undermine their long-established status, and the innovators had to contest against the deep-seated tradition of subservience to age and to high rank. An example of the persuasive problems with which Ōkuma contended is the controversy in 1868–69 over construction of telegraphs and railways:

> It is almost impossible for men of today to form an idea of how ridiculous, how absurd, and yet how persistent was the popular prejudice against the two most important branches of modern communication. A latent anti-foreign sentiment also added not a little to the outburst of the tempest. Improvements of communication by wire and rail, it was said, were detrimental to the interests of the realm because they served to facilitate foreign invasion. Iron coin was still in circulation; and when it was known that rails to be used for the new means of transport were made of that metal people were furious because, they said, it would degrade the status of money. A third and a more specious objection was that the person of the Emperor would be desecrated were he to travel in a carriage run on two pieces of metal.[47]

Ōkuma had no power simply to override such feelings; he had to neutralize them by persuasion. The audience he dealt with was not the general populace, which was not to be consulted, but the entrenched bureaucracy and, particularly, the elder statesmen. The method he pursued to overcome their conservative negativism was to overwhelm it with a floodtide of public opinion. In 1878, following the assassination of Ōkubo, Ōkuma and his associates called national conventions of the Society of Patriots in 1878, 1879, and 1880. "These were attended by thousands of delegates representing nearly one hundred local societies, and monster petitions were prepared, calling for the immediate opening of an elective national assembly."[48] The council of state promptly enacted laws restricting public meetings and the formation of political societies. In response, the young liberals commenced to tour the provinces, giving public lectures before local clubs and at other public gatherings. This was a new form of political activity in Japan, for in the early years of Meiji speech-making was an unknown art, and it was even found necessary to invent a word for it.[49] The principal influence in the development of public speaking as a persuasive force in politics came from Fukuzawa Yukichi, who will be discussed in the following section. But among the early and successful speakers was young Marquis Shigenobu Ōkuma.

"It ought to be remembered that Japan at this time was as yet without a representative assembly and that, therefore, the rulers of the country transacted business in their closets or at the council board."[50] After

Ōkubo's death, Ōkuma was recognized as the senior member of the cabinet. "Now sitting at the head of the council table Ōkuma was able and willing fully to display his extraordinary powers."[51] Politically, Japan was in ferment; public opinion, for the first time, was having a visible effect. Proponents of liberal reform went outside the government to arouse public support, using "the sharp weapons of pen and tongue." Along with speech making, newspapers were established, chiefly as propaganda organs for politically minded individuals. "The agitators, availing themselves of the modern tactics of propaganda, showed themselves capable of appealing to the discontented feelings of the nation."[52]

Decisive action could only be taken by senior members of the government, among whom Ōkuma was the most powerful. Largely because of the persuasiveness of his friend Fukuzawa, Ōkuma in 1881 presented to the council of state a paper calling for establishment of a parliamentary system, based on elections contested by political parties. The first elections were to be held within two years. This proposal was stormily opposed by the conservative faction, and Ōkuma came under heavy attack. At this juncture a scandal broke out concerning the sale of public works on the northern island of Hokkaido to private interests. Ōkuma was absolved of blame since he opposed the sale, but the public distrust of government that the incident aroused weakened his position. At this time the emperor decided on a seventy-day tour of the nation and took Ōkuma with him. During his absence from the capital his enemies connived to require his resignation. As his biographer writes, "And thus the mighty statesman fell. It was a great fall indeed. It had the effect of changing the whole face of national politics. The event is truly regarded with the Korean controversy, as one of the two most important political changes of the new Japan."[53] Ōkuma left the position of power that he had held for three years. The event was an end but also a beginning.

In announcing Ōkuma's resignation to the public, the emperor also proclaimed that in 1890 a parliament would be elected. Ōkuma's followers quickly planned the organization of Japan's first real political party, named the Reform party, with Ōkuma at its head, to contest for seats in the parliament.[54] Two other parties, the Liberty party on the Left and the Teisei party on the Right, were also formed. To a meeting in Meiji Hall, Tokyo, on 16 April 1882, Ōkuma made his inaugural speech as president of his party, advocating a moderate program of gradual liberalization. He also issued a written report to guide the party, in which he said:

> I have always kept the great work of political reform before my eyes. . . . Nevertheless, we should not be too sanguine in our hopes. Reforms can only be accomplished with profit by means that do not cause disruption of society. Look at what the so-called disciples of

Rousseau have done in Revolutionary France. We should not be foolish enough to reenact the part played by the Jacobins.[55]

Ōkuma from time to time addressed large audiences on behalf of his party, but he had not yet "developed those wonderful powers [of public speaking] which later proved the greatest of his talents." His personality is well depicted in Lebra's revisionist biography:

> Ōkuma was a paradoxical man. . . . The paradoxes he posed were more than something flowing out of the complexity of the man. They derived also from the paradoxes of his age. . . . Within a society beset by tensions Ōkuma added further contradictions and paradox through the eccentricity of his own character.
> Ōkuma was both popular and unpopular; in his popularity lay the causes of his unpopularity. His most notable traits as a politician were the charismatic appeal which made him popular, and his courage, optimism, and willingness to take risks, which sometimes led him to ignore the consequences of his actions. . . .
> Much of Ōkuma's political behavior was generated by great faith in the common man and awareness of the implications of public opinion and the media. These qualities and his extrovert nature made him beloved by the public, but led his fellow oligarchs to denigrate him.[56]

One of Ōkuma's postretirement activities was his founding of Tokyo College, which afterward grew into the prestigious Waseda Univesity. In February 1888 he was recalled to the government, as minister of foreign affairs. The particular charge given to him was to accomplish basic changes in the unequal treaties that curbed Japan's independence. "His return to office was hailed with shouts of joy by the nation"—partly because this signalized a triumph for public opinion, and partly because the people had confidence in his ability to renegotiate the treaties in a way suitable to Japan's new power. Revision of the treaties proved, however, to be virtually impossible, and Ōkuma attempted to compromise by agreeing to the continuance of trials of English citizens accused of crimes in Japan by English judges, with the provision that they first become naturalized Japanese citizens. The proposal was rejected on all sides and Ōkuma's resignation from the government was effected at the end of 1889.

As a direct consequence of the unpopularity of this proposal, Ōkuma was assaulted by a man with a bomb who injured him so seriously that his right leg had to be amputated. Ōkuma sent a gift of money to the man's family, as a sign that he recognized the right to freedom of political opinion, however drastic its results. The incident was far from the end of Ōkuma's public life. Following the election of the first parliament of Japan in 1890, Ōkuma organized the Progressive party, which drew strong support for its policy of denouncing the government's submission to restraints on its expansionist program after its quick and decisive defeat of China in the winter of 1894–95.

Once again Ōkuma was summoned to office as foreign minister. He accepted only after the government met his three requirements: (1) that only individuals supported by public opinion be appointed to cabinet positions; (2) that freedom of speech, of the press, and of the right to hold public meetings be assured; and (3) that the rule of "careers open to talent" be put into effect. His appointment was hailed joyously by the press and in public meetings, while his critics grumbled that "he knew how to play to the gallery." And so he did. "Ōkuma amazed statesmen of the old school by coming out among the people and speaking from the platform. For a Cabinet Minister to address public meetings was regarded as below his dignity; but Ōkuma did not scruple to brush away this punctilio. He as Foreign Minister was glad to avail himself of opportunities to state his views squarely and frankly before public audiences." In similar vein, he initiated the practice of speaking as a cabinet minister in the parliament. It was on 16 February 1897 that, at the age of fifty-nine, he made his first parliamentary speech. "It was a surprise to members because they had never heard such an honest, straight-forward utterance from the lips of a Cabinet Minister. Here again Ōkuma opened up new ground. It was not so much because he said many wonderful things but because he chose to take his hearers into his confidence that his speech scored so great a triumph."[57]

Because of his prestige and his practice, as well as because of the earnest teaching of his friend Fukuzawa Yukichi, public speaking became an agency of political effectiveness in the new Japan. In this practice Ōkuma continued, both in the Opposition and again as prime minister, until the end of his life, in 1922. Typical were his speaking engagements during the election campaign of March 1915 (when he advocated strengthening the military as a prelude to entering the war against Germany).

> Ōkuma entered upon the election campaign with an energy, industry, and enterprise that had never before been seen in a Prime Minister and in a man of near eighty. He travelled all over the country; he addressed meeting after meeting; he spoke from the railway carriage window to the crowd assembled on the platform. His speeches made into gramophone records were reproduced at the meetings which he could not attend. . . . Never had a Prime Minister enjoyed so enthusiastic a popularity as Ōkuma in this campaign. He was the idol of the people in the true sense of the word.[58]

Continuing to make frequent speeches into his eighties, he was the most-sought-after speaker of the day. He was also a voluble and vivid conversationalist, and his comments were reported in a book entitled (in translation) *Ōkuma's Armchair Talks.* As his biographer writes, "Ōkuma was glorious and mighty when his tongue was agoing; and his tongue was always agoing."[59] He died quietly, at the age of eighty-four, well short of his proclaimed goal of one hundred twenty-five years but able to look back on a fullness of vigorous activity of most unusual duration, beginning in his late twenties when he was commissioner of customs at Nagasaki. He received a public funeral as one of Japan's most remarkable men.

A specialist in the study of Japanese political leadership concludes about him that his "speeches were an inseparable part of his personality." He describes Ōkuma's speech making vividly and with discernment:

> As an orator, he often shared the platform with others and so there are several good accounts of his speech-making style. When he mounted the platform, his clean-shaven face was always set in a firm expression, his broad mouth arched downward in a forceful curve. Even on his first leisurely glance at the packed crowd, the intensity of his bearing already dominated the hall. Ōkuma's voice was not clear or sharp, but rich in resonance; effortlessly parading his extensive knowledge as he unfolded his deft and original arguments, he captivated large audiences by the sheer dynamism of his performance. Adroit in timing and intonation, when he rose to the climax of his peroration he would gesticulate vigorously or pose for a moment with both hands held out over the heads of the audience. Sometimes he thrust out his right hand suddenly like a flash of lightning to emphasize a point or brandished a clenched fist here and there as a sign of his determination.[60]

Adding to this description, the critic goes on to say that Ōkuma "was most noticeably in his element when attacking political enemies," that "on such occasions his overbearing and menacing tone was repellent to some people in the audience," and that "intelligent listeners often found his arguments shallow and irresponsible." His rashness sometimes prompted him to make promises he had no intention of fulfilling. For some he was a demagogue; for others, an autocrat; but to the great mass he was what passing years have proved him to have been—a true father of Japanese democracy.

Perhaps Tsunoda sums him up best of all. More than other leaders, Tsunoda says of him, "he represents that characteristic of Meiji Japan which perhaps best accounts for its rapid progress along Westen lines: its capacity to hold contending forces in dynamic balance and foster the growth of new and varied activities contributing to the national welfare—in short, its diversity in a vital unity."[61] What this means is that Ōkuma helped Japan to become westernized in its methods while retaining the central traditional values. This provided a stabilizing strength that held the society together while it was beset by a bewildering series of major changes. For the first decades of the Meiji Reformation, this mode of putting new wine in old bottles helped to make the transition acceptable. Fundamentally, however, it was self-defeating. New attitudes had to replace the old. And for this most fundamental aspect of the Reformation movement, leadership was supplied primarily by the friend of Ōkuma's who had encouraged his early liberalism—Fukuzawa Yukichi.

Fukuzawa Yukichi: Intellectual Pioneer of the Reformation Period

If Europe had shifted suddenly from the feudalism of 1200 to the modernism of 1900 within the space of a single generation, the transformation would have been scarcely more rapid or more complete than the miraculous changes that swept through Japan between 1858—the year in which Fukuzawa Yukichi went to Tokyo—and 1901, the year of his death. Many individuals of great ingenuity, courage, and foresight combined to accomplish this sudden modernization. The greatest single credit, however, must go to the simple but industrious and amazingly purposive educator who never held political office but never rested from teaching, persuading, and guiding the people of Japan into a new world.

The success of Fukuzawa derived from two factors—the clarity of his vision of what the Japanese must do, and his tremendous persuasive ability to get them to do it. What Japan needed, as he understood it, was not only material transformation from an agrarian to a technological society but also a spiritual conversion from stultifying hierarchy to individualistic independence. While statesmen labored to bring to Japan armaments and factories, the telegraph and railways, the postal system and financial institutions, Fukuzawa perceived clearly that civilization does not consist only of material things but also of a way of thinking. In his most mature book, *Gakamon no susume* (The encouragement of learning) the opening sentence is: "It is said that Heaven does not create one man above another man, nor does it create one man below another." All men are equal. "Whether daimyo or laborer, the importance of life is the same." Instead of the four classes, society consisted of "all people under one ruler." Only thus could Japan rise to equality with the great powers of the West, for "independent individuals make for an independent country."

Such ideas were the absolute antithesis of the deeply implanted and centuries-old Japanese traditions. Fukuzawa relates an incident from his youth that helped him to gain such insights. He and some friends, all from the lower order of samurai, waited in the cold for an hour for a ferryboat, and when it came a warmly and richly dressed upper-level samurai swept by them to take the boat for himself, while they were forced to prostrate themselves on the ground before him; then they had to wait in the cold for another hour. Such a system, Fukuzawa felt, was not civilized. When he found that no such class inequality prevailed in the West, he realized that foreigners were not barbarians. Civilization, he wrote in his 1872 book, "begins in doubt." There must be a questioning of established ways. Subservience must be challenged. Minds must reach out beyond the known to search for new answers. This was the innovative teaching that struck deep into the heart of Japan.

Carmen Blacker, in her insightful study of Fukuzawa, credits him above all others for showing "the incompatibilities of the old ways of thinking with the new age." No one equaled his call "for a new scheme of values, a new practical morality in ordinary everyday life, a new view of the past and its influence on the specious present, and a new theory of political obligation."[62] Beasley concluded that Fukuzawa's books "became for many the only reliable guide in an otherwise uncertain world."[63] Tsunoda judged that "no other Japanese in those turbulent pre-Restoration years had such a wide vision."[64] Sandra Davis, studying intellectual change in the Meiji period, found that "Fukuzawa's call for independent spirit and for self-respect combined with his stress on the practical and material aspects of life and set the tone for the mainstream of early Meiji thought."[65] Today, Fukuzawa's homilies seem simple truisms; but to newly opened Japan they were sunlight from another world.

On one theme Fukuzawa's liberalism was even in advance of that in the West. This was his defense of women's rights. He did not advocate votes for women, but he did demand a revolutionary improvement in their status. In his *Nihon Fujinron,* published in 1885, he bluntly described the treatment accorded to the typical Japanese woman: "At home she has no personal property, outside the home she has no status. The house she lives in belongs to the male members for the household, and the children she raises belong to her husband. She has no property, no rights, no children. It is as if she were a parasite in a male household." Among the reforms he recommended were equality of opportunity for jobs and the same freedom for sexual satisfactions that were accorded to men. He denounced the misunderstanding of the Confucian system that resulted in respect for men, contempt for women.[66]

In order to propagate his ideas, Fukuzawa used all the avenues that were available and invented new ones as well. He wrote books and magazine articles and pamphlets in endless profusion. He started a school, which grew to be Keio University. He founded and edited a newspaper. He seized every opportunity to converse with men of position and influence. And he taught the Japanese that it was possible—and desirable—to make public speeches.

There was no word for public speaking in Japanese; Fukuzawa had to invent it: *enzetsu.* He also invented a word for debate, *tōron,* combining the terms for *dispute* and *opinion.* Mori Arinori, a friend of Fukuzawa's who was also active in advocating westernization of the country, was convinced that the Japanese language was wholly unsuitable for talk addressed to large numbers of people. Mori and Fukuzawa belonged to a select society of some thirty-three intellectuals called the Meirokusha, which was dedicated to modernizing Japan. Fukuzawa urged that they give public speeches to spread their ideas, but they retorted that such a process was impossible. On 16 November 1874 the Meirokusha met at a restaurant in Tokyo to exchange ideas, as they did regularly. Fukuzawa and a few comrades had been practicing speech making privately in their homes, and Fukuzawa determined upon a daring experiment. He described what happened as the members gathered for their dinner meeting:

> I stood up and said, "Gentlemen, give me your attention. I have something to say. Please seat yourselves around the table." I stood near the edge of the table. This happened to be at the time of the Japanese punitive expedition to Formosa in 1874. I spoke about this for from thirty minutes to an hour and then sat down. When I questioned them as to whether they understood what I said, they all undestood very well indeed. I concluded that to say that one cannot make speeches in Japanese was either blind credulity or cowardly evasiveness. Had not my recital, which they admitted they understood, been a speech? This was my victory for the idea of speech-making.[67]

A few months later, on 1 May 1875, Fukuzawa inaugurated on the campus of Keio University his Enzetzu-kan, or the Hall of Public Speaking, where the first speeches heard by the Japanese public were presented.[68] In his autobiography, Fukuzawa merely mentions his "using public speaking as an entirely new form of communication" along with such other "radical innovations" as collecting tuition and discarding samurai swords.[69] Nevertheless, he considered it to be important and wrote extensively in his effort to promote this new mode of influencing public opinion.

Like Ōkubo and Ōkuma, Fukuzawa was born on the island of Kyushu, and like Ōkubo he came from a poor family of the lower samurai. The Fukuzawa family fell into even deeper poverty when Yukichi was just one year old, for his father died and his mother was left with the care of five children. This may have proved fortunate for Yukichi and for Japan, for his father, with a deep hatred for the subservient life of a lower-class samurai, had determined to save Yukichi from it by making him a Buddhist priest. The Fukuzawa children did not play with others outside their home and were almost the only ones in the town who did not see the plays presented in the local theater. Yukichi did not even start school until his fourteenth or fifteenth year. In the school the new students (mostly much younger than he) were taught early in the morning by more advanced students.

During the afternoons they all discussed books they were reading. Fukuzawa comments that "perhaps I was somewhat talented in literature, for I could discuss a book with the older student who had taught me the reading of it earlier in the morning, and I was always upsetting his argument. This fellow knew the words well, but he was slow to take in the ideas they expressed. So it was an easy matter for me to hold a debate with him.[70] In this way he developed his lifelong characteristic of independent thought. Like Ōkubo and Ōkuma, Fukuzawa left home to go to Nagasaki to study Dutch, and, also like them, he found a little later that this language was useless, so he turned to the mastery of English.

Young men with such linguistic accomplishments were scarce, and Fukuzawa was therefore given an opportunity in 1860 to go as a servant to San Francisco for a month of wide-eyed observation. The following year he was chosen for a govenment-sponsored inspection trip to seven European capitals and spent almost an entire year in eager study of European life. He took notes on everything: hair styles, clothing, buildings, utensils, ideas, governmental systems, factories, social conduct—all indiscriminately jotted down. Everything was new, and to him everything was of almost equal importance. He crammed his mind full of the ways of these peoples of the West. And he was deeply impressed. They seemed to be successful. They were prosperous, happy, and well behaved. The notion that the East was civilization itself, surrounded by barbarism, withered in the face of such facts. Fukuzawa was converted to modernism and detemined to do all he could to carry his people with him into this new realization.

Upon his return to Japan on 11 December 1862 he suffered the shock of finding Japan in the strong grip of antiforeign sentiments. For a known internationalist such as he, life was becoming dangerous. He then burned some of his notes to prevent their being found and he remained in his home, afraid to go out on the streets. He took to drinking heavily, became a retainer of the shogun, and in general retreated from his westernized views. Then in January 1867 he was again selected to accompany a committee that was sent to America, and the group spent six months there. His earlier enthusiasm fully returned. He curbed his drinking, opened the school that grew into Keio University, and wrote his book *Seiyo Tabi Annai* (Guide to travel in the Western world), which became enormously popular, with a sales figure of at least 250,000 copies. The book was deliberately noncontroversial, dealing not with social or political ideas but simply informing the Japanese about the manner of life in America. In quick succession he produced more essays, pamphlets, and books, mostly plain and simple descriptions of Western institutions and manners. Only later, after the antiforeign movement was ended or submerged and after his fame served as some protection, did he shift to sharp criticisms of Japan's outmoded customs and to praise for egalitarianism. He never, however, felt wholly safe, for assassination remained a political device of respectable standing.

Fukuzawa's purposiveness in crusading to revise Japanese thinking and the country's way of life was remarkable. But even so, accident played a large part in his career. As he attested, he did not go to Nagasaki to study Dutch for any reason at all except to escape from his miserable poverty at home; and when he wrote his first book on the West it was not from any urge to reform his own country or even to earn money but simply because it was something to do. His first trip abroad, to San Francisco, was no more than a boyish adventure. Even on his yearlong official trip to Europe, he had little purpose or discrimination in his note taking. During the revolutionary struggles that overthrew the shogunate and restored the emperor to centrality in the state, Fukuzawa remained quietly apart from the struggle, apparently with no great interest in which side won. It was only after the amazing success of his *Seiyo Jijo* (Guide to the West) that he began to take himself seriously as a national reformer. It took a while for this self-evaluation to sink in, but by 1870 or thereabouts Fukuzawa urgently set forward on his course.

"I felt as though . . . I must try to change the whole people's way of thinking from its very foundations," he wrote. Then he clarified his aim:

The Confucian civilization of the East seems to me to lack two things possessed by western civilization—science in the material sphere and a sense of "independence" in the spiritual sphere. I see now that this is the reason why Western statesmen govern their countries so successfully and Western businessmen are so successful in their commerce and industry, and why people are so patriotic and their family circles so happy.[71]

In order to render his ideas effective, Fukuzawa worked hard to commumicate them with simplicity. He would call in his housemaid and read to her what he had written, in order that he might change any word or expression that she did not readily understand. He had no literary pretensions or desire to win fame as an author. All he wanted was easy understanding. and this he achieved so well that the seventeen pamphlets that he wrote between 1872 and 1876 had a total sale of at least 3,400,000 copies. His newspaper, in which his writings were published serially, gave them wide and immediate circulation. Following the Restoration, neither his pen nor his tongue was often unemployed.[72]

He had no interest in holding a government position, realizing that if he did so, even on a high level, he would be constrained to represent official policies rather than to exercise freely his own opinions. Government, he well knew, is critically important in its role of shaping affairs, and he wrote many books on such topics as the rights of the people, diplomatic relations, the need to decentralize power, public security, and reverence for the emperor. But even more basic than government is education.

What must most fundamentally be achieved, he was convinced, was to change the thoughts, the beliefs, the feelings of individuals. He devoted his life tirelessly to education. And he was sure that communication was the most powerful weapon that could be employed. In his autobiography, Fukuzawa wrote that his early ambition had been merely to learn about Western culture and to earn his living. But after the Restoration, he felt a new urgency:

> I must take advantage of the moment to bring in more of Western civilization and revolutionize our people's ideas from the roots. . . .
>
> Consequently, I renewed my activities with "tongue and brush," my two cherished instruments. On one side I was teaching in my school and making occasional public speeches, while on the other I was constantly writing on all subjects. . . .
>
> A man may grow old, but while he has his health, he must not sit idle. I too intend to do all within my power as long as life and health are granted me.[73]

Fukuzawa's interest in public speaking commenced in the spring of 1873, when he was shown a copy of a curious American booklet called *American Debation* [sic]. Within a few days, in collaboration with two friends, he produced a small book, *Kaigiben* (How to hold a conference), which appears to be the first book on public speaking to be published in Japan. What Fukuzawa presented was "a format for group discussion." In the preface he stressed its importance:

> The learning of group organization is not unlike the military drill of soldiers. Even a million brave warriors, if undisciplined, will lose a war. The people today are no different. Though a man may possess supreme eloquence, great wealth, the political genius of a Franklin, or the scholarly mind of a Newton, he will be of no value to the world unless he is able to solve problems through the method of group discussion.[74]

The book not only describes parliamentary rules but also adapts them directly to Japanese problems. For example, he devoted twenty-eight pages to depicting the problems of villagers whose roads are in need of repair. He shows in detail how they should meet to analyze their problem and to consider various possible ways of solving it, and then reach a decision through orderly discussion. He concludes that this same method serves the needs of scholars in their meetings, of businessmen, and even of women and children. It is in this book that Fukuzawa first presented his

newly coined word *enzetsu*, meaning speech or oration, which he formed
by combining the characters for *tongue* and *explain*.

Promptly Fukuzawa organized a society for the study of public speaking, and its first meeting was held on 27 June 1874. The biweekly meetings
were first held on the second floor of a building beside Fukuzawa's house,
then on a houseboat moored in the river. In the evening the ten members
would gather, draw lots for taking sides on a question, and practice
debating it. They also read English-language books on speech making, and
they listened on street corners to storytellers to note their vocal intona-
tions and gestures. When they felt confident enough to speak in public, the
Hall of Public Speaking on the Keio University campus was opened and
each of the ten made a brief congratulatory speech. This speech hall still
stands, preserved by orders of the government as a national monument,
"the first building of its kind to have ever been established since the
founding of Japan."

The inauguration of public speaking in Japan coincided with a period of
turbulence over the rising issue of political rights. First, in 1874, came the
demand for a popularly elected national assembly. Then political parties
began to take form, contesting vigorously for support. As some gains were
made and others denied or delayed, radical speakers assailed the government. After the establishment of the Diet, members sought to shift power
from the cabinet to the parliament. An active movement for women's
rights developed. In religious matters, in 1869 the government established
an organization to promote Shintoism, while both Buddhist priests and
Christian evangelists were also trying to win converts. Such issues
aroused heated public interest; and meetings, some of mammoth size,
were held all around the country at which speakers advocated proposed
policies.

One result was that in June 1875 a severely restrictive set of libel laws
was proclaimed to limit freedom of the press. Almost a decade and a half
later, on 31 December 1887, the government suddenly proclaimed a Peace
Preservation Law curbing freedom of speech. The Tokyo police quickly
rounded up some 570 political speakers and writers and exiled them from
Tokyo. For what proved to be a long generation, public speaking lan-
guished in Japan, and what remained dealt only with noncontroversial
subjects. Only after the Pacific war ended in 1945 was there a new beginning of vital public discussion. Fukuzawa, like Ōkubo and Ōkuma, had to
leave his innovative program to be carried forward in later years by new
leaders under new circumstances.

Conclusion

The massive changes that renovated Japan during the Meiji period were
guided by a new breed of leaders who realized that the complete revision

of government must be supported by fundamental changes in the culture of the people. No longer, as in the past, could there be government merely by proclamation. Instead, there had to be an effective process of communication that would not only go from the top down but also from the people up to the national administration and out through all the prefectures and communities. This was the essence of the new Japan, indispensable for the remaking of the society and the emergence of what was virtually a new nation.

Two other points must also be kept in mind. In addition to the leaders who aroused public opinion and utilized it as the dynamic force that impelled modernization, there were also large numbers of technicians and administrative experts who selected from around the world what they conceived to be the best features of Western progress and who skillfully adapted these innovations to Japanese circumstances. Their contributions were indispensable, for without them the newly aroused dynamism of public opinion would have been of little avail. The second point of consequence is that modernization of attitudes did not and could not possibly suddenly and completely prevail. Not surprisingly, as the nineteenth century ended and the twentieth century began, there was a militaristic reaction that appealed to the deep substratum of Japanese psychology. Notably, this occurred after the death of the three leaders who provided much of the dynamism for change. As they realized, their work could not be complete.

Naturally, it could not all be done within a generation or two. Cultural roots are deeply implanted, and one of their basic characteristics in Japan, as in Asia generally, is respect for tradition. Ōkubo Toshimichi was especially concerned with strengthening Japan. Shigenobu Ōkuma was similarly intent on doing all he could to magnify Japanese pride and self-regard, along with expanding broadly the base of public support for governmental policies. Among the three, Fukuzawa Yukichi was notably the one dedicated to reshaping the Japanese spirit—toward democracy, toward equality, and toward innovation and acceptance of many Western values; but, like the others, he sought also to intensify the sentiments of ethnic pride. The stimulation that they and their associates provided during the period of Reformation did not turn the Japanese away from their vision of special greatness but nurtured methods and attitudes that would make that greatness more real.

As the Reformation period reached its height, near the end of the century, the inrush of European imperialism in both north and south Asia fortified an accompanying Japanese ambition for military, territorial, economic, and cultural expansion. Such ideas were given sustenance by the new industrialism, which was able to support an extensive military establishment. The new constituion adopted in 1889 was written by oligarchs and imposed upon the people a system of imperial absolutism that led directly to the 1904 attack against Russia, the seizure of Korea, the 1931 conquest of Manchuria, the 1937 invasion of China, and, finally the waging of the Pacific war.

Nevertheless, the new liberalization proved to be too sturdy to be destroyed. During the lifetime of the innovative leaders, matters did not always go as they wished. As all three of the trio noted near the end of their lives the tasks they set for themselves were incomplete and needed the further guiding influence of new leaders. After them came a period of retrogression.

But the concept of leadership that derives from the will of the people, and that reflects their wishes as well as guides their affairs, was firmly rooted. This is the principal legacy they left the nation. They were members of a unique generation, and what they accomplished through persuasive communication set a standard that, once again after World War II, revolutionized Japan. The American occupation under the command of General Douglas MacArthur, like the penetration into Japan by Commodore Matthew Perry, had profound effects. But the most lastingly effective impulsions to change were, and had to be, Japanese. The real makers of modernized and democratic Japan were not foreigners but the country's own leaders, communicating with the people in ways they could understand.

The definitive transition from the old to the new Japan, reflecting both domestic and international influences, is the following statement from the historic 1 January 1946 radio broadcast by Emperor Hirohito: "The relationship between the people and me is bonded by mutual trust and respect, but never by mere myth and legend. It shall not, therefore, be based on the fictional concept that the emperor is a living god and that the Japanese people are superior to other people and have a destiny to rule the world." Their destined way turned, thereby, from militaristic ambitions to economic endeavors. Through this transition the new nation took form.

2

China's Advance toward Modern Nationalism: A Diversity of Ways

While Japan was rapidly becoming unified, modernized, and strong, China remained divided, undeveloped, and weak. Progress was made under leaders whose visions were persuasively supported; but there was no massive surge forward to match that of Japan. The problems of the two countries were different and so was the character of their leadership. China emerged into modernism not suddenly and not fully but by fits and starts; each move forward was stimulated and guided by a particular kind of leader, and each leader had a goal and a method different from those of the others. For all of them the need was to communicate their ideas with sufficient effectiveness to unite the people. But for China unity was long delayed.

The leaders who had the most direct influence in the emergence of China into modernism and nationalism were K'ang Yu-wei, Sun Yat-sen, Generalissimo and Madame Chiang Kai-shek, Mao Tse-tung, and Chou En-lai. Each one was quite different from all the others, in personality, in aims, and in methods. What they had in common was their effort to make the inchoate mass of China into a nation that would serve the needs of its people and have the strength to stand independently in the international arena. Much larger than Japan, much more populous, and with a far longer tradition of cultural superiority, China nevertheless lagged far behind Japan in attaining modernity. The contributions of successive leaders were impressive but proved to be not enough.

Perhaps one reason is that the early nationalist leaders in China lacked something of the clarity of purpose, the strength of will, and the comprehensiveness of vision of those who guided Japan's transformation. Perhaps the Chinese people were less malleable, partly because they were not as dissatisfied with their old system as were the Japanese. There surely were other reasons as well. China, being vastly larger than Japan and more diverse in its parts, was harder to unify. As yet another factor, in China the "barbarians from the West" came gradually, nibbling at the edges of the kingdom rather than appearing suddenly and dramatically as did Perry in

Japan in 1853. Consequently, the reaction to them was less cohesive. Overriding all, the Chinese, more than any other people in the world, were especially averse to change because of their confidence that the civilization they enjoyed was the best that was attainable.

The Chinese lived by precepts that they implicitly believed. They had a social system that strongly favored stability yet provided, through the Confucian examination system, some opportunity for upward mobility by the most able and ambitious. The standard of living for the bulk of the people was low but was seldom questioned, for it was as it always had been. For some four thousand years China had been the "middle kingdom," the unchallenged center of civilization, not just for the East but for everywhere, for everything outside was assumed to be barbarian.

Things were as they were. Things were as they had been for multiple centuries. Things were as they were described in the ancient classics and as they were supposed to be. Things were as they always would be—for neither in Chinese philosophy nor in Chinese social and political systems was there provision for change. Even in Europe the idea of "progress" was an eighteenth-century invention of the French Encyclopedists—and its disintegrative influence had not penetrated the Far East. "Leave well enough alone" was a lesson that did not need to be taught. It was taken for granted. Very few dreamed of doing anything else.

When change came it was neither invited nor welcomed. It came in the form of gunboats and landing parties. It came as opium wars aimed to sell the Chinese what they did not want, with payment guaranteed by foreign management of their customs revenues. The decadent Manchu (Ching) dynasty was too weak to offer resistance; and the frantic uprising known as the Taiping rebellion was subdued by superior Western gun power. The floodgates were opened by the surprisingly easy victory of Japan in the 1894–95 winter war, after which Western nations rushed in to grab extraterritorial control of the major seaports along the Chinese coast.

The modernization of China was impeded by a deep and general sentiment of antiforeignism. It was difficult for the Chinese to discriminate between good and bad aspects of Western civilization, since all the invading strangers were bad in their several ways. Christian missionaries sweepingly denounced as paganism and superstition the whole gamut of their sacred and ancient beliefs. Merchants backed by gunboats sold them shoddy goods in return for gold, jade, jewels, spices, and silk. Diplomats made demands enforced by military power. Through it all was a humiliating assumption by the invaders of racial superiority. The famous William Henry Donald, who served faithfully in sequence the Manchus, Sun Yat-sen, and Generalissimo and Madame Chiang Kai-shek, told of the shock he felt when he arrived from Australia as a new reporter in the office of the *China Mail* in Hong Kong. A paper fell to the floor, and Donald was about to pick it up when the editor stopped him, clapped his hands, and shouted, "Boy! Pick up that paper!" A gray-haired Chinaman shuffled forward, picked up the paper, and handed it to Donald, saying "Here, master."[1] The Chinese saw little reason for adopting the ways of the West.

But there were leaders who saw different needs and different ways of meeting them. Leaders become leaders partly because they see what the people do not, and partly because they have special skill in imposing their ideas upon others or in winning the willing acceptance of them. These were the characteristics of the leaders who in differing degrees and in their own ways brought about the gradual transformation of Chinese society.

K'ang You-wei: Idealistic Theorist

The first of these leaders, and perhaps the most self-confident of them all, was a farmer and self-taught scholar from a small village near Canton, K'ang You-wei. As a youth he won local admiration for his scholarship and independent mind. He studied the Confucian classics, as did all Chinese who studied at all, but with a difference. Far from contenting himself with memorization, he looked for the centrality of meaning. What he found was that Confucius did not teach simple conformity and subordination, but that he greatly valued and sought to nurture individual merit and the ability to lead not by force but by being right. He was equally impressed by Confucius's stress upon harmony and his hopeful vision of a time to come when the Greater Harmony would peacefully unite all the world. In addition, K'ang studied Buddhism and developed a compassionate love for all mankind as he accepted Gautama's insight that everyone is caught in a trap of pain and suffering from which the only escape is abandonment of selfishness and inclusive love for all.

When he felt ready for it, K'ang made the long trip to Peking, via Hong Kong and Shanghai, to take the third-degree examination for political office. This was his first view of the world outside and he was aroused to seek broader knowledge. He bought every book he could find about the countries of the West and carried them back to his village, where he studied and meditated on the significance of this new way of life. Then he went to Japan for further study and for observation of the effects of Western influence on the society.

In rapid succession during the next decade he produced a series of books: *Renovation of Japan, Life of Peter the Great, Constitutional Changes in England, History of the Greatness and Decadence of Turkey,* and *Confucius as a Reformer.* With the attention he won from the popularity of these books, he founded the Higher Learning Reform Society, which attracted a membership of leading intellectuals and middle-rank officials serving the Grand Council. As always happens, his own understanding was clarified by his writings, for communication demands not only clarity of comprehension but also consideration of what the ideas mean to those at whom the writing is aimed. He evolved from being a student to become a prophet.

It was born in upon him with the force of an apocalyptic vision that a day of salvation for mankind was dawning, and that he had a leading part to play. First "a new China must be made" in which the full force of Chinese universalism and glorification of social harmony might shine forth, and then he and his fellow students must "take responsibility for the whole world."[2]

In 1891, at the age of thirty-three, K'ang left his scholarly isolation, as Confucius had done, and established himself as a teacher in a suburb of Canton, welcoming any who wished to learn. His most famous disciple, Liang Ch'i-ch'ao, described K'ang's teaching:

He made Confucianism and Buddhism and Sung and Ming philosophy the essence, and history and Western learning the application. What he aimed at was the inspiration of men's souls and the widening of their wisdom. . . . Every day he would be in the classroom for four or five hours, discussing one branch of learning or one particular matter; tracing its development and success or failure, looking at every side from the past to the present and illustrating it by comparisons with Europe and America. Also he went to the full lengths of his idealism, holding up some noble standard with its advance and decline, in the past and the present, in China and abroad: all in order that the learner might grow in the freedom of idealism, and the power of discrimination be born.[3]

During the four years in which he conducted his school, K'ang worked out his *Ta T'ung* philosophy, advocating world peace and world unity. In a book that was published after the fall of the Manchus, K'ang analyzed the many kinds of suffering in the world, many of them deriving from the virtually constant wars, and he concluded that the virus of nationalism was the principal cause. Therefore, the efforts of mankind must aim to break down the barriers between nations so that all peoples would be ruled by a world council composed of representatives from all countries. In his book he expressed neither admiration for nor condemnation of the West but shifted easily in his discussion from China to Europe, seeing all mankind as essentially akin. He granted that Western nations had developed ways of serving the needs of the common people, but he found this guidance also in Confucius and Mencius. What chiefly impressed him was that the West had devised governmental forms for making the will of the people effective, including representative parliaments, secret ballots, and just laws. With this understanding came a determination to leave his study and to struggle to achieve reforms, for he agreed with the doctrine taught by his favorite philosopher, the Neo-Confucianist Wang Yang-ming (1472–1529), that "to know is to act."

K'ang was introduced by the imperial tutor to the young emperor Kuang hsu, who had just come of age and was eager to assert his independence from the stern control of the empress dowager Tzu Hsi. On 3 January 1898, the emperor ordered K'ang to attend a conference that lasted for three hours, with all the principal ministers of the court in attendance. To a reporter for the *China Mail* K'ang described what happened. After noting that "I was received with all respect," he added: "I had to say that everything in China must be reformed and follow Western civilization."

> I could see that the majority of them were against reform. . . . The first thing I suggested was that China should have a properly constituted judicial system—that a foreigner should be engaged to work conjointly with myself and some others to revise the laws and the government administrative departments. That I hold to be the most important change. . . . Unfortunately, the Emperor has been pushing on the other reforms before preparing the way for them. That has contributed to bringing about the present crisis.[4]

The "present crisis" was the impending financial collapse of the government, brought about by corruption and inefficiency in construction of railways and collection of taxes, and by general incompetence. For these conditions members of the Grand Council, who listened to K'ang, were responsible. Of course they did not like what he was saying. A principal among them reported to the emperor: "He is talking nonsense; he speaks about changing the ways of our ancestors!" Even so, as K'ang recorded,

> The outcome of the conference was that I was ordered by the Emperor to submit my proposals to him in the form of a memorial. . . . I advised the Emperor to select young, intelligent men, well imbued with Western ideas, to assist in the regeneration of the Empire, irrespective of their position, whether they are lowly born or of high degree; that they should confer with the Emperor every day and discuss the measures for reform, first devoting their energies to a revision of the laws and administration.

As before, the ministers did not like what K'ang proposed, which in effect was that they be displaced. K'ang sent the emperor two of his books, on the reforms in Japan and on Peter the Great. On 16 June the emperor again called him in for a conference.

> The Emperor said to me: "Your books are very useful and very instructive."

I practically repeated what I said in my memorial about the weakness of China being owing to the lack of progress.

The Emperor said: "Yes; all these conservative Ministers have ruined me."

. . . I asked him to look at the difficulties Japan had to overcome before she could reform on modern lines. . . . I repeated to him what Peter the Great did to make Russia powerful, saying, "You, the Emperor, I would ask you to remove yourself from the seclusion in which you live. Come boldly forward and employ young and intelligent officials."[5]

K'ang's persuasiveness was successful. Between 11 June and 6 September, known as the Hundred Days of Reform, the young emperor issued a series of decrees creating a translation service, naval and agricultural colleges, and a public budget; dismissing conservative officials; abolishing sinecures; and instituting similar reforms. The last of these decrees was a plea for support:

In promoting reforms, we have adopted certain European methods. . . . But our statesmen and scholars are so ignorant of what lies beyond our borders that they look upon Europe as possessing no civilization. . . . The cause of my anxiety is not fully appreciated by my people, because the reactionary element deliberately misrepresents my objects, spreading the while baseless rumours so as to disturb the minds of men.[6]

The result of this revolution by decree was failure, for neither K'ang You-wei nor the young emperor had troubled themselves to organize support for such massive changes. The empress dowager joined the court conservatives, and with control over the armed forces they carried out a *coup d'état* in September. The reform leaders were arrested and the emperor was imprisoned, to remain a forgotten figure until his death on 15 November 1908, just one day after the death of the empress dowager. K'ang You-wei and a few of his closest associates escaped into exile in Japan, where he remained until his death. His ideas, however, did not die but were an inspiration for many years to the small group of intellectuals who continued to yearn for modernization and for formation of a unified world government.

Sun Yat-sen: Father of the Chinese Revolution

The enigma of Sun Yat-sen, along with his undoubted importance, has led to a long list of books attempting to explain him. The vigor of his influence is manifest in the fact that both Communist and Nationalist China acclaim him as their founding source, while they also ignore or reinterpret his ideas. To one China expert, Sun Yat-sen "belongs partly to two worlds and fully to neither. . . . Plans hatched from Western ideas he only half understood inevitably failed in a China he understood no better."[7] Miss Lyon Sharman, who was born in China and who loved it and knew it well, found it difficult to interpret Sun because just nine years after his death, "the real man" was "being obliterated by a legend," with both the Communists and the Kuomintang treating him like "a lacquered god," above any criticism.[8] Nathaniel Peffer found him to be blinded by egotism as well as "gullible beyond imagining and credulous past understanding," yet possessing "irresistible magnetism."

> I have never known anybody [he wrote] who has been face to face with Dr. Sun who has not been impressed with him. . . . Nothing about him strikes you till he talks—in a low and uninflected tone with rapid flow of words. Then his poise, his dignity, his enthusiasm, and, above all, his utter sincerity record themselves on your memory forever.[9]

His longtime secretary said of him that "he dreamed of Utopia, of establishing a sane and orderly government that was benevolent to the people." And the method by which he hoped to establish it was persuasion, not force.

> In public speaking he was a ready and eloquent speaker. He could get up before an audience and speak for hours on a stretch. His speeches were not flowery [but] were inspirational and stirring in grass roots language, a quality easily understood and appreciated by the masses . . . I have to add that in his speeches he never used strong and abusive language and on issues of politics he never exhorted his audience to use violence. Neither would he start the shouting of slogans such as are so commonly resorted to at most political gatherings and demonstrations of the present day.[10]

The "engima" of Sun Yat-sen is twofold, involving (1) the nature of his ideas, which make him the patron saint of both Communist and anti-Communist Chinese, and (2) his revolutionary methods, which aimed to accomplish a drastic reshaping of China while avoiding or deemphasizing the use of force. Except for the first twelve and last nine years of his life, he lived mostly outside of China, spending twelve years abroad getting an education and another three decades in travels or brief residence in Europe, America, Japan, and Southeast Asia. He better understood how to appeal to foreign audiences for support than how to forge unity among his own people; yet, even so, the magnetism of his influence stirred the depths of Chinese society. He could not govern China, but he did govern its spirit and at least after his death, commanded its loyalty.

Sun Yat-sen (or Sun Wen, as he was known in his early years) was born on 12 November 1866 in a small village near Canton. His family was poor, but his father was the chief leader among the villagers, and Sun's elder brother went to Hawaii where he became modestly prosperous. When Sun Wen was twelve, his brother came from Hawaii to take him there to get a Western education. After five years of study in the worldstream of democratic and progressive ideas, and after being converted to Christianity, Sun quarreled with his brother and returned to his home village. There he was unable to settle down into the old patterns but became a troublemaker, inducing youths to desecrate a shrine to a local deity. At the age of eighteen he married a girl selected by his parents and enrolled in the Canton Hospital Medical School. Shortly, to escape from his problems at home, he transferred to a small college of medicine for Chinese in Hong Kong where, after five years, he graduated with a degree in medicine and surgery. During these years he also studied Mandarin Chinese and read widely in Chinese history. Thus at the age of twenty-seven he had a cursory Western education, was fairly proficient in Chinese history, and had prepared for the medical profession. His problem was that under British law he could not practice medicine in Hong Kong, and under the Portuguese law he was barred from practice in Macao.

His initial impulse, like that of K'ang You-wei before him, was to reform the Ching monarchy. In 1894 he went to Tientsin to present a memorial to the venerable viceroy Li Hung-chang, demanding (1) full development of the abilities of the people through education; (2) full development of natural resources, agricultural and mineral; (3) rapid and widespread industrialization; and (4) the unhampered flow of commerce, including abrogation of the treaties giving foreigners control over China's customs offices. He also recommended himself for a position in the government that would enable him to help institute these reforms. "Western languages, literature, politics, customs, mathematics, geography, physics, and chemistry," he wrote—"these I have had an opportunity to study in a general sort of way. But I paid particular attention to their methods of achieving a prosperous country and a powerful army and to their laws for reforming the people and perfecting their customs." Despite the timeliness of his petition and the impressive array of his presumed qualifications, Sun was not personally received by the viceroy. He did not get the job he sought. And his petition was brushed aside.

More important than he could have realized at the time was a meeting Sun had in Shanghai, on his way north, with a well-to-do but otherwise undistinguished merchant named Charlie Soong, whom he met at the Moore Methodist Church in the International Settlement. Soong was destined to play a key role in the history of modern China, partly through his patronage of Sun Yat-sen, but chiefly through the influence of his three daughters—one of whom became Sun's second wife years later, while another married a young militarist named Chiang Kai-shek and the third became the wife of China's wealthiest banker, H. H. Kung. A friendship between Sun and Soong quickly developed, and Sun stopped again at the Soong home on his way back from Tientsin. Charlie Soong arranged to have Sun's rejected memorial published in the September–October issue of Shanghai's *Review of the Times*—the first occasion on which Sun's views were presented to a broad "audience." There is no evidence that this brought Sun any special advantage; but his friendship with Charlie Soong definitely did, for thereafter Soong paid many of his travel expenses and introduced him to influential secret society chiefs. This was a distinct turning point in Sun Yat-sen's life; from then on he was to be not a reformer but a revolutionary.

When the futility of the Ching dynasty was displayed in Japan's easy victory over China in 1894–95, Sun took part in one of the sporadic uprisings against the monarchy in Canton, then escaped to Hong Kong. From there he went on to America and thence to London, to be with his friendly mentor, Dr. James Cantlie, who had just retired from the faculty of the Hong Kong Medical College. In London Dr. Sun's career very nearly came to an end, for he was kidnapped by staff members of the Chinese legation, who intended to return him to China to be executed. Through the efforts of Dr. Cantlie, who aroused the British government, Sun was rescued.

By this time, Dr. Sun had firmly learned a number of lessons: that the Chinese monarchy could not be reformed but must be replaced; that the new government should be egalitarian and representative, like those of the West; and that the principal requirements for revolution were twofold—to arouse the spirit of the Chinese masses and to win the sympathetic support of peoples (if not the governments) of the West. For such a major undertaking he had few resources—not wealth, or high status, or an organized following, or recognition as a leader either by his own people or by foreigners. What he did have was determination and the understanding that his only chance for success was to impress people with the force of his own ideas and his own personality. Opportunities were opened for him by the publicity given to the narrow escape in London. The incident also markedly increased his self-esteem and self-confidence. Sun himself attested that the event "shook the entire country, agitated Europe, and every country in the world." As one of his biographers wrote, "Thus, a few weeks before his thirtieth birthday, Sun was suddenly propelled onto the international stage as a celebrity."[12]

For the next several months Sun remained in London, reading in the British Museum from the works of Marx, John Stuart Mill, Huxley, Adam Smith, and Henry George. He readily accepted ideas of socialism, social justice, and human rights. He commenced giving speeches to groups of Chinese and to foreigners, always seeking to clarify his own ideas. He also began to organize secret societies of Chinese, pledged to liberate and renovate their homeland. With small resources—getting small gifts from friends, working in restaurants, and in general living precariously—he traveled in Europe, back to America, and on to Japan. In 1899–1900 he became involved in the Filipino revolt against the United States, and, in 1900, in an ill-planned revolt in China. Through his speeches and his secret societies, and by forming ties with labor unions, he became recognized as a leader of China's revolutionary movement. Always abroad, begging for funds, speaking to revolutionary groups, feuding with rivals, and encouraging sporadic local uprisings in China, Sun managed to keep in the forefront of the revolutionary sentiment. As a student of his career concluded, "Ultimately Sun's major contribution to the Revolution was his optimism. . . . And when the Revolution did break out, he was recognized as 'undoubtedly the prime mover.' "[13] Along with his persistence and his optimism, however, even more significant was the polarizing effect of his program, which he summarized as the Three Principles of the People. These were the rallying point, and they have continued to represent the principal current of his influence.

These principles, which Sun claimed emerged from meditation on Lincoln's phrase, "government of the people, by the people, and for the people," he formulated gradually during the years of his travels, while he was clarifying his ideas by developing them in speeches. The principles are that (1) China must have equality in the world community of nations; (2) the Chinese people must rule themselves democratically; and (3) there should be provisions for improving the social and economic welfare of the people. All three were goals without precise form or the means for accomplishing them. Sun was particularly vague about the third goal, but apparently chiefly had in mind fair taxation and decent working conditions in industry. He had no evident appreciation of the massive problems of China's enormous farm population. A fair assessment is that Sun Yat-sen was neither an organizer nor a philosopher but was a superb agitator.

In his autobiography, *Memoirs of a Chinese Revolutionary,* first published in 1918 and reissued in Taipei by the China Cultural Service in 1953, Sun wrote in chapter 2 that "understanding is difficult; action is easy." This was his lifelong credo. He was not an activist but a formulator of ideas. Much like K'ang You-wei, he believed that knowledge itself is action—that once people rightly understood a situation, they would react to it appropriately. Whenever in his own life he violated the principle, he came to regret it. Naturally, his revolution-minded followers wanted action, and sometimes he had to yield to their insistence. First in 1895, then in 1898, and eight times afterward, Dr. Sun authorized armed uprisings, none of which had any real effect. As has been noted, Sun himself took part in the 1895 uprising—and barely escaped with his life. For the others, he remained abroad, raising funds, sending supplies, and issued orders. The effect he was having was well stated by a journalist, George Lynch, in 1901: "When I went through southern China in October [1900] for the purpose of seeing something of the Rebellion, which was in progress near Canton, I was perpetually hearing of Sun Yat-sen. He was the organizer, the invisible leader, the strange, mysterious personality whose power was working it all." Lynch finally found Dr. Sun, living in Yokohama incognito and animated with optimism:

> He talked long and interestingly of his aims and projects. He has a good following of what he calls modernized young Chinamen, who have been educated in England, Honolulu, and in Japan, and among them men who are sufficiently wealthy to supply the requisite funds. . . .
> Seldom have I met a more interesting personality. There was that inexplicable something about him that stamped him as a leader of men, a personal magnetism about him that affected one strangely, a singleness of purpose to the end for which he was devoting his life that compelled admiration.[14]

Despite failure after failure, and in the face of seemingly insurmountable difficulties, Dr. Sun continued to animate his followers, assuring them calmly that "success will come to any measure that conforms with the natural laws, that follows the course of human understanding, that keeps in step with world trends, that answers the people's needs, and that has been discovered by men of superior intelligence."[15] Instead of always asking him "What shall we do?" Sun told them, they should persist patiently and systematically in trying to understand China's problems. Once their understanding was clarified, the requisite actions would follow necessarily and easily.

In 1906 Sun Yat-sen found another friend who would have great influence in his career, an American, Paul Linebarger, who was a circuit judge in the Philippines and who encouraged and counseled Sun throughout the remainder of Sun's life. Meanwhile Sun went on, tirelessly, from country to country, eating in greasy restaurants and staying either with friends or in shoddy rooming houses while soliciting funds and enlisting recruits. His persuasive speech and his courageous determination were his only assets, and his efforts were successful. He managed always to raise money enough to keep the revolutionary groups supplied with at least a minimal amount of materiel. Finally, on 11 October 1911, the Ching dynasty was toppled by revolutionary groups with which Sun Yat-sen had no direct communication.

He was on a train, traveling from Denver to Chicago, when he bought a newspaper in St. Louis and read that the revolution had succeeded, that the Republic of China was proclaimed, and that he was named its provisional president. With his customary calmness, he proceeded on his fund-raising mission, going on to Europe before returning to China. He arrived in Shanghai on Christmas Day, and his presidency was confirmed on 29 December.

On 12 February 1912, Sun resigned, to turn the office over to the commander of China's regular armed forces, Yuan Shih-k'ai, who had served the empress dowager well before deciding to cast his lot with the revolutionists. The circumstances were tangled but Yuan had the real power. Sun Yat-sen was no doubt reluctant but had no choice. At a meeting of his political followers, the Kuomintang (National People's party), in Shanghai on 5 October 1912, Sun described Yuan as "really a man of ability. . . . Some people in the south still distrust him, but I definitely believe in his sincerity. . . . In order to govern the Republic one must have a combination of new ideas, old experience, and old-fashioned methods. Yuan is just the right man."[16] Within a few months Sun had ample reason to change his mind.

In the meantime, Sun did what he did best—make speeches. As two of his biographers point out, "Public speaking was not at that time an established custom in China. Sun's public speeches were a modern development. His long years of speech-making outside of China had been superb preparation." Then they quote a description of his platform manner:

> He does not care to use the dramatic eloquence which appeals to the imagination and the passions of the masses, and which is usually found in political and religious reformers of the ordinary kind. . . . He spoke quietly and almost monotonously with hardly any gestures, but the intent way in which his audience listened to every word—his speeches occupy often three and four hours—showed me the powerful effect which he was able to exercise.[17]

Sun's change of mind about Yuan Shih-k'ai came quickly and was shared by most of those who had supported the revolution, both inside China and abroad. Yuan never was in favor of a republic; as a military man and as a monarchist, he distrusted democracy and saw no way to rule except by strength. With the army under his command he felt it was safe to dissolve the republic and to declare himself emperor on 1 January 1916. But this proved so unpopular that in March he restored the Republic. The imbroglio ended with Yuan's death on 6 June. After a long period of disorders and disunity, Sun Yat-sen was elected president of the Republic and was inaugurated on 5 May 1921. By this time Japan had sought to protect its interests in China by submitting a list of twenty-one humiliating demands. North and south China were separated. Warlords had taken advantage of the disorders and lack of government controls to establish their own armies to enforce their own administration in the provinces.. The Republic of which Sun became president was able to exercise authority over only a small area in the south of China, was deeply in debt, and had neither internal resources nor foreign allies.

These were the circumstances when the Communists seized power in Russia and, in 1920, established Communist parties in the various Asian countries. Sun Yat-sen was of course interested in the Russian Revolution and was sympathetic to its idealistic aims. In 1919 the Soviet Union issued a "Manifesto to the Chinese People" and claimed to be their only ally in their struggle for national freedom. In 1921 Lenin sent an emissary to Sun with a promise of the kind of help that was not available from other nations. In a fit of discouragement with his Western friends, Sun declared that "we no longer look to the Western Powers. Our faces are turned toward Russia."[18] He was grateful when the Soviets returned to China some of the territorial concessions that had been wrung from it by the Tsarist government. And he received cordially the diplomatic and military help that the Russians tendered. He appointed Chiang Kai-shek to military command and sent him to Moscow for a four-month study tour, after which the Whampoa Military Academy was established with Russian instructors. On 20 January 1924, Dr. Sun opened the first national congress of the Kuomintang, with women for the first time in Asia admitted as political delegates; and on Sun's recommendation, Communists also were allowed to be members. But Sun advised the congress that communism and the Soviet system could not be applied to China.

The question of Sun Yat-sen's relationship to communism has been endlessly debated. Beyond question he was sympathetic to its aims and grateful to the Soviet Union for its help. It seems equally clear that he never favored communism for China. What he really sought was assistance from any source, while insisting meanwhile on Chinese independence. At a meeting of the Kuomintang Executive Committee, he drew on a blackboard a large circle that he labeled "Kuomintang." Inside it he drew smaller circles labeled "Capitalism," "Communism," "Socialism," and "Marxism," among other isms. Then he explained that China had its own problems that were peculiar to its situation and history. Consequently it would have to work out its own solutions while learning all it could from all manner of foreign experiments.[19] To a Japanese reporter who interviewed him in November 1924, Sun said: "In China where industry is not yet developed, class war and the dictatorship of the proletariat are unnecesary. So today we can take Marx's ideas as a guide, but we cannot make use of his methods."[20] In a lecture to the Kuomintang membership on 10 August 1924, he declared that the concept of "class struggle" was meaningless in China, since "we should be aware that China's trouble is poverty, not unequal distribution of wealth."

What Sun Yat-sen did feel to be of the highest importance he showed clearly by his behavior during the last year of his life. His government was a shambles, his people were distraught by internal warfare and poverty, and his country was hard-pressed by Japan while neglected by its allies. He himself was dying of cancer and knew he had little time left. What above all should he do? What he did was to make speeches. He called together in weekly meetings some thousand officials of his party and government and delivered to them a series of lectures called the *San Min Chu I*, on the meaning of his Three Principles of the People.[21] This was his final and definitive heritage. It is these principles that are cited by both the Nationalist and Communist Chinese as the foundation on which they have built. Taken down by stenographers as they were delivered extemporaneously, these lectures have been reprinted again and again, both in Chinese and in many translations, as the veritable bible of Chinese nationalism.

The style of these lectures is plain, hortatory, expository, repetitive, and animated with examples drawn from ordinary life and observation. They illustrate, too, the most salient feature of Asian rhetoric: respect for tradition, for learning, and for the person of the teacher-leader, who does not have to prove his point but need only make it clear. A simple passage, typical in its style, will show the quality of Sun Yat-sen's reasoning—which some critics have derogated as simple-minded but which has the unanswerable strength of common-sense realism:

> What is the Principle of Nationalism? Looking back over the history of China's social life and customs, I would say briefly that the Principle of Nationalism is equivalent to the "doctrine of the state." The Chinese people have shown the greatest loyalty to family and clan with the result that in China there have been family-ism and clan-ism but no real nationalism. Foreign observers say that the Chinese are like a sheet of loose sand. Why? Simply because our people have shown loyalty to family and clan but not to the nation—there has been no nationalism. The family and the clan have been powerful unifying forces; again and again Chinese have sacrificed themselves, their families, their lives in defense of their clan. . . . But for the nation there has never been an instance of the supreme spirit of sacrifice. The unity of the Chinese people has stopped short at the clan and has not extended to the nation.[22]

The quality—but not the influence—of Sun Yat-sen has been disparaged by many. Perhaps the most insightful of his biographers found him "not a very original or profound thinker" and concluded that he was "disturbing because of the limitations of his mind."[23] An anonymous Englishman wrote scathingly that "it will be demonstrated that during his lifetime his chief claim to fame, or infamy, was his destructiveness; that on no single occasion did he display any real constructive ability; and that the political philosophy with which he appears to have infected the China of today is a sham and is based upon theories and arguments unworthy of a kindergarten pupil."[24] But even this harshest of critics could not avoid the fact that Sun's ideas have indeed "affected the China of today." Both in Taiwan and on the mainland, Sun Yat-sen is revered as the "founding leader." But, in both parts of divided China, there are also reservations about what he stood for. These are represented in a speech in Peking on 12 November 1956 in which Mao Tse-tung helped celebrate the ninetieth anniversary of Sun's birth. "Many great figures in history," Mao said, "who guided the march of events in a positive manner, had their shortcomings. Like them, Dr. Sun, too, had his shortcomings. We must explain this in the light of historical circumstances so that people may understand it. We must not be too exacting with regard to our predecessors."[25]

To some degree, diminishing as the years pass, Sun Yat-sen has been to modern China what Confucius has been throughout Chinese history. T'ang Leang-Li was speaking for the generality of his countrymen when he wrote: "As Confucius is the prophet of traditional China, Dr. Sun . . . may be regarded as the creator of the new China."[26] A Western liberal found him analogous to Woodrow Wilson, describing him as "a brave and honest theorist, inexorably wedded to policies at odds with life's nasty facts."[27]

It is true that Sun's Three Principles were scarcely advanced at all in his lifetime. Neither were they advanced significantly under the direction of his designated successor, Chiang Kai-shek. They remained, however, China's inspiring guidelines, and in later years two of them, at least—a status of equality in the world community of nations and a substantial improvement in the welfare of the people—have been realized. Perhaps more significantly, Sun Yat-sen's life of steadfast and courageous endeavor provided the Chinese people with a national hero and a legendary patriot as a focal point of sentimental unity. This was much for a village boy of simple parentage to achieve. Without him China would be poorer indeed. "The tendency of this movement," Dr. Sun told his followers in his 1924 farewell lectures, "is like the current of the Yangtze or Yellow River; it turns in many directions either to the north or to the south, but eventually flows eastwards, and nothing whatever can hinder it." It is this optimistic glow, more than Sun's program, that, in the words of Gustav Amman, "has given the initial impulse toward a new rise of Chinese consciousness, the momentum of which will never rest, toward a reorganization of the political and economic life of the Chinese continent."[28]

The Kuomintang Period: Nationalism on the Defensive

The aftermath of World War I both intensified Chinese nationalism and brought it under fire. As *New Youth,* an influential magazine launched in Shanghai in 1915, declared in its first issue: "The world continually progresses and will not stop. All those who cannot change themselves and keep pace with it are unfit for survival and will be eliminated by the process of natural selection." How fit would the new Republic of China prove to be? Disunited, weak, and uncertain of its direction, its prospects were not good.

International politics bore heavily on the Chinese. In 1915 Japan forced Yuan Shih-k'ai to accept proposals known as the Twenty-One Demands, which granted Japan extensive territorial rights in China, control over important mines, a veto over foreign investments in special areas, a special role in Manchuria, control over some railways, and employment of Japanese advisers in financial, political, military, and police matters. In 1917 China proposed to England, France, and Italy that the 1915 agreement with Japan and all extraterritorial rights to Chinese ports be abrogated, along with renunciation of all the unequal treaties that had been imposed on the country; but the Allies refused to accept this request. As German defeat impended, China requested of the Allies that the rights over Shantung Province that Germany had exacted be restored to China, but the Council of Foreign Ministers concluded that these rights should be transferred to Japan.

The spirit of nationalism had, however, been nurtured in China to such strength that nongovernmental forces began to be effective. To reduce the general illiteracy, Professor Hu Shih of Peking University launched a national Literary Revolution, including a simplification of the written language. In May 1919 students representing thirteen universities staged what came to be known as the May Fourth Movement to insist upon equality for China in dealings with other nations. Peking University librarian Li Ta-chao, viewing the Russian Revolution as the start of a new era for humanity, launched a program of New Asianism designed to combine all Asia in a socialist unity. Young intellectuals started a New Village Movement that repudiated the old class hierarchy. Culminating these initiatives, in March 1919 university students organized a Mass Education Speech Corps to take these new ideas directly to the people in nationwide meetings.

The chief enemy of Chinese nationalism, and the principal barrier to national communication, was warlordism, which dominated the country from 1916 to 1928.

For those twelve years, China was politically fragmented, divided among a host of warlords, large and small. Some controlled a district or two, some ruled a province; the most powerful exercised authority over two or three provinces. A national government continued to exist in Peking. . . . For most purposes, however . . . it was the creature of whatever warlord or warlord clique ruled the capital and its environs.[29]

As another student of the period put it, "Every petty military satrap was doing his utmost to squeeze more wealth, as well as endless manpower, from the peasantry for the support of his swollen ambitions."[30]

These were the general circumstances when Sun Yat-sen reorganized his political party, the Kuomintang, in 1924. The platform adopted by the party in its January meeting provided for "1) alliance with the Soviet Union in foreign affairs; 2) collaboration with the Chinese Communist Party in domestic affairs; and 3) creation of a strong base among the workers and peasants."[31] The party copied the Communist party system of organization, with strong centralized control on a base of local cadres that disciplined members and communicated the demands of the leadership to the local communities. This party, like Chiang Kai-shek who came to head it, was both liberal and reactionary in its nature. As Clubb pointed out, "Modern Chinese rulers have proved congenitally unable completely to divorce themselves from the thought patterns of emperors who governed China when it was dominant in Asia, and all the rest of the world was inhabited by 'barbarians.' "[32] This ethnicity was expressed by Sun Yat-sen in his lecture on "The Machinery of Government," which he delivered to his Kuomintang audience òn 26 April 1924:

For thousands of years China has been an independent country. In our former political development we never borrowed materials from other countries. China had one of the earliest civilizations in the world and never needed to copy wholly from others. Only in recent times has Western culture advanced beyond ours, and the passion for this new civilization has stimulated our revolution. Now that the revolution is a reality, we naturally desire to see China excel the West and build up the newest and most progressive state in the world. We certainly possess the qualifications necessary to reach this ideal, but we must not merely imitate the democratic systems of the West. These systems have become old-style machinery.[33]

Sun warned that foreign controls still kept China as a "semi-colony." This feeling stimulated anti-Japanese, anti-British, and general antiforeign sentiments in the decades after Sun's death. Chiang Kai-shek, in his turn, sought to face both ways: toward Western nations as friends and also away from them as underminers of Chinese sovereignty and as checks upon his own authority. To the list of foreign enemies Mao Tse-tung added the United States and, eventually, the Soviet Union.

Chiang's career was stormy, autocratic, harsh, weak, and eventually ended in at least partial futility. In some respects it was also highly successful. He has been interpreted as villainous by his critics, as heroic by his admirers. A balanced description presents him as purposive if not always effective:

Generalissimo Chiang Kai-shek, ruler at Chungking, is a remarkable character. Hard, shrewd, almost humorless, he is capable of studied urbanity and courtesy. . . . His tall, trim body is a contrast to the softness of some of his pudgy political generals. He is abstemious. He neither drinks nor smokes, and his handsome semi-foreign homes are not palaces. He is no mystic; he is Chinese and trusts to reason and not to intuition. He is no fanatic; ideas are things to be used, not to be victimized by. . . . He is not an intellectual; he is a politician. . . . He has cooperated with anyone who seemed useful to him, for as long as it seemed worthwhile.[34]

Sterling Seagraves, in his *Soong Dynasty,* portrays Chiang as akin to Hitler and Mussolini in dictatorial brutality, as drunken and licentious before and sometimes during his marriage to Mai-ling Soong, and as a gangster and hoodlum in his basic character. H. H. Chang, who served in Chiang's government, considered him an ideal sage and model states-man.[35] I had a thirty-five minute personal interview with the Generalissimo in 1956 and found him to be highly intelligent, as well as courteous and mannerly, despite whatever he lacked (was it strength of will, ruthlessness, cunning, or charismatic magnetism?) that kept him from uniting the turbulent Chinese nation and from winning the devotion of the masses of the people. As a leader he was no less an enigma than was Sun Yat-sen.

Born 31 October 1887 into a moderately well-to-do family living in a small town a little south of Shanghai, Chiang was reared by his mother, after his father's premature death. With five children to support, Mrs. Chiang made the necessary sacrifices to send her favorite son first to the Shinbo Gokyo Military Academy and then to the Japanese Military College in Tokyo. In Tokyo he met Sun Yat-sen, and when the 1911 revolution succeeded, Chiang returned to China to lead a small force that captured Hanchow, after which he was promoted to regimental command. When Sun was elected president of the Republic in 1921, Chiang resigned from the army to serve on his staff in Canton. Two years later Sun sent him to Moscow to study military and political tactics for four months. When Chiang was leaving Moscow, Trotsky said to him, "Patience and activity are the two essential factors for a revolutionary party, and the one complements the other."[36] It was advice that Chiang sought to incorporate into his own guiding principles. Chiang disliked what he saw of communism, but he did admire Trotsky's military genius. After his return he was named director of the Whampoa Military Academy, which was built with Soviet funds and organized in the Soviet manner. Chou En-lai was named as Chiang's assistant, to keep a supervisory eye on administration. At this time Chiang's view of Russian communism, much like Sun's, was that "our alliance with the Soviet Union, with the world revolution, is actually an alliance with the revolutionary parties which are fighting in common against the world imperialists to carry through the world revolution."[37]

After Sun's death, Chiang was named commander in chief of the armies of the Republic and waged successful warfare against dissident forces in the north. When his army captured Nanking, his contingent of Communist soldiers committed outrages against the civilian population, apparently in a deliberate attempt to discredit Chiang. Chiang then turned against his Communist allies in Shanghai, killing some five hundred of them and imprisoning many more. His break with communism was now complete, for which reason he began getting favorable notices in the European and American press. But within the Executive Committee of the Kuomintang, Communist members were conniving to have Chiang dismissed as army chief. Abruptly, on 12 August 1927, Chiang resigned, issuing a lengthy statement explaining why he had worked with the Communists and was now determined to wage war against them: "Chinese Communists tried to outdo the Russians in their plots and conspiracies. What was the result? By professing to be Kuomintang members in a halfhearted fashion and adopting deceptive methods they have tried to disorganize our military and party affairs."[38]

He withdrew to live in a Buddhist temple beside his native village, where he received a steady stream of visitors and adherents. One visitor was Miss Mai-ling Soong, to whom Chiang was married on 1 December. The two had long been acquainted. They were very different: She was thirteen years his junior and had been educated in Macon, Georgia, and at Wellesley College. She was a devout Methodist and so Americanized that, as she wrote, "the only thing oriental about me is my face."[39] Chiang was a Buddhist, did not speak or read English, and was already married to a second wife (which marriage he conveniently ignored). Concerning Mai-ling's personality, her college classmates recalled that "she kept up an awful thinking about everything. She was always questioning, asking the nature of ideas. She was a stickler for truth, and resented any discovery that she had ever been fed any conventional misinformation."[40] Chiang considered the marriage into the powerful Soong family to have political significance, and on their wedding day he issued a revealing statement: "The work of the Revolution will undoubtedly make greater progress, because I can henceforth bear the tremendous responsibility of the Revolution with peace at heart. . . . From now on we two are determined to exert our utmost for the cause of the Chinese Revolution."[41] And so they did.

Within ten days following the marriage Chiang was restored to command of the armies and in addition was given control over the Government Council. His first act was to break diplomatic relations with Russia. He announced that China would be governed by military power until full control over the country was achieved. Then there would be a period of "political tutelege" to prepare the way for eventual democratic elections. After this, constitutional government would be instituted. In short, the people were to be ruled by force rather than by persuasion. For a time this system appeared to work. Armed rebellion was suppressed and on 4 October 1928 a constitution was adopted by the Government Council, and Chiang was named president.

The real problems remained to be solved. The Kuomintang was deeply divided into right-wing and left-wing groups. Both the Soviet Union and Japan were pressing demands upon China. The budget was deep in deficit and the soldiers could not be paid. The warlords continued to demand independence. The nation was woefully weak economically, the people were largely illiterate, and there was no adequate means of countrywide communication. A climax came in 1931 when Japan seized Manchuria and parts of northern China. Despite the problems, "the government of Chiang Kai-shek . . . gave China its best administration in a century."[42] This is probably true, for it was a century of chaotic disintegration.

Instead of going to war with Japan, Chiang undertook a two-pronged effort to strengthen China. One part of his program included asserting control over China's customs revenues, speeding industrialization, expanding transportation facilities, and developing a stronger educational program. The other part consisted of a relentless war against the Communists who, in 1931, held some three hundred thousand square miles in south-central China. He dealt them defeat after defeat, with the result that the remaining Communist troops were forced into the "Long March" in 1934–35 that covered six thousand miles; some twenty thousand of them survived to reach their remote base at Yenan. After this, in 1936, left-wing soldiers of the Chinese army captured Chiang and demanded that he abandon his war against the Communists and instead launch war against Japan. Chiang scornfully refused to treat with them, saying they had to choose between killing him or accepting him as their commander in chief. His captors freed Chiang, fearing that otherwise the Kuomintang would come wholly under control of its right wing and might even unite with Japan to expel communism from China.

A new turn of affairs began on 7 July 1937, when Japanese troops seized the Marco Polo Bridge, a vital railway junction near Peiping. Even then Chiang sought to avoid war, but Japan pushed ahead. On 9 August the

Japanese captured both Peiping and Tientsin, announcing that they had come to "protect" the people. Chiang was forced to make peace with the Communists, who placed their armed force under his command as the Eighth Route Army, although it retained its separate identity with its own Communist officers. One other condition the Communists imposed was that Chou En-lai be admitted to Chiang's government as chief of propaganda. In this post Chou organized an extremely large propaganda organization designed to accomplish the twofold task of converting the Chinese people to communism and convincing foreign newsmen and diplomats that the Chinese Communists were "agrarian liberals" who were oppressed and misrepresented by the "corrupt and reactionary" Kuomintang. Chiang rendered this propaganda objective easier by intensifying the brutal activities of his secret police apparatus.

In 1939 when the Soviet Union signed a pact with Nazi Germany, the Soviets ceased to require the Chinese Communists to cooperate with Chiang, and open warfare broke out between the two Chinese groups. Under attack from both the Chinese Reds and the Japanese, the Republic was driven back to a new capital in Chungking. Then the Western powers, in order to avoid war with Japan, closed the Burma Road, the only route over which vital supplies could be delivered to Chungking. After Pearl Harbor, the U.S. Congress voted to provide $500 million in military aid for China, but delivery of supplies was possible only for the small amounts that could be flown in over the Himalayas. The Chinese generals were so weak and corrupt that resistance to Japan was minimal. The American embassy in Chungking became convinced that Chiang must be forced to establish a coalition with the Communists. Meanwhile, at Yenan, Mao Tse-tung was steadily building his military strength and popular support, and Chou En-lai was winning the propaganda battle for both diplomatic approval and domestic Chinese acceptance of communism.

The period of greatest success for Chiang Kai-shek and his wife had been 1933–37, while his campaign against the Communists was succeeding and before the Japanese attack. Both of them did a great deal of speaking. This was their major effort to strengthen their leadership through communication with the people.

Madame Chiang was active in the YWCA and in the Shanghai Child Labor Commission. She founded schools for Children of the Revolution and converted the Officers Moral Endeavor Association into a series of discussion clubs. "Today a large part of her work is in public speaking," her biographer pointed out.[43] Initially shy, she soon became mistress of the platform and became widely known not only in China but especially around the world. Her principal themes were denunciation of opium, dirt, and poverty, along with advocacy of women's rights, social reforms, and acceptance of personal social responsibility. These speeches had far less effect in China than they had on foreigners. As another of her biographers found, "May-ling had negligible impact on the Chinese people, but attracted enormous attention among foreigners. Wherever she went, she spoke to foreign missionaries and to women's clubs. . . . She marshalled the foreign wives, the church groups, and the missionary men to her side."[44]

After the outbreak of war with Japan in 1937, Madame Chiang spoke often to the American people, both via radio and on visits to the United States. Her speeches were not conciliatory but blunt, with overtones of irony and sarcasm. Assailing America's continuing support for Japan, she said:

Tell me, is the silence of Western nations in the face of such massacres, such demolition of homes and dislocation of businesses, a sign of the triumph of civilization with its humanitarianism, its code of conduct, its chivalry, and its claims of Christian influence? Or is the spectacle of the first-class Powers, all standing silently in a row as if so stupified by Japan that they do not utter a reproach, a forerunner of the collapse of international ethics, of Christian guidance and conduct, and the death knell of the supposed moral superiority of the Occidental?[45]

In another radio program addressed to Americans that was broadcast on 1 April 1940, her sister, wife of the wealthy banker H. H. Kung, said soothingly, "When I am speaking to America I know that I am speaking to truly sympathetic friends of China. We have evidence of that sympathy in a much-needed practical flow of contributions to our relief funds." Following her, Madame Chiang, in contrast, very forthrightly declared, "We of China ask that a stop be put to one of two things: either the Congressmen, who are the lawmakers of America, should stop expressing horror at aggression, or they should stop encouraging aggression by permitting gasoline, oil, and other war materials to go to Japan."[46] Madame Chiang had no intention of veiling her real meaning behind soothing words. She was still the Wellesley girl, outspoken and fluent, with nothing oriental about her but her face.

Generalissimo Chiang's effort to strengthen his leadership through communication and persuasion commenced in early 1934 with his launching of the "New Life Movement." His aim was to unify and raise the morale of the people through appeals to the traditional Confucian virtues of propriety, justice, integrity, and conscientiousness (*li, i, lien,* and *ch'ih*). "To look back at the civilization of the past," Chiang told the people in his radio address on 19 February 1934, "is the best way to improve present trends of thought, and what has been handed down to us from the civilization of 5,000 years is the crystallized result and handiwork of years of pioneering experience." He identified the deadly sins as self-seeking, concern for "face," cliquishness, defeatism, and evasion of responsibility. To replace these he outlined eight guidelines for right living:

1. Regard yesterday as a period of death, today as a period of life. Let us rid ourselves of old abuses and build up a new nation.
2. Let us accept the heavy responsibilities of reviving the nation.
3. We must observe rules and have faith, honesty and shame.
4. Our clothing, eating, living and travelling must be simple, orderly, plain and clean.
5. We must willingly face hardships. We must strive for equality.
6. We must have adequate knowledge and moral integrity as citizens.
7. Our actions must be courageous and rapid.
8. We must act on our promises, or even act without promising.[47]

In the midst of military disasters, social disintegration, hardships verging on mass starvation, and venality in the very structure of the government, Chiang chose to preach cleanliness, courtesy, and self-respect. From the perspective of Westerners, this New Life Movement and the speaking Generalissimo Chiang and his wife did in supporting it were signs of their utter futility. Within the Chinese tradition, however, this movement was typically and healthily correct. Confucius's basic teaching was that when evils afflict the state, individuals can do their part by setting their own lives in order. In any event, the Chiangs believed sufficiently in their movement to devote considerable attention to it.[48]

In addition to their own frequent speeches, they organized two hundred groups of students who were given training in public speaking and were sent around the country lecturing on the movement. Thirteen lecture centers were established. The birthdate of Confucius, 27 August, was dedicated to meetings and speeches on behalf of the New Life Movement. Nationwide rallies were organized, with banners bearing such slogans as "Be Prompt," "Don't Crowd," Keep in Line," "Don't Spit," "Be Neat," "Kill Flies and Rats." Opium suppression became a principal concern of the movement. For two years enthusiasm mounted; but it was already diminishing when the outbreak of war in 1937 diverted attention from it.

Six or eight years later, while Chiang's government was barricaded in the mountain fastness of Chungking and he, like the whole population, was desperately weary of what seemed an endless war, Chiang continued to speak frequently to audiences of officials (as Sun Yat-sen had done), but he did so almost mechanically.

These speeches, delivered in a high-pitched voice of quite extraordinary monotony, so that the words had a hallucinatory effect, were always variations on the themes of Dr. Sun Yat-sen's three principles. He spoke without notes and most of his audience knew what he would say during the speech after hearing the first words. He never entertained any new concepts, never permitted himself the least deviation from the accepted doctrine. . . . He was the ancient sage endlessly repeating the unchanging tablets of the law, following a ritual that had been handed down through the centuries.[49]

In short, his speaking was typically Chinese in the traditional mold, not aiming to arouse emotional fervor, simply taking acquiescence for granted.

The Generalissimo also spoke frequently to his troops, again with morale building as his aim. An extract will suffice to show how he combined self-castigation, exposition, logical deduction, muted emotional appeal, and hopeful prophecy. The speech was given to soldiers going to battle, but it seems aimed instead at the intellectuals, domestic and foreign, who would read it later. It was carefully calculated to show that eventual victory would emerge from current defeat:

> How can we resist the enemy? . . . We are not fit to be called a modern state . . . Dr. Sun plainly told us: "China occupies the status of a semi-colony." What is a semi-colony? It is a country which is oppressed or protected by a group of nations, thus becoming a common colony of them all. . . . Because of the fact that China is virtually a semi-colony, Japan wishes to swallow her alone. First of all, she must conquer the world. As long as Japan is unable to conquer the world, she cannot destroy China or dominate Asia. . . . Internationally and diplomatically, we stand for justice and righteousness, whereas Japan represents suspicion and enmity. If we could strengthen ourselves, we would find friends all over the world. No matter how powerful Japan is militarily, she is already placed in isolation.[50]

The defeat of Japan in 1945 proved that these views were at least partly prophetic. The general tenor of the speech also supported Dr. Sun's principle that understanding is more urgent than action. Why, then, was the outcome so detrimental to Generalissimo and Madame Chiang Kai-shek and to the cause of democracy in China? Perhaps it means that Sun Yat-sen was wrong—that understanding, however clear and correct, cannot substitute for prompt and decisive action. Another reason of perhaps even greater significance was stated by a biographer of Chiang who concluded his account by saying: "But he had nothing to match the technique of relentless mass persuasion which Mao developed."[51]

The lesson of 1949, when Chiang was forced to withdraw from mainland China to the refuge on Taiwan, is that leadership without effective communication to build a base of popular support proves, in words borrowed from Sun Yat-sen, to be no better than a rope of loose sand. Persuasive communication might not have saved Chiang Kai-shek's rule over China, but the lack of it surely proved to be decisive. Where he sought to lead, the people did not choose to follow.

Mao Tse-tung (Mao Zedong): Master of Mass Persuasion

As the Pacific war drew to its end in the mid-forties, China remained neither united nor modernized. Some new kind of leadership was needed. K'ang You-wei was powerfully attractive to a small group of intellectuals, but he lacked mass appeal. Sun Yat-sen was a master image-builder, at his best in face-to-face persuasion, but he was not able to deliver his message to the deeply divided Chinese people. Generalissimo and Madame Chiang Kai-shek failed to win the favor of the population. Their successor, Mao Tse-tung, so well mastered mass propaganda that he swept China into nationhood if not into modernity. It is in these terms that an anti-Communist Chinese historian assessed Mao's accomplishments:

In retrospect one has to agree that there has always been a myth surrounding Mao. He was acclaimed a genius, a revolutionary prophet, and the "creator of New China". In the remotest corner of the huge country, no household was complete without his portrait on the wall and his works on the table. Even toddlers were taught to thank him for everything—a sweet, a bowl of rice or a toy. If ancient emperors were accepted as Sons of Heaven, Mao was Heaven (God) itself. On the strength of the all-prevailing propaganda apparatus, the Mao cult was firmly established. Fed on the ignorance and superstition of the ordinary people, it became a religion and a way of life.[52]

Essentially the same point was made by an editor of Mao's speeches and writings, who said that "for Mao, as for every other revolutionary, the central problem which subsumes all the others is that of combining effective leadership with broad participation, in order to achieve a radical transformation of society." In this, as the editor added, Mao was following the teachings of Lenin, but with a significant difference:

Lenin had defined democratic centralism in terms of organizational principles: freedom of discussion, but absolute acceptance of decisions once adopted; consultations with the rank and file, but absolute obedience of lower organs to higher organs. Mao, too, accepts these principles, but characteristically he poses the problem not only in terms of organization, but in terms of communications. . . . [Mao's system] implies that only if people are consulted will they subsequently be in the right frame of mind to accept the decisions of the leading organs once they are elaborated, and to work willingly and wholeheartedly for their implementation.[53]

Like Lenin and Stalin, Mao used the stick to beat his people into compliance. He also used the carrot of personal advantage to win their eager aquiescence. How he did this is illustrated by a speech he made to his troops as they were set to make a raid into Sichuan Province in January 1928: "The gentry and the landlords are stinkingly rich there, piles of silver dollars lie asleep under the floorboards, waiting for us to make good use of them. When we get there we must deal the wicked gentry heavy blows, take the money and mobilize the masses."[54]

This is how Mao Tse-tung won China: with a combination of ruthless force, appeal to the self-interest of his adherents, and a constant flow of direct and two-way communication. Of the three, the last was probably the most effective. Chiang Kai-shek had used the other two, but without the third he had not succeeded.

A vital account of how Mao won his persuasion campaign after 1949, when he had full political control, is related by a Catholic missionary priest, Father Eleutherius Winance, in a book of reminiscences entitled *Communist Persuasion*. Father Winance remained in China after the Communist takeover in order to care for his parishioners. He was soon jailed and afterward sent out of the country. Meanwhile he observed what amounted to a nationwide conversion of the population to communism. Partly, this was accomplished by new laws enforced by relentless police power. But far more fundamentally, the conversion was through an all-encompassing system of persuasion. What the people were to know and what they were to think about affairs was presented to them by a vast, well-integrated, uncontradicted panoply of information services—schools, newspapers, radio programs, films, public speeches, wall posters, books, and periodicals. Every source of information relayed the same stories, with the same interpretations. This vast pressure upon the minds and the feelings of the people was difficult to resist or to doubt. But, as Father Winance observed, there was yet another factor that he believed to be decisive. That was the mandatory discussion meetings, held weekly or even thrice-weekly, in which all Chinese were required not only to listen to what the government wanted them all to hear but also to rise in the meeting to state and to restate an eager and complete acceptance of the truth and the significance of what was being said. As Father Winance concluded, no one is strong enough to resist such persuasive campaigns, in which only one truth is uttered and in which that version of truth is repeated voluminously and monotonously from all sides, plus the vital factor that the individual is required to utter the same message in his own words and with his own emphasis. This was the Mao Tse-tung pattern of persuasive communication.[55]

Mao had a hard-headed peasant practicality that led him to undertake any task by doing first what lay immediately at hand. It was in this way that he set about taking his persuasive campaign to the people, during the years in which he was rising in power but still was far from attaining complete control. He began with his own army troops. To them he stressed three principles that they were to follow: (1) establish unity among officers and soldiers, with all bearing similarly the hardships and sharing the rewards of their campaigns; (2) maintain unity of the soldiers with the people by refraining from exploiting them and by helping them in all available ways; and (3) seek unity even with the enemy by attempting to win the allegiance of soldiers who were captured.

The next goal was recruitment of the intellectual elites, such as "lawyers, journalists, and teachers, students of the humanities and social sciences, philosophers, novelists and poets . . . men with a vision of the future and men who speak and write well."[56] In order to win their allegiance, there had to be focal points to attract them. In part these were slogans and goals that emphasized the good life that would come to China after it was cleansed of its "exploiters". With such points from which to start, the intellectuals could spell out the details. Beyond this there had also to be organization. Basically, the Communist party (officially inaugurated on 1 July 1921) served this function. As early as 1931 "the Chinese Communist Republic," based in a remote portion of south China, had been proclaimed. There were annual conventions in which emergent leaders could meet and find guidance. In addition, since public attention centers upon personalities more readily than on abstract issues, special efforts were made to emphasize the transcendent merits of "the great leader," thus developing what came to be known as the personality cult.[57]

By these and other means—including Mao Tse-tung's penchant for presenting his views and his programs in lengthy speeches—persuasion was developed as a key factor in the governing of Communist China. So important was it that many experts agree that "of all the ways of characterizing the first decade and a half of the Chinese Communist regime the one that may be most likely to elicit consensus among the widest range of observers is to stress Peking's efforts to mobilize mass activities and participation."[58] As to how this was brought about,

> the broad picture that emerges centers on Mao. . . . Acting in accord with his consciously held beliefs as well as his more primordial sentiments and manipulized to an undeterminable degree by the bureaucracies over which he presided, Mao constantly intervened in the decision making processes to bring fresh policy initiatives to areas of concern to him and to give renewed vigor to languishing pet programs. The major way in which he brought his will to bear was to convene informally a small group of party officials. There, he heard the range of opinions of his associates in remarkably lively policy debates, and then

he issued a summary of his views, which he expected to be translated into action.[59]

Along with utilizing every resource to spread his own ideas, Mao also took care that contrary ideas would not be heard. Although he repeated again and again that his government was "democratic" and truly represented the people, he carefully defined democrats as those who agreed with his policies. In defining what kind of rule he planned for China, he wrote on 30 June 1949 a brochure, *On the People's Democratic Dictatorship,* in which he excluded from civil rights all whom he considered to be enemies of the people. "That is, the right of reactionaries to voice their opinions must be abolished, and only the people are allowed to have the right of voicing their opinions." In justification of this policy, he argued that "here, the method we employ is democratic, the method of persuasion, not of compulsion. When anyone among the people breaks the law, he too should be punished, imprisoned, or even sentenced to death; but this is a matter of a few individual cases, and it differs in principle from the dictatorship exercised over the reactionaries as a class."[60] His reasoning was devious and obscure but his conclusion was clear. There was one truth, only one truth, and that was his.

His vision of truth came to him not suddenly but over a span of years while his mind was maturing. He was born into a well-to-do farming family in Hunan on 26 December 1893. His parents were illiterate and his father was domineering and unfeeling. Nevertheless, Mao was able to attend school at intervals, when education did not interfere with work on the family farm. During a brief period in middle school he commenced to read avidly about Western civilization. Between 1912 and 1918 he attended the Hunan Normal College, where he spent every available hour in the school library. "During this time," he later recalled, "my mind was a curious mixture of ideas of liberalism, democratic reformism, and Utopian Socialism. I had somewhat vague passions about 'nineteenth century democracy', Utopianism, and old-fashioned liberalism, and I was definitely anti-militarist and anti-imperialist."[61]

In 1918 he left home and went to Peking as propagandist for a pacifist organization. In 1920, inspired by his reading of Karl Marx and his admiration for the Russian Revolution, he joined with seventeen comrades to found the Chinese Communist party. When a schoolmate argued with him that China could be modernized better through democratic freedom than by Communist totalitarianism, Mao replied: "If the leaders have no power, it is impossible to carry out plans, to obtain prompt action. The more power the leader has, the easier it is to get things done. In order to reform a country one must he hard with oneself and it is necessary to victimize a part of the people."[62] Stuart Schram, a careful analyst of Mao's political theories, called him "an admirer of violence in the service of justice," and quotes from his works what he considers to be Mao's guiding justification for the ruthlessness of his rule: "A revolution is not the same as inviting people to dinner. . . . A revolution is . . . an act of violence whereby one class overthrows the authority of another."[63]

In 1950, after Mao had gained control over the whole of continental China, Western newsmen found more about him to admire than to condemn, more to like than to dislike. Typical is the following assessment:

> Now turning 57 [he is] somewhat taller than the average Chinese, with a moon face and an increasing poundage that is dissolving the sensitive, almost feminine, facial features of earlier years. What kind of man is he? Even in the days when Mao was accessible to Western journalists, he emerged as a complex, many-sided personality that defied a pat characterization. There was the individual Mao, the omnivorous reader, the keen appreciator of ideas, the lucid pamphleteer and orator, who spoke with almost Jesuitical logic and who wrote essays on education, art, and literature as well as a manual on guerrilla warfare. On the other hand, there was the Mao who doted on his small daughter and who, like many Chinese, was deathly afraid of flying in airplanes. There was a bluff, gregarious, down-to-earth Mao, who could speak the idiom of the peasant; who tended his own tobacco patch and who once took off his trousers to make himself more comfortable during a military conference. A diffident Mao, who asked for "advice" from his interviewers; the romantic Mao; and the aloof and sometimes mystical Mao. Above all, transcending these many aspects of his personality, today as in the past, there is the shrewd, coolly calculating, patient and utterly realistic Mao, steeled in revolution.[64]

To this description it should be added that Mao was careless and disheveled in his dress, with his clothing loose-fitting and with his socks often falling down over his shoetops. In his speech he freely interjected racily profane terms common among the peasantry. He refused to speak over the national radio since his Hunan vernacular would lessen the image he sought as the father figure of all China. He was indeed Chinese to the core, with the typical characteristic of his generation of both revering the traditional past and reaching beyond it to a new and different future. Only twice in his life, and then briefly, did he leave China—in 1950 and in 1957 for trips to Moscow. He spoke often and spoke well, with an air of easy authority and confident assurance, explaining what the people should understand and believe about a wide range of subjects. Most importantly, he defined what he meant by patriotic devotion, as the standard around which all the people should rally. When China became his to rule, he addressed the first plenary session of the Central Committee on 21 September 1949, triumphantly asserting that "China has stood up!" Their triumph, he claimed, was complete:

> Henceforth, our nation will enter the large family of peace-loving and freedom-loving nations of the world. It will work bravely and industriously to create its own civilization and happiness, and will, at the same time, promote world peace and freedom. Our nation will never again be an insulted nation. We have stood up. Our revolution has gained the sympathy and acclamation of the broad masses throughout the world. We have friends the world over. . . . The era in which the Chinese were regarded as uncivilized is now over. We will emerge in the world as a nation with a high culture. Our national defense will be consolidated and no imperialist will be allowed to invade our territory again. . . . Let the domestic and foreign reactionaries tremble before us.[65]

The promising start of Mao's rule was soon disturbed by the entry of China into the Korean War in November 1950. From his point of view it proved to be a sound decision, with results that abundantly compensated for the extensive loss of Chinese lives. The century of humiliation marked by Western invasions, seizures of territory, and multiplied forms of insults was fully avenged by the success of the Chinese Communists in forcing the United Nations to abandon its proclaimed goal of reuniting Korea. Henceforth the Chinese had a national hero who defended their sovereignty and their dignity against the combined force of seventeen nations. This was the foundation upon which was erected the image of Mao's invincibility and transcendent superiority. It was an image that had to be massively supported by an extremely large propaganda apparatus, for it conflicted with palpable evidence of inhumane severity and dictatorial suppression of individual rights. The people had little to celebrate and much of which to complain.

In February 1957 Mao sought to allay the widespreading dissatisfactions of the populace by announcing a new policy of freedom of discussion that urged everyone to set forth new ideas for improving conditions under the slogan "Let a Hundred Flowers Bloom." Mao was badly shaken by the enormity and vigor of the protests that broke out against his totalitarian rule, and within six weeks he made another speech, "On the Correct Handling of Contradictions among the People," in which he abruptly declared that "the days of national disunity and turmoil which the people detested have gone forever." During the remainder of that year the government systematically rounded up and punished those who had dared to accept the invitation to speak their minds. In February of the following year, Mao once again undertook to accomplish revolutionary goals by slogans. Calling for a "Great Leap Forward," he demanded a sweeping renovation of society, with impossible goals for production of grain, steel, and all manner of products. In what came to be called the Cultural Revolution, the intellectual elites were stripped of their jobs and sent into the country to work on farms, and a frenzied period of persecution by the youthful Red Guards was unleashed to ferret out and punish everyone who deviated in speech or in act from the pursuit of Mao's impossible goals. Idealism had by now yielded to force, with Mao proclaiming that "Political power grows out of the barrel of the gun. Our principle is that the party commands the gun, and the gun shall never be allowed to command the Party."[66]

Excesses of this magnitude could not continue, and Mao's power began to erode. Surrounded by evidence of failures, Mao turned against one after another of his chief associates and agents, blaming them for what was going wrong. When he died on 9 September 1976 the government and the party were in disarray. After great, if only partial, success had come failure. The transition Mao Tse-tung guided toward nationalism and modernization advanced and then retreated, with the essential repairs waiting to be made by others after he was gone.

Enrica Collotti Pischel, in a brilliant study of Mao's rise and decline, assigns priority in both stages to his mode of communication. First he rallied the people through his skill in sloganeering; then he lost authority because persuasive simplification did not suffice to solve the complex problems.

> Mao has elaborated a whole series of themes whose effectiveness with the Chinese masses can scarcely be appreciated by a European. This capacity for fertile and popular syntheses constitutes a fundamental instrument in the effort to call forth and direct the revolution in China, and also, within certain limits, for carrying over part of the momentum of the revolution to the period of peace and building of socialism. But it is of less and less weight as the technical and objective problems of building socialism come to take precedence over armed revolutionary struggle. In a more complex society, . . . Mao's "simplifications" lose part of their effectiveness.[67]

It was unfortunate both for Mao and for China that he did not abide by the political theory he set forth in his speech of 27 February 1957, before an audience of eighteen hundred of China's elite. Briefly he toyed with liberalism, and then abandoned it. Perhaps today the trend in China is toward the sentiments set forth by Mao in that speech:

> Even in a Communist country, conflicts of interest must arise. The state might want more centralism, the people more democracy. The state might pay more attention to overall and longterm interests, the people to

their immediate wants. . . . All this was inevitable and should not cause worry. . . . Discussion, not force, was to be the method by which disputes were to be solved.[68]

Unfortunately, for himself and for China, he did not believe this deeply enough.

Chou En-lai: Prophet of Chinese Nationalism

Chou En-lai, who was Communist China's chief spokesman to the outside world and also its most effective propagandist to its own people, was born in January 1898 and died in January 1976, some five years younger than Mao Tse-tung but otherwise almost his exact contemporary. The two worked together in the closest harmony, differing greatly in their personalities but very much akin in purpose and ideology. Mao was a born leader; Chou was equally suited to be the top aide and chief assistant. Both were skilled propagandists—Mao in formulating and stating ideas, Chou in engineering their acceptance. A veteran China hand, reporting for the *New York Times,* believed that Mao became an abstract deified mythic figure, whereas Chou was "the real folk hero . . . a revered and sympathetic leader to turn to in time of trouble." Continuing this analysis, Fox Butterfield wrote on the first anniversary of Chou's death:

> Part of Chou's appeal was that he seemed to embody all the virtues the Chinese admire and used to associate with a Confucian gentleman. He was intelligent, kind, gracious, and modest, shrewd without being scheming, ambitious and forceful without being overbearing. He was also a good diplomat and conciliator, ready to repair the damage done by Mao's more apocalyptic style.[69]

A Western journalist described Chou in terms that Westerners admire, two years after Japan's 1937 invasion of China, while Chou served as the liaison between Mao Tse-tung and Chiang Kai-shek:

> His manner was lively, almost gay; and he moved his hands in deft, sudden gestures. He spoke current English with perfect ease, but with an occasional French turn of phrase or a French word to help out a sentence. Dark eyes were youthful and animated, and lit up as soon as he began to talk. He had an unaffected charm, and the power to convince of the born orator.[70]

In the spring of 1954, at the Geneva Conference on Korea and Indochina, I observed him in action over a period of weeks, while he dominated both the formal conference sessions and the even more important daily press conferences. Despite the important roles played by the American, British, and French delegates and the special appeal of the North Korean, South Korean, and Indochinese delegations, Chou En-lai was unquestionably the star performer and the focus of attention. The cause he represented—trying to convince the world that the war in Korea was caused not by a Communist but by a South Korean attack—kept him in a palpably impossible situation. As a veteran news reporter said to me, "Everyone tells lies. I do. You do. It's natural and it's easy. But it surpasses understanding how Chou En-lai can look us all in the face, with that remarkable innocent expression of his, and lie deliberately day after day, when he knows that we know that he knows he is lying. That is difficult. But he makes it seem easy."

Unlike Mao, Chou was no peasant. He was born into an aristocratic family of no great wealth but was raised in succession by two wealthy and influential uncles, after his father's premature death. As his biographer says, he was the most sophisticated among Communist world leaders and the most durable, holding high party posts and receiving considerable international attention for more than half a century. He proved to have high survival value, coming through the tangle of relations between the Communist party and the Kuomintang, and afterward the brutal period of the Cultural Revolution, with his reputation unscathed and his position secure. Like the other central leaders in China's revolutionary transition, Chou En-lai was an enigma difficult for the West to understand; little of his personal life was known even to the Chinese. Stories about him in the world press bore such headlines as "Red China's Gentleman Hatchet Man," "The Elastic Bolshevik," "The Rubber Communist," and "The Chinese Sphinx."[71] Not much is known about what Chou was really like.

His grandfather was a high official under the Ching dynasty. His father was a brilliant teacher. His mother was a well-informed and critical-minded lover of literature. The 1911 revolution captured Chou's imagination and swept him into liberalism. In middle school and at Nankai University in Tientsin, both of which were partly supported by the Rockefellers and by missionary funds and were strongly influenced by Christianity and other Western ideas, Chou learned English and read Darwin, Mill, and Rousseau, along with Chinese history. When the United States offered to use its share of the Boxer Rebellion indemnity to educate young Chinese in American schools, Chou eagerly applied and was despondent at not being selected. Had he been chosen, recent Chinese history might well have been different. During his four years at Nankai, Chou did exceptionally well in languages and social studies and surpassed his fellows in passionate discussions of the international issues raised by World War I and by internal Chinese problems as Yuan Shih-k'ai betrayed the Republic, and the country fell into political chaos.

At the age of nineteen Chou graduated from Nankai in the year of the

Russian Revolution, went to Japan to enroll in Kyoto University, and commenced to study communism. Like many in his generation he was distraught by the urgency of China's political, social, economic, religious, and cultural changes and was humiliated by the pressures exerted by Japan and Western nations. One evening among friends Chou burst into a speech that marked a new beginning in his life:

> You cannot salvage China with strong leadership alone. You must have strong followers to support the leadership. You have to start with a complete re-education of the younger generation—and the older generation if that's possible—of the students, the workers, even the peasants. You must have them all with you before you can push a revolution to success. And without a revolution, China cannot be saved.[72]

He followed this speech with action by organizing student groups to agitate against the Allied powers for their refusal to stand by China against Japan, and by commencing a series of hotheaded editorials in the student newspaper, of which he was editor. In September 1919 police raided the newspaper office and Chou was taken to a cold, damp, windowless prison cell where he remained for four winter months. It was then that he became a Communist and a revolutionary. Years later, in commenting on the experience, he said that it was like jumping out of bed on a winter morning. "It was chilly at first but much warmer later because of the chill."[73] When he was released from prison he went to Paris to continue his education and to start organizing Chinese overseas branches of the Communist party. He earned his living as an automobile mechanic, while editing a magazine called *The Red Light,* trying to unify the various groups of Chinese in Europe, and mediating their disputes. His abilities were maturing:

> The united front Chou tried to achieve in Paris was not a complete success, but his approach became a respected hallmark of his later statesmanship. In a heterogeneous assembly his tact and quick thinking never failed to set him above the rest. Always the master of the situation, particularly a confused and violent situation, he chose the line for the crowd to follow. At times he did not hesitate to launch a severe attack on his opponents, but immediately after the attack he always softened his voice to explain away the point in dispute, emerging in triumph as a resourceful peacemaker.[74]

In 1924, Chou returned to China, eager to help Sun Yat-sen stabilize the Republic. Sun appointed him political deputy to Chiang Kai-shek for the Whampoa Military Academy, which Sun hoped would become China's West Point. With this appointment Chou was in the center of the troubled alliance between the Chinese Communist party and the Kuomintang, and between China and its domineering Soviet ally. During the next ten or fifteen years Chou was deeply embroiled in trying to interpret Moscow's demands to the Chinese Communists and in explaining to the Soviets why conditions in China prohibited the country from adhering closely to the Russian patterns. When in the 1930s Mao Tse-tung finally rebelled against the Moscow-dictated "city strategy" (including both concentration on organizing industrial workers and launching direct military attacks against Chiang's fortified positions) and decided instead to base his program on the peasantry, Chou En-lai went along with him and became thenceforth Mao's principal propagandist and front man.

It was in 1927 that Chou En-lai broke decisively away from Chiang Kai-shek and the Kuomintang. In that year, under Chiang's orders, Chou went to Shanghai to organize the communication and transportation workers and to call them out in a general strike that enabled Chiang to capture Shanghai without a battle. Within a month Chiang decided (rightly enough) that Chou's geniune loyalty was to the Communists and ordered that he be arrested and executed. Chou escaped and commenced an underground campaign against Chiang. When Chiang was captured by Communist troops at Sian in December 1935, it was Chou En-lai, acting in accord with Moscow, who negotiated his release. After Japan's invasion of China in 1937, Chou sought to achieve a working allegiance of the Communists and the Kuomintang against Japan, and these efforts led to this appointment as propaganda minister under Chiang after the United States entered the war against Japan. In this position Chou was very successful both in converting masses of Chinese to communism and in convincing the United States and European nations that Chinese communism was not only distinct from the Russian brand but was in effect little other than liberal agrarianism.

When the People's Democratic Republic of China was proclaimed in September 1949, Chou En-lai was named foreign minister and busily set about winning advantages for Communist China at the Geneva and Bandung conferences and on special diplomatic missions to India, Burma, and throughout Africa. In all this, Chou sought to enlarge the famous dictum of Clausewitz that "war is the continuation of foreign policy by other means." Chou broadened and sharpened the concept by declaring that "all diplomacy is a continuation of war by other means."[75] The diplomatic means he used were camouflage, deception, encirclement, and, when necessary, direct denunciation or attack. Far more than is customary in diplomacy, Chou achieved much through the sheer force of his own personality.

His general attractiveness has seldom been questioned. Chiang Kai-shek called him "a reasonable Communist."[76] Foreign newsmen were intrigued by "his sparkling eyes, the rapid shifts of those bushy, expressive eyebrows and the ironical quirk of the wide mouth."[77] Freda Utley "found it hard to believe that Chou En-lai, who charmed me as he did everyone else, is a liar and a cheat."[78] Ping-Chia Kuo, counselor of the Foreign Ministry in Chungking, who had many dealings with Chou, noted the "skillful blending of threat, suspense, and cool calculation"[79] that Chou manifested in conferences with diplomats of other nations. A veteran *New York Times* correspondent, Tillman Durdin, issued a warning that during the war years was not often heeded: "At the beginning Chou overwhelms you by the force of his personality and his clever arguments. But after hearing him month after month and year after year, you realize you can't trust what he says. He has contradicted himself too often."[80]

The cleverness in argumentation on which Durdin commented is well illustrated in a single paragraph from a long speech that Chou delivered on 15 June 1956 to an audience of thirteen hundred delegates to the First National People's Congress, in Peking. As was typical of his speaking, his "real audience"—the one he most wanted to influence—was the world outside of China, particularly, in this case, the Congress of the United States:

China is a newly risen nation. We know that a newly risen nation, especially one which is a great power, often cannot be fully understood by other countries within a short period, and frequently arouses apprehension. If to this fact are added the calculated slander and instigation by certain quarters, such lack of understanding and such apprehension could even be aggravated. But slander and instigation will not stand the test of facts, and apprehension and lack of understanding can also be removed through observation and actual contact over a comparatively long period. In this conviction, we have always welcomed people in all walks of life from all countries to China and we have tried our best to meet their requests during their visits. We do not exaggerate our achievements, nor do we hide from them our shortcomings. We hope that by observing the concrete process through which the Chinese people are moving from backwardness to an advanced state, they will see that the Chinese people have oriented themselves in the direction of peaceful construction and that they urgently desire peace. What we seek is not praise but mutual understanding and trust. We also sincerely hope that, without reservation our guests will point out our shortcomings so that we can improve our work. It is possible that some among those who originally harboured suspicions about us will retain their suspicions. We shall not be disappointed at this, for we are convinced that through continued observation and contacts they will gradually understand us better. We certainly welcome a change in the attitude of those who were originally prejudiced against us or hostile towards us, but if they retain their original attitude, it will be no loss to us.[81]

The persuasive pattern was carefully contrived. China was misunderstood. The fault lay with hostile slanderers. China welcomed investigation and would gladly abide by the judgment of observers. It would also welcome criticism from which it might learn to improve. The Chinese want nothing but to be understood. They realize that some critics are unfair—and "if they retain their original attitude, it will be no loss to us." It all seemed so natural, so reasonable, that it could not be denied—if only it also were true.

Persuasion was the principal instrument of the Communist leadership, as Mao Tse-tung and Chou En-lai thoroughly believed, and in working at it together, in their separate roles, they were masterful. Madame Sun Yat-sen, a perceptive observer of the process, pointed out the potency of ideas that are persistently and persuasively disseminated: "It is not the gun but the ideological make-up of the man behind the gun that determines the outcome of any conflict."[82] Another Chinese observer of the Communist persuasive program believed that it was based on the ancient traditions of hierarchy and acceptance rather than a belief in individual assertiveness. As he phrased it, the guiding principle behind the mass propaganda was that "man's mind is . . . plastic, and passive, powerless against the mould-ing force of the society moving according to a 'law' nobody can change and only some can understand."[83] Mao Tse-tung had no doubt that it was by persuasive communication that China was won and controlled. As he said: "In settling matters of an ideological nature or controversial issues among the people, we can only use democratic methods, methods of discussion, of criticism, of persuasion and education."[84] He neglected to mention what at other times he freely admitted, the brutality of his brain-washing techniques, deceptive spread of misinformation, strict cen-sorship, massive execution of disbelievers, and intensive control systems.

What Chou En-lai accomplished is indicated in the judgment of him by the United States secretary of state Henry Kissinger, who called him "the greatest statesman of our era."[85] It was Chou En-lai who initiated the "ping-pong diplomacy" that eventuated in President Richard Nixon's his-toric trip to China in 1972. From his youth until his death, his was a guiding voice, shaping the responses to Mao's policies, both inside China and around the world.

Conclusion

From K'ang You-wei to Sun Yat-sen and Chiang Kai-shek, then on to Mao Tse-tung and Chou En-lai, China proceeded in a tortuous course from semicolony to united nation. The leadership that guided develop-ments depended on modes of persuasion that were suited to the Chinese situation. China is a crowded land, inhabited by a fifth of the world's population. It is a land of cities and villages, where individuals live crowded together.

It is this fact of living always submerged in a crowd that, in the judgment of an able Chinese scholar, makes the Chinese more receptive than other peoples to mass movements and mass propaganda. As he points out, "There is next to no privacy; private life consists nearly entirely of public life, and the need for psychological adjustment to one's environment is forced on the mind in every minute of one's existence."[86] In such an environment, individualism is necessarily subordinated to the group. As Sun Yat-sen pointed out, Chinese history had been dominated by "familyism" and "clanism"—and was in search of nationalism to transcend such local ties. Because of the communal nature of Chinese life, harmony was considered to be the greatest need, greater than personal advantage and greater even than justice. There must be agreement; there must be consensus; there must be acceptance of whatever seemed to satisfy the group. Peer pressure and authority were effective guidelines.

Such factors made the masses unusually susceptible to persuasion, especially when it came from an authoritative source and appeared to be acceptable to the group. As I found in my own study of the roots of Chinese culture: "Uniqueness and individuality were regarded as eccentric, to be condemned not admired. The personality type favored by the Chinese was not that which attracted attention to itself by being different but that which manifested the wisdom of conformity to the social norm." Along with this there developed another characteristic that made the Chinese people pliable under masterful persuaders:

> It also was a cardinal characteristic of traditional Chinese culture that no one person could possibly be intelligent enough or experienced enough to develop a particularized insight that could be equal to the understanding clarified through the multiplied intelligence and experience of past generations. The authority of a venerated past, as distilled in the words and acts of great sages and revered historic personages, came to exercise a dominant role in Chinese culture. The authority of tradition came, thus, to have a more convincing effect than even direct observation and personal experience. It was more likely that a person would be wrong about what he thought he saw or felt than that the condensed and evaluated wisdom of the past could be misleading. Hence, proverbial sayings were often quoted and were heard with respect.[87]

As all students of recent Chinese history agree, the centralist controls exercised by the Kuomintang and then by communism represented not a break with the past but a continuation of the age-old tradition of rule by the emperor. K'ang You-wei, Sun Yat-sen, Chiang and Madame Chiang Kai-shek, Mao Tse-tung, and Chou En-lai all sought to align themselves with this concept. Power flows from the center. Guidance must be provided from the top. This was the theme on which nationalism developed in modern China.

3

India: The Way to and from Satyagraha

In India the development of modernization and the emergence of nationalism posed very special challenges for leaders to confront and surmount. The making of any nation involves a vast complexity of problems, both internal and external. A goal must be set. Popular enthusiasm to support that goal must be aroused. Means must be discovered or devised that will prove to be workable and effective. In India problems such as these were magnified. It is a high tribute to the Indian character that leadership of the right kind and of the required ability proved to be available.

Different circumstances in Japan, and then again in China, produced types of leadership that could not have solved the problems in India. The deeply implanted social structure of India, the abysmal poverty and lack of economic development, cultural factors that opposed modernization, and devoted or even fanatic adherence to beliefs and practices that defied unity combined to magnify the difficulties. That both modernization and national independence could be achieved within a generation or two seemed incredible. Yet both have been won—by impressively persuasive leadership. What is no less impressive is the emergence of leaders who differed as much among themselves—in their personalities, their methods, their programs, and their policies—as they did from national leaders in other parts of Asia.

Indian Disunity

Indian civilization is older even than that of China, and its traditions were deeply and firmly established. Unlike Japan and China, India never had been a nation. What it did share with them was a cultural dislike for much that Western civilization represented. Along with this, however, there was also a reluctant feeling and understanding that the Western world's general characteristics had to be accepted and at least partially adopted.

What Asians found least compatible with their own traditions was the egotism, the individualism, the competitiveness, the emphasis on self, the striving for personal advantages on earth and for the salvation of a person- alized soul after death that contrasted Western civilization with China's humanistic, hierarchal, and communal modes of thought. India was dif- ferent. Its belief in Karma (or individual responsibility) and the trans- migration of souls made its social psychology as individualistic, in its own special way, as that of the West. But it was not the Western kind of individuality. What attracted Asians generally to the West was the over- whelming evidence of its success, not only in accumulating wealth and power but also in creating and sharing temporal satisfactions and well- being. Those who sought to lead the people had first of all to attain their own understanding of what new synthesis should be sought and then of how to get it accepted. In Japan the audience that mattered was chiefly the Japanese people themselves. In China it was not only the Chinese people but also their potential, or desired, or overbearing allies. In India's pro- gression toward nationhood the audiences that had to be persuaded were primarily Great Britain, world public opinion, and the very diverse, deeply divided, and largely illiterate masses of the people.

The magnitude of what happened almost surpasses comprehension. A weak and divided people without military organization, without diplo- matic support, and without industrial or economic strength had to displace the rule of Great Britain, which had been in effect for two centuries. One explanation is that this took place simply as a part of the dissolution of colonialism in most parts of the world. Colonialism, however, did not disappear automatically, and its end did not derogate from the necessity for leadership able to guide and shape the nationalism that took the place of colonial subordination. In India what had to be overcome was not only British strength but the multiple weaknesses of India. Sun Yat-sen found divided China to be no more cohesive than a rope of loose sand. Yet in comparison with India, China was by far more unified, more cohesive, more amenable to political leadership.

India was a geographical expression, the name of a subcontinent. As Ali Jinnah said in his speech to the Muslim League conference in 1922, "It must be realized that India never was a country or a nation." There was an encompassing Indian culture but it was not nationalistic. In one sense it was universal, incorporating not only all mankind but all sentient beings; and in another sense it was sharply, and deeply, and decisively, divisive. The Buddhism that developed in India was pushed out into other coun- tries. Hinduism was not nationalistic and did not encourage political practicalities. Hinduism was not a simple entity but was broken apart into contentious sects. Meanwhile, millions of Indians were not Hindu but Muslim, or Jain, or Sikh, or adherents of other smaller faiths, all inher- ently and aggressively inimical to one another.

Indians speak some five hundred different languages, of which fifteen, spoken by the largest number, are mutually unintelligible.[1] During six generations of British rule, English became the second or even the first language of a small elite class of aristocrats, officials, and merchants who also assimilated aspects of European culture. But this had the effect of dividing the natural native leaders from the bulk of the population. Linguistic differences continued to be a major barrier to the communication between Indian leaders and the people.

Another kind of divisiveness was the existence of the independent princely states. According to an expert on constitutional government in British India,

> The Indian States presented a unique problem, and a highly complex one, in the progress to independence. They varied enormously, from principalities the size of France to petty estates unworthy to be ranked as political entities yet neither part of British India nor subordinate to any other government. . . . Some of the States were ancient monarchies . . . others were fragments from the breakup of Mogul dominion . . . a few were deliberate creations of the British.[2]

Queen Victoria's proclamation in 1858 declared that "We shall respect the rights, dignity and honour of Native Princes as our own," but it also decreed that "the States were to have no dealings with each other on any political matter." The states were in some degree united by railways, trunk highways, and the telegraph and postal systems. They remained separated, however, in their administration, in their laws, and in the aims and ambitions of their rulers. No one could speak for their people except their own hereditary rulers, and it was difficult for any outsider to speak to them on questions of nationality. The states were effective barriers to unity.

The linguistic, cultural, and political characteristics that separated the Western-educated elite from the people of India were enhanced by a dilemma with which the British colonizers had to deal. What should they do about Indian cultural practices, some of which were repugnant to outsiders? Such practices as the burning alive of widows on the funeral pyres of their husbands, the betrothal of newly born children, and marriages by the age of ten or twelve were among many that were deplored by the British public as cruel and barbaric.[3] But they were deeply meaningful to Indians, and the British Raj (the colonial government) permitted their continuance on the ground that foreign rulers ought to interfere as little as possible with native culture. Westernized Indians were caught in the heart of this dilemma. When many of them adhered loyally to the culture of their ancestors, their Western education made them feel both guilty and ashamed, which led to mingled feelings of disgust for their own society and people and distrust of themselves as split personalities, incapable of being true both to their ancient traditions and to their modernized understanding. The confusion that they felt about themselves was fully matched by the skepticism concerning them that was felt by the general Indian public. All this was a handicap that had to be overcome by leaders seeking to communicate with followers and to persuade them to support nationalistic programs.[4]

Even more deeply and sharply divisive was the Indian system of caste. For many centuries the population was divided according to membership in one or another of three major castes and, beyond this, into some three thousand subcastes, or *Jatis*. Individuals were born into a caste and could leave it only by death. Marriage outside one's caste was prohibited, and between members of different castes social relations were distant, merely formal, or nonexistent. Caste membership dictated the kinds of employment available to individuals, the manner of their dress and adornment, even their methods of eating and of personal toiletry. Modes of speech were special for each caste, and communication from one to another was strictly governed by traditional rules. Far more decisively than the class distinctions that have been common in all parts of the world, and that were particularly rigid in pre–Meiji Japan, India's caste system stratified and fragmented the society.

These various kinds of divisiveness, singly but especially cumulatively, made leadership across the spectrum of India's diverse societies incredibly difficult. Nationalistic leadership was inhibited not only by these problems but also by widespread illiteracy and by a severity of poverty that made it difficult for the mass of the people to be interested in anything other than their immediate and pressing needs. Yet despite all the handicaps, leadership on a national scale did develop, and it did so in profusion, involving large numbers of leaders, and with impressive effects.

A major factor that favored communicative leadership was that members of the top caste, the Brahmins, were the religiously and socially designated speakers and leaders to whom the people were to listen and whom they were, in general, to obey. Another consideration is that traditionally the culture of India has been oral, with meanings shaped and shared in direct, face-to-face communication, thus enhancing the influence of revered or highly regarded leaders. Still another factor is that from time immemorial, public speaking and debating on fundamental issues were central parts of Indian life.[5] This is a cultural factor that has persisted in modern times. As a student of the Indian scene points out: "The techniques of agitation were thoroughly developed in pre-independence days. The simplest agitation is the public meeting, where inflammatory speeches are made, a petition is promoted, and a long protest procession, with banners and loud-speakers, winds its way through town."[6]

Inasmuch as the principal function of members of the Brahmin caste was to be opinion makers in the community, inevitably there were a great many leaders who sought to guide the transition of India to nationalism and modernity. One biographical compendium lists forty-seven of them,[7] and an equally long list of others could readily be compiled. India was far from lacking in leadership, even though one name, one man, one personality, came to transcend all the others.

Mohandas K. Gandhi, who came to be called the Mahatma (or the saintly one) and Gandhiji (or the revered Gandhi), was by far the most influential of them all. But had it not been for his associates, his influece might have been more hurtful than helpful. His crusade involved disastrous ideas that had to be curbed and reshaped by others. This is why the nationalist cause proceeded for a time toward satyagraha (civil disobedience, or soul-force) and then away from it.

Other leaders whose influence was most effective included Sri Aurobindo Ghose, a zealous mystic; Subhas Chandra Bose, a militant extremist; Manabendra Nath Roy, whose career ranged from revolutionary militarism to international communism and finally to liberal humanism; Jayaprakash Narayan, a close associate of Gandhi, whose devotion to social justice led him from Gandhism to Marxism and then back to Gandhism; Motilal Nehru, who did much to strengthen the Congress party; and Jawaharlal Nehru, Motilal's more famous son, who was drawn away from his early leaning toward communism by admiration for the effectiveness of Gandhi's theories of nonviolence, and who rejected Gandhi's primitivist and religious emphasis in order to develop a more realistic program of democratic and industrial socialism. All of these merit serious consideration. But the campaign to liberate India and to renovate Indian society can be traced through the leadership of Sri Aurobindo, Gandhi, and Jawaharlal Nehru, with deviant tendencies led by Roy and Bose. Their intelligence, their dedication, and their moral fervor provided the Indian people with a heritage to greatness that is an inspiration also for the world. All of them were keenly aware that they did not and could not have stood alone. Organization was necessary, and for this they had sturdy and capable help.

The Indian National Congress

"The History of the Congress is really the history of India's struggle for freedom."[8] The Indian National Congress provided two essential kinds of opportunities for Indian leaders to communicate with the people and thus to make their leadership effective. For one thing, it was a political party with local units in every section of the country, in the boroughs of every city, and in virtually every village, thereby comprising a channel through which the leaders could deliver their messages to the population at large. In addition, it was also a central forum, holding annual conventions at which prospective and acknowledged leaders confronted one another face to face to debate the issues and to contend for victory for themselves and their ideas. It served, therefore, much the function of the British Parliament, plus the organizing function of the major British political parties. Yet it was an appendage of the government, not a key part of it. It is unique to India, and it provides a unique setting for a study of national leadership that depends upon persuasive communication. Paradoxically, the Congress was organized not by Indians but by a Briton.

In March of 1885 Mr. Allan Octavian Hume, a Scot who had retired from the British Indian Civil Service and who was frustrated by the lack of qualified Indians to serve in subordinate positions in the Raj, wrote a letter to Indian leaders inviting them to meet the following December to organize an all-India congress. The country was ready for it. Some 475 newspapers were in circulation, mostly in provincial languages. Schools and universities were established, spreading ideas of democracy. Political organizations were established in Bombay, Calcutta, Madras, and some other places. Hume thought it would be useful if these organizations sent representatives to an annual meeting, where social problems would be discussed under the chairmanship of a British official, with political issues kept off the agenda. As its historian notes, from this modest beginning, "it soon became a powerful and authoritative exponent of the political ambitions of the people of India."[9]

During its first decades the speaking in the Congress generally dealt with problems that the delegates felt the British should and could solve. The speeches consisted of

a reasoned appeal to the authorities for the redress of grievances and a moderate demand for the new concessions and privileges. This frame of mind soon developed into an art. Forensic talent on the one hand and richly imaginative and emotional eloquence on the other were soon brought to bear on the task that lay before the Indian politicians. An irresistible statement of facts followed by irrebuttable arguments to prove the justice of the popular cause are to be met with everywhere in the speeches supporting the Congress resolutions and the addresses delivered by Congress Presidents. The burden of these utterances was that the English people are essentially just and fair, and that if properly informed they would never deviate from truth and the right.[10]

In this spirit, the Congress was hailed as a great and useful institution by both the Indian leaders and the British. It was a forum in which proposed reforms could be considered in a spirit of mutual trust. It was in this spirit that a delegate declared in 1893 that "we happily live under a Constitution whose watchword is freedom and whose main pillar is toleration"; and five years later another said, "The educated classes are the friends and not the foes of England—her natural and necessary allies in the great work that lies before her."[11]

The change of mood in India may be traced to some degree to the Japanese victory over Russia in 1904–1905, which greatly enhanced the self-confidence of Asians. Even earlier, however, dissident voices began to be heard. In the 1893 Congress, for example, delegate Pandit Malaviya pointedly referred to the worsened economic conditions under English rule:

> Everyone sitting here is clothed in cloth of British-make—almost every-one—and wherever you go, you find British manufactures and British goods staring you in the face. All that is left to the people is to drag out a miserable existence by agricultural operations and make infinitesimal profit out of the little trade left to them. In the matter of the Services, in the matter of trade, our people are not enjoying one-hundredth part of the profit and gain which they used to enjoy fifty years ago. How then is it possible for the country to be happy?[12]

The dissatisfactions, however, went little further, in the main, than to petition for increased benefits. Only a few radicals, denounced by most of their own associates as "extremists," were venturing onto new ground. Their demand was not yet for independence, but for autonomy—for home rule under the British Crown. This was the new spirit that was aroused and that grew as it spread.

A Patriotic Mystic: Sri Aurobindo Ghose

At the 1906 convention of the Indian National Congress party, one of the delegates, Bar Gangadhar Tilak, made a rousing speech in which he defined a developing attitude, identified viable means for communicating it, and set forth the goal to be attained:

> One thing is granted, namely, that this government does not suit us. . . . We are not armed and there is no necessity for arms, either. We have a stronger weapon, a political weapon, in boycott. We have perceived one fact, that the whole of this administration, which is carried on by a handful of Englishmen, is carried on with our assistance. We are all in subordinate service. This whole government is carried on with our assistance and they try to keep us in ignorance of our power of coopera-tion between ourselves by which that which is in our own hands at present can be claimed by us and administered by us. . . . Self-govern-ment is our goal; we want a control over our administrative machinery.[13]

This speech inspired a young man who in a brief span of four years won for himself a position in the Indian independence movement akin to that held by K'ang You-wei in China—that is, he lighted a flame that served the whole people as a guiding inspiration. Aurobindo Ghose was born in Bengal in 1872, the son of a westernized wealthy doctor who was determined that his son should grow up completely Europeanized. The boy was sent at the age of five to a convent school and then for thirteen years, until he was twenty, he studied in England, removed from all Indian influences. In 1893 he returned to India to serve in the British Civil Service. Here his father's hopes for him were disappointed. Aurobindo felt himself so alienated from his Indian fellows that he flung himself into intense study of Hindu literature, philosophy, and history. By the time he heard Tilak's speech he was saturated with Indian thought. Because of his British education, with its nationalistic culture, it was natural for him to think of India as a nation. With youthful zeal, he became overnight a fanatic nationalist.

Aurobindo led a large Bengali delegation to the 1907 Congress party convention, and for the next three years he poured out a stream of fervent speeches and journal articles that not only aroused a large national following but also were inspirational for Gandhi. Their theme was clear-cut:

> We wish to kill utterly the pernicious delusion that a foreign and adverse interest can be trusted to develop us to its own detriment, and entirely to do away with the foolish and ignoble hankering after help from our natural adversaries. . . . Whatever our hands find to do or urgently needs doing, we must attempt ourselves and no longer look to the alien to do it for us. And we would universalize and extend the policy of defensive resistance until it ran parallel on every line with our self-development. We would not only buy our own goods, but boycott English goods; not only have our own schools, but boycott government institutions; not only organize our league of defense, but have nothing to do with the bureaucratic executive except when we cannot avoid it. . . . Passive resistance may be the final method of salvation in our case or it may only be the preparation. . . . In either case, the sooner we put it into full and perfect practice, the nearer we shall be to national liberty.[14]

In a speech that he made soon thereafter in Bombay, Aurobindo was swept into a passion of religious fervor:

> Nationalism survives in the strength of God and it is not possible to crush it, whatever weapons are brought against it. Nationalism is immortal; Nationalism cannot die because it is no human thing, it is God who is working in Bengal. God cannot be killed, God cannot be sent to jail. . . . Have you got a real faith? Or is it merely a political aspiration? Is it merely a larger kind of selfishness? . . . You are merely instruments of God for the work of the Almighty. Have you realized that? If you have realized that, then you are truly Nationalists; then alone will you be able to restore this great nation.[15]

The religious sanction that Aurobindo sought engulfed him. A Hindu holy man advised him to abandon all thought so that supra-mental power could fill him. He left his wife and his home in Bengal to spend the remaining forty years of his life in solitary meta-meditation and in writing. His influence continued to the point that India as a whole began to transcend its many divisions, so that individuals of all languages, of all faiths, of all castes were becoming part of the same nation. This was a great step that had to be taken, and no one else managed it as decisively as Aurobindo did. After this lesson, it was easier for Indians to feel themselves bound together—except, as it turned out, that the split between Hindus and Muslims was not bridged but accentuated. And for this, Aurobindo himself was at least partially to blame.

In contrast with his constructive accomplishments, he made one basic mistake. That was his assumption that the nation was a religious entity—that it was a creation and an instrument of God. Far from separating religion from politics, Aurobindo proclaimed and emphasized their indivisible unity. Politics, he taught, must be brought to the religious test. Only political action that was motivated and directed by religious faith, he insisted, could succeed. This, too, was a theme that proved to be attractive to Gandhi. It came to dominate the Indian independence movement.

No doubt the zealousness it inspired gave powerful impetus to the mass enthusiasm that was aroused. Unquestionably it inspired the selfless spirit of sacrifice that induced great numbers to set aside their daily tasks and to accept the punishment, including hunger, thirst, beatings, and imprisonment, that resulted from the vast demonstrations, marches, and boycotts, and the violations of British laws.

But it had the tragic effect of identifying political policies with religious beliefs. This not only led to the partition of India into two hostile nations but also to holy wars and massacres involving not only Muslims and Hindus but also Sikhs and adherents of other faiths. In India from ancient times, to be intensely and inclusively religious in thought, feeling, and action was embedded in the culture.[16] Partly because of the preaching of Aurobindo, and in more urgent degree from the teaching and example of Gandhi, religious dedication became a hallmark of Indian nationalism. Other leaders, notably M. N. Roy, Subhas Bose, and Jawaharlal Nehru, perceived the danger in this religious-political unity and sought to avoid it. But their programs introduced problems of different kinds.

Their careers were intertwined, and these men influenced one another as well as the course of events. Mahatma Gandhi was the center around which they revolved, either to support or to oppose his measures and his methods. As a leader who guided the emergence of India as a nation, Gandhi by no means stands alone, but his personality towered over and dwarfed the others. How he lived and what he lived for has been endlessly discussed in an outpouring of books. But all accounts agree in stressing his spiritual depths.

Mohandas K. Gandhi: Prophet of Nonviolent Resistance

Gandhi belonged to a family that was aristocratic, wealthy, conservative, and orthodox in its devotion to Hinduism. Transcending this background, he made a career of befriending the poor and the outcast and of leading a revolution against constituted authority and tradition, while living and working in sympathetic rapport with Christians and Muslims. Yet fundamentally he remained true to his ancestral Hindu traditions and loyalties. Gandhi was a revolutionist not for modernism but in significant ways against it. Both his aims and his methods were derived largely from India's past. Yet nothing like him had been known in India or anywhere else. He was an anomaly who made his own rules, lived according to his own standards, and won scores of millions of converts to his unnatural and demanding principles. Gandhi looked the twentieth century in the eyes and did not like what he saw. And he convinced many in his own country and around the world to seek with him the visionary purity of a primitivistic past.

Gandhi was born on 2 October 1869 into a family that on his father's side, had supplied three generations of prime ministers for princely states. His father was sternly dutiful; his mother, deeply religious. As a child he was very shy, unsocial, and with little intellectual curiosity or indication of any special abilities. At the age of thirteen he was married by parental choice to an illiterate girl and became a passionate, jealous, and tyrannical husband. As a high school student he became a secret meat-eater—in violation of the most sacred canons of his religion—and he stole money from the family servants with which to buy cigarettes. "Moreover," as he later recorded, "I was a coward. I used to be haunted by the fear of thieves, ghosts, and serpents. I did not dare to stir out of doors at night. Darkness was a terror to me. It was almost impossible for me to sleep in the dark, as I would imagine ghosts coming from one direction, thieves from another and serpents from a third."[17] This was the unpromising beginning out of which, at the age of eighteen and already a father, he left for England to commence the study of law.

During three years of study in England, Gandhi undertook to make three speeches, each a dismal failure. As a secretary of the Vegetarian Society, he wrote out a brief speech for a debate on the qualifications for membership, but he was so embarrassed that the president had to ask someone else to read it for him. Then he accepted an invitation to speak at a public meeting held to promote vegetarianism. Again he wrote a brief speech, but when he arose to read it, "My vision became blurred and I trembled, though the speech hardly covered a sheet of foolscap." While a friend read it for him, Gandhi sat "ashamed of myself and sad at heart for my incapacity." The third experience was at a party he gave for a few intimate friends when he was leaving England. After dinner, several arose to make brief speeches, and Gandhi was expected to speak, as the host. "I had with great care thought out one which would consist of a very few sentences," he recalled. But he could not proceed beyond the first sentence.[18] During two years of unsuccessful law practice in India, after his return home, he was no more able to meet the urgent demands for oral discourse. In 1893, he left for South Africa, glad to leave the scene of his failures in India and assured of a substantial fee for what he was promised would be an easy case in Natal. Thus far, both personally and professionally, his life had been largely a failure.

There were, however, mitigating aspects. A veteran English lawyer had directed his interests in what proved to be the right direction by assuring him that knowledge of the law was of little value; that what was needed instead was a close acquaintance with human nature.[19] His own readings in religion, including the Bhagavad-Gita and the New Testament, led him to the conclusion that "morality is the basis of things."[20] He was led by admiration for the writings of Tolstoy and Thoreau to believe that moral force could and should be used to overcome entrenched social evils. When he arrived in South Africa, intending only a brief stay, he was intellectually and spiritually prepared to respond strongly against what he observed of the pattern of discrimination against the Indian minority there. How he responded to these injustices determined the future course of his life.

After a period of unprecedented success at the bar, when his income rose to three thousand pounds a year, he underwent a regime of *bramacharya,* or self-discipline, and surrendered his law practice to devote himself entirely to leading a nonviolent movement for Indian rights. He established "Tolstoy Farm" as a refuge where Indians might live simply, close to the soil, without dependence on machines, and free from English dominance. He was several times imprisoned for encouraging Indians to violate the laws limiting their civil rights. Twice he was beaten: once by Europeans for his civil disobedience activities, and once by Indians for his insistence upon nonviolence. During the Boer War and again during the 1906 Zulu rebellion, he abandoned his pacifism to organize an ambulance unit in support of the British, for he felt that in these conflicts they were in the right. In 1913, he led a mass demonstration of two thousand Indians who refused to obey a law requiring their special registration as aliens with limited political privileges. Prime Minister Jan Christian Smuts developed a deep respect for Gandhi, and the discriminatory law was repealed. Finally, in 1914, after some twenty years in Africa, he returned to India with a philosophy and a method by means of which he hoped to assist his nation to independence. He was ready, finally, to commence his real career.

The goal he set was *swaraj,* or self-rule, for India. The method was to be satyagraha, which directed individuals to join together in a mass movement of nonviolent civil disobedience.

Gandhi became a leader in the Indian National Congress party, but was far from dominating it. A significant majority favored gradual reforms and ultimate independence when India should be "ready." This group concentrated upon urging the English to build more schools and hospitals and to admit more Indians into the civil service and to higher positions in the colonial government. Opposing them, Gandhi insisted that any acceptance of British rule was compromise with evil. In 1919—to protest the Rowlatt Acts, which prohibited Indian meetings and free speech—Gandhi called for nationwide noncooperation, including the withdrawal of all Indians from English schools and hospitals and from all government appointments.

The agitation that he unleashed led to massive mob violence. Gandhi admitted his "Himalayan miscalculation"[21] in failing to realize that the masses were not yet sufficiently self-disciplined to be able to protest peacefully. He came to understand that an individual may passively resist civil authority on the basis of moral conviction but that a nationwide movement requires in addition careful organization and hour-by-hour direction of mass actions. After the 1919 riots he was condemned by the British for launching the movement and by Indians for calling it off when violence erupted.

During the next several years Gandhi preached passive noncooperation, but the chief result was the arousing of passionate resistance to the English, which led to frequent outbreaks of violence. In 1922, he was condemned to six years imprisonment—though the British judge expressed personal admiration for him, declaring: "There are probably few people in India who do not sincerely regret that you should have made it impossible for any Government to leave you at liberty."[22] Because of his ill health, threatening the dire event of his death in prison, the English released him within six months.

Gandhi now found himself in the midst of agitation that he had sought to avoid. Ever since 1918, he had made strenuous efforts to reconcile the Hindus and the Muslims, urging forbearance and tolerance upon both groups. While he was in prison, riots broke out between adherents of the two religions. In December 1924, in New Delhi, Gandhi underwent a three-week public fast in an effort to quiet the conflict. But his troubles were multiplying in the form of opposition not only from outside but also within the Congress party. In 1925, the party adopted a formal policy of cooperating with the British in a program of gradual reforms. In protest, Gandhi withdrew from all political activity.

For the next four or five years he worked among the villages on behalf of the Indian weaving trade and the abandonment of "untouchability." During this period he became a frequent public speaker, urging his views in village after village as he traveled through India by train, by car, and on foot. Typically, his speeches were given from a sitting posture, while a silent and attentive crowd stretched far around him, trying to see when they could not hear. A close observer of his speeches thought that "what makes him irresistible" is that "he is so convinced of the righteousness of his cause that others cannot help believing it too."[23]

One of his most sophisticated auditors was Jawaharlal Nehru, who was drawn irresistibly to Gandhi against his better judgment. "The mind struggled with these new ideas," Nehru noted, "often put out without much method or logic. But the whole system reacted to them and grew under their impress. Was it the personality of Gandhi that did this or the force of the ideas that he represented and that he translated into action? Was it the rare spectacle of a man whose thought and word and act were so closely co-related as to form one integrated whole"?[24]

An American missionary who was won to Gandhi stressed his sophistication, both in his methods and in his ideas, and his dedicated idealism.

> Every word was carefully chosen. Every gesture was deliberate. His body was well poised, but his eyes seemed like flashes of fire, and his lips were burning coals. Never did I see more clearly in any personality such absorbing love for men, and I have seldom heard more refreshingly scientific and practical suggestions for social improvement and growth. . . . He crouched there against the wall, a picture of passionate patriotism, consumed by his spirit till his very body dwindled and left only a soul—the soul of India.[25]

Another missionary wrote: "On one such occasion, during the night of an eclipse of the moon, I watched an audience of nearly one hundred thousand peasant people, men and women, who had gathered from all the countyside to listen to his simple words. . . . The sight of Mahatma Gandhi was regarded by each and all of them as itself a purification and an act of religion."[26]

Nehru concluded that it was both the personality of Gandhi and his ideas that revolutionized India.

> He was like a powerful current of fresh air that made us stretch ourselves and take deep breaths; like a beam of light that pierced the darkness and removed the scales from our eyes; like a whirlwind that upset many things, but most of all the working of people's minds. He did

not descend from the top; he seemed to emerge from the millions of India, speaking their language and incessantly drawing attention to them and their appalling condition.[27]

Gandhi was beyond doubt a rare individual—one whose beliefs so completely dominated his life that he acted fully and unconsciously according to them. He believed in love toward all men, including his enemies—and practiced it. He believed that determined faith will accomplish miracles of regeneration, and he acted on that belief. He trusted that reasonable men cannot long oppose a sensible idea that is supported by sacrificial and widespread action. He thought that the ideal of brotherly accord can be made to be more appealing to masses of people than violent conflict. And he felt that government would grant to people what they wanted if only they demanded it consistently, reasonably, and with virtual unanimity. For Gandhi, the Sermon on the Mount outlined a set of working principles that can and should be put into effect. And he was not unaware that the opposition he had to overcome was eminently fairminded. "An Englishman," he wrote, "never respects you till you stand up to him. Then he begins to like you. He is afraid of nothing physical: but he is mortally afraid of his own conscience, if ever you appeal to it and show him to be in the wrong."[28]

It was on the basis of these convictions that Gandhi resumed nationwide leadership in India after the National Congress party split asunder in reaction to Great Britain's Simon Commission, which sought to pacify the Indians with a program of reforms. In April 1930, Gandhi led a gigantic "march to the sea" to make salt in the seaside marshes, in violation of the government salt monopoly. Thousands of the marchers were arrested and Gandhi was returned briefly to prison. To pacify the millions who pursued a policy of passive noncooperaton at Gandhi's behest, the British freed him and joined with him (on 5 March 1931) in the Delhi Pact, which promised a large measure of self-government for India. Within months, for what seemed to them evidence of Indian incapacity, the British restricted self-rule, and in 1932 Gandhi, again protesting, was again imprisoned. The MacDonald Labor government, then in office, adopted what it considered the liberal policy of guaranteeing separate political representation for the "untouchables"; but Gandhi felt that this perpetuated the social discrimination directed against them and commenced a "fast unto death" in protest against the policy.[29] Again released from prison when his fast seemed about to cause his death, Gandhi devoted himself for several years to pleading with the Indian people for fair and equal treatment of the "untouchables," or Harijans (children of God as he renamed them). Several times more he resumed his fasts, on these occasions not in opposition to the British government but as a dramatic means of appealing to the conscience of the Indians.

The outbreak of World War II precipitated increasing disagreement within the National Congress party. Gandhi favored "moral support" of the British, in return for an unconditional promise of independence at war's end. Other Congress party leaders demanded immediate independence. In early 1940, the party was in turmoil, and Gandhi launched a mass-disobedience campaign to deny the British any benefits of Indian cooperation while still "permitting" them to use Indian soil as a base for their war operations in the Far East. The Cripps Mission, in 1942, attempted to resolve the differences by assuring India independence at the close of the war; but Gandhi, changing his mind, joined other Congress party leaders in rejecting this offer as a "postdated cheque." In August 1942, riots and demonstrations were unleashed throughout India in the wake of a Congress party demand for immediate independence. Thousands of Indians were arrested, including Gandhi and his wife, and Mrs. Gandhi died in prison. Gandhi underwent a three-week fast in 1943, but the British this time refused to bow to his demand. In 1944, seriously ill, he was released from prison.

At this time he directed his principal attention to one of India's most deeply troublesome problems—the bitter division between Hindus and Muslims. Gandhi (and the Congress party majority) insisted that India must be granted independence as a united nation, with the dispute between the Muslims and Hindus to be settled afterward by a plebiscite.[30] In the summer of 1946, terrible slaughter resulted from nationwide fighting between these two religious populations.

During 1946–47, Gandhi, at the age of seventy-seven, trudged barefoot from village to village, pleading for unification and for toleration of religious differences. In the spring of 1947, the Congress party and the Muslim League agreed to accept independence as two separate nations, and the date for independence was set for 15 August 1947. Bloody Hindu-Muslim riots were anticipated in Bengal and Calcutta but were forestalled by Gandhi's pleas, enforced by another fast. Riots did, however, erupt in the Punjab, and Gandhi hastened to Delhi, which was swept by waves of hatred. Gandhi sadly admitted that his teachings of nonviolence had failed to achieve their effect; but he continued his pleas for mutual tolerance and for the granting of equal rights to members of all religions within the borders of both new nations. In January 1948, he underwent another fast in Delhi on behalf of fair treatment for Muslims.

On 30 January 1948 all India, and indeed the world, was stunned by the assassination of Gandhi by a Hindu fanatic, who viewed him as a threat to Hindu dominance in India. Nehru announced the news in a radio broadcast that began: "Friends and comrades, the light has gone out of our lives and there is darkness everywhere."[31]

Gandhi's personality was admired, almost revered—sometimes even venerated—around the world. But perhaps only in India and among Indians in Africa could he have been a major influence; and even there the high regard for his person did not always extend to his policies. Sir Winston Churchill, strong advocate of empire, not surprisingly considered him a "seditious fakir."[32] Gandhi himself, always half-amused, half-irritated, by the extravagant adulation he received,[33] wryly declared that "people describe me as a saint trying to be a politician, but the truth is the other way around."[34]

The objectives to which Gandhi devoted his life were *swaraj*, independence for India, and *sarvadaya*, a rather vague and broadly inclusive concept of improved welfare for all the people. Included in sarvadaya were such goals as elimination of caste and of "untouchability," which he called Hinduism's greatest curse; prohibition, for he thought alcoholic drink the direct cause of many sins; chastity, even within marriage; vegetarianism; and protection of cows, which he considered "one of the most wonderful phenomena in the human evolution" and "the gift of Hinduism to the world."[35] Among the methods by which he hoped to see these objectives accomplished were satyagraha, or peaceable noncooperation; *bhoodan*, or the giving away of all that one possessed to the poor; hand-weaving—and along with it a strict boycott against not only textiles but also all other foreign-made goods; self-support through family-centered handicrafts, in order to eliminate the use of machines; and a decentralization of political government, economic processes, and social organizations.

With such a program Gandhi was an anomaly and often a trial to his most devoted associates. Nehru wrote while Gandhi was at the height of his influence that "Very few persons in India accept in its entirety his doctrine of nonviolence or his economic theories."[36] The great Indian poet Tagore mingled admiration for Gandhi with flat rejection of his basic premise. Renouncing the whole program of noncooperation, Tagore declared, "The present attempt to separate our spirit from that of the Occident is tentative of spiritual suicide. . . . No nation can find its own salvation by breaking away from others."[37] Gandhi's most ardent advocates were disturbed by his constant stance of anti-intellectualism, leading him again and again to appeal from the "mind" to the "heart."[38]

Still, month after month, year after year, Gandhi patiently continued his teachings—constantly reiterating that what he proclaimed was an ideal that might never be attained but that at least set the believers upon the right path. In a speech to the YMCA at Madras on 16 February 1916, he said what he had already said many times, and what he was to keep on repeating until his death: "*Ahimsa* [nonviolence] really means that you may not offend anybody, that you may not harbor an uncharitable thought even in connection with one who may consider himself to be your enemy. . . . If we resent a friend's action or the so-called enemy's action, we

still fall short of this doctrine. . . . That does not mean that we practice
that doctrine in its entirety. Far from it. It is an ideal which we have to
reach, and it is an ideal to be reached even at this very moment, if we are
capable of doing so."[39]

In this vein his campaign continued. "To revile one another's religion, to
make reckless statements, to utter untruth, to break the heads of innocent
men, to desecrate temples or mosques, is a denial of God," he declared.[40]
Charges that his idealism was impractical, as illustrated by, for example,
the professions of "brotherhood" by Communists in contrast with their
ruthless behavior, he brushed aside with such comments as: "I have never
believed in the Bolshevik menace."[41]

His method was to avoid argument, to say what he had to say and to let
the matter rest. As an Indian biographer accurately reported, "To millions
he was the incarnation of God."[42] To Jan Christian Smuts, whose policies
Gandhi staunchly opposed in South Africa, he was one of the great men of
the world.[43] To Rabindranath Tagore, he was the incarnation of "mental
despotism," incalculably threatening to the welfare of the Indian people.
"An outside influence seemed to be bearing down on the people," Tagore
warned, "grinding them and making one and all speak the same tone,
follow the same groove. Everywhere I was told that culture and reasoning
should abdicate, and blind obedience only reign. So simple is it to crush, in
the name of some outward liberty, the real freedom of the soul!"[44] And to
all the criticism Gandhi replied, "But who am I! I have no strength save
what God gives me. I have no authority over my countrymen save the
purely moral."[45] He refused any position of authority in the National
Congress party. He never held political office. He renounced both wealth
and aristocratic position. His weapon was persuasion, and in wielding it he
was astute.

As a practitioner of persuasion, Gandhi was neither naive nor unskilled.
His early incapacity in speech was turned by him into an advantage. "My
hesitancy in speech, which was once an annoyance," he wrote, "is now a
pleasure. Its greatest benefit has been that it has taught me the economy of
words. I have naturally formed the habit of restraining my thoughts. And I
can now give myself the certificate that a thoughtless word hardly ever
escapes my tongue or pen."[46] He was utterly sophisticated in his handling
of the huge crowds that heard his speeches—or at least that saw him as he
crouched against a wall, dressed only in a loincloth, uttering his thoughts.
"Nothing is so easy as to train mobs," he told his lieutenants, "for the
simple reason that they have no mind, no meditation."[47] He developed a
twofold method of polarizing his audiences to reduce opposition and
enhance unity of response: he had them sing national songs and shout in
unison three selected slogans.[48] He knew that a nationwide campaign
must progress through successive stages, and he advocated that the first

groups to be influenced should be those "who have hitherto moulded and represented public opinion."[49] And always—most importantly of all—he managed with consummate skill to impose his own personality upon the mind of the masses. One of his major methods of doing this was to conduct in public a "fast unto death"—a visible process of suffering on behalf of his ideas and beliefs, with the constant threat that his life might end, his personality disappear, unless he got what he wanted. It was a prime example of the Indian rhetorical method of being, not doing; of communicating with the whole of one's self, not just with words.[50]

His greatest persuasive influence, however, came not from his methods or even from his personality, but from the nature of his program. Indians who were discontent with British rule could espouse terrorism, which was antithetical to their religion and also seemed doomed to failure; or they could support the constitutionalist demand for reforms, which proved to be substantially futile. Gandhi proposed a third mode of revolution— nonviolent resistance—which offered a means of active opposition without the commission of overt acts of lawless fury. It appealed strongly to those who wanted to be both respectably conservative in behavior and radically revolutionary in pursuing their goal. It was something almost new under the sun: a genuinely religious means of attaining political ends.

Mahatma Gandhi was a marvelous phenomenon unfolded upon the world's stage. He sought to practice religious doctrines that others, however devout, honored only with words. He called upon and won millions to follow, at least partially, where he led. A frail and fallible man, subject to all the limitations of his fellows, he yet was able to seize the imagination of the world, to enshrine himself through the adoration of whole populations, to exercise effective power in overthrowing the might of the British Empire, and to direct the sentiments of the Indian people in ways that were in part wonderfully constructive, in part anachronistically primitive. His influence, for good and for bad, was enormous in his own day; and admiration for his spirit is scarcely less after his death. No man in our time has come closer to deification. And to none was the irony of this more apparent than to Mohandas K. Gandhi himself.

Jawaharlal Nehru: Pilot of Indian Independence

When a ship is in dangerous waters, the captain may temporarily relinquish his command to a pilot who is especially qualified to deal with the dangers. In a sense, this situation is analogous to the relation between Gandhi and Nehru. There was never any doubt in the mind of Gandhi, Nehru, or the Indian masses and politicians that Gandhi was the real power in the Indian independence movement. But Gandhi himself fully realized that he lacked both the will and the skill to manipulate the political forces that had to be maneuvered day by day and month by month to reach the successive stages within the overall movement. To shift the analogy, Gandhi was the master strategist; Nehru was the field commander who developed and directed the tactics. Yet, like other simplifications, this depiction of Nehru as the instrument for carrying out Gandhi's purposes conceals as much truth as it reveals. Nehru was concurrently an independent force—sometimes supporting Gandhi, sometimes opposing him. In some respects the two men were so akin that they simply reinforced one another. In other respects they were deeply, diametrically, different.

Concerning the long-range goals of independence for India and improved welfare for the Indian masses, they agreed wholly. Temperamentally, Gandhi and Nehru shared an enormous capacity for unselfish sacrifice and for undeviating courage amid decades of failures. Both, too, emerged from inarticulateness to charismatic power to influence the Indian populace. But the differences were fully as significant as the similarities.

To millions around the world Gandhi seemed a saint, even godlike. In part this was because of his massive unconcern for practicalities, his utter conviction that ideals can be made to work not only for individuals but for nations. Nehru always impressed detached observers, both in India and around the world, as being more shrewd than saintly. In 1936, when Gandhi had to intervene to prevent a mass revolt against Nehru within the Congress party, Gandhi privately but sternly told him: "They have chafed under your rebukes and magisterial manner and above all your arrogation of what to them has appeared your infallibility and superior knowledge." Even so, Gandhi reassured him, "they know you cannot be dispensed with."[51]

A 1937 anonymous "portrait of Nehru" pictured him receiving the plaudits of the crowd. First, "his pale, hard face was lit up with a smile"; then, "the smile passed away and the face became stern and sad. Almost it seemed that the smile and the gesture accompanying it had little reality; they were just tricks of the trade to gain the goodwill of the crowd whose darling he had become. Was it so? Watch him again. Is all this natural, or the carefully thought out trickery of the public man? Perhaps it is both." The sketch concluded: "Men like Jawaharlal, with all their great capacity for great and good work, are unsafe in a democracy. He calls himself a democrat and a socialist, and no doubt he does so in all earnestness . . . but a little twist and he might turn into a dictator."[52] The analysis is disturbing because it is convincing—but its sting is converted to bewildered admiration for the subject when it becomes known that the author of this critique is none other than Nehru himself. Can a man be dangerous to the state when he has so much self-knowledge and so much candor in self-criticism? On the other hand, could it be that Nehru spoke ill of himself to confound and undermine his critics? Few who knew Nehru doubted that he was sophisticated enough to employ the most subtle means for achieving his ends.

Nehru was so much the introvert that he never tired of self-analysis. He knew himself for what he was: an intellectual and an aristocrat who hated poverty as it can only be hated by one who has never known it, and who served the people without ever conceiving himself as one of them. "I took to the crowd," he wrote, "and the crowd took to me, and yet I never lost myself in it; always I felt apart from it. From my separate mental perch I looked at it critically, and I never ceased to wonder how I, who was so different in every way from those thousands who surrounded me, different in habits, in desires, in mental and spiritual outlook, had managed to gain good will and a measure of confidence from these people."[53]

Time and again he restated the essential fact of his character: that he could not establish intimacies but that he was most truly himself when he was playing the role of the sad, tired leader who sacrificed himself to do for the people what they could not do for themselves. To his biographer he described himself as "like a schoolmaster . . . just trying to get them to think and to understand."[54] Revealingly, he confessed, "With a large crowd I speak my intimate thoughts always more than in a small committee. I feel I have a sense of communion with them, although I am very different from them."[55]

Nehru was indeed different. He was born on 14 November 1889, the only son of Motilal Nehru, a wealthy, strong-willed, extremely talented and conspicuously successful lawyer-aristocrat. For eleven years he remained the only child and was egregiously spoiled. The Nehrus had two swimming pools, a stable of fine riding horses, the first motor car in India, and a palatial residence, and they were highly honored by both the Indian and the English communities. Young Nehru was educated at home by private tutors and was often a silently attentive auditor while his father entertained the most scintillating company in their intellectual community of Allahabad. The language of the home was English, and Nehru grew up so much the English lad that when he later wrote about his homeland it was under the title *The Discovery of India.* To ensure Nehru's success within the Anglo-Indian system (within which Motilal had prospered hugely), he was sent through Harrow and then Cambridge. Urdu, the language of his province, became his second language; Hindi he confessed to knowing no better than he knew Latin. In all externals he was the model English aristocrat. Yet he had none of the qualities of extrovert bonhomie with which he might have pushed his way comfortably into English society. He belonged, at Cambridge, to the Majlis, a special society for Indian students. Actually he never was fully English and never became fully Hindu, but remained "a queer mixture of the East and the West, out of place everywhere, at home nowhere."[56]

Along with the pampering and the spoiling, however, his father taught him a strong sense of integrity and of duty. What he was to be dutiful toward, though, was slow in developing. Returning from England in 1912, he merely toyed with the practice of law and quietly entered the fringes of Anglo-Indian politics. He married in 1916 but continued to be supported by his father.

It was not until 1920 that Nehru was "awakened" to his real mission in life. He accepted the invitation of a group of peasants to visit their village for a few days—and was "filled with shame and sorrow. . . . A new picture of India seemed to rise before me, naked, starving, crushed, and utterly miserable."[57] He had met Gandhi in 1916, but had not been much impressed by him.

Now, however, in 1920—with Gandhi taking a bold stand within the Congress party for a new policy of peaceful noncooperation as a means of forcing the British to restore India's independence—Motilal, the elder Nehru, took the courageous course of moving from the reformist to the revolutionary wing of the Congress party; and Jawaharlal moved with him. From this date forward he was to be India's most ardent revolutionist—far more so than his father, far more consistently so than Gandhi. And he was as effective as he was ardent, particularly in the speeches with which he aroused the fervor of the Indian masses.

Like Gandhi, Nehru as a youth was virtually inarticulate. In the Majlis and also in the Magpie and Stump society in Cambridge, Nehru paid fines rather than obey the rule that called for a speech by each member every term. As a young lawyer he rarely pleaded a case, and he avoided occasions calling for oral advocacy. It was not until 1915 that he made his first public speech—and at its conclusion he was embraced on the platform, not because he had spoken well but because he had dared to speak at all. It was during his visits to the villages in 1920, when the villagers begged him to say something to them that would give them hope in the midst of their miseries, that his power of speech unfolded. "These peasants took away my shyness from me and taught me to speak in public . . . I could not possibly avoid addressing these peasant gatherings, and how could I be shy of these poor unsophisticated people? I did not know the arts of oratory, and so I spoke to them, man to man, and told them what I had in my mind and in my heart."[58]

From this time onward Nehru's flow of speech seldom stopped, and almost always it was this same extemporaneous type: an artfully artless mode of thinking out loud as his thoughts and feelings developed. Chester Bowles found him "the most articulate man I ever heard in personal conversations."[59] Vincent Sheean thought him, "as far as I know, about the most indefatigable public speaker in existence."[60] No other world statesman (except, perhaps, Gladstone) has ever spoken so much. As prime minister he generally spoke at least once a day to some audience, large or small. Unfriendly critics accused him of being the chief publicity officer for his administration. A friend admitted that perhaps "he speaks too often. But leaders have to spend a good part of their time capturing the imagination of the people."[61]

During the crucial campaign of 1936, when Nehru had to counter a good deal of opposition from within his own party, he traveled about fifty thousand miles in four months, making a dozen speeches a day, "apart from [those to] impromptu gatherings by the roadside." Carrying his own public address system with him, he spoke to audiences that ranged upward to a hundred thousand and averaged twenty thousand. To get to them he traveled by airplane, train, automobile, truck, horse-drawn carriage, bullock cart, bicycle, horseback, steamer, paddle-boat, and canoe. Sometimes he penetrated distant fastnesses by elephant or on camelback. Some areas he could reach only on foot. His own estimate is that in those 120 days he spoke to ten million listeners.[62]

A *New York Times* reporter assigned to India during Nehru's years in power wrote: "I have watched, dozens of times, the ragged crowds gaze steadily at Nehru for more than an hour, never taking their eyes from his face, hardly moving as they listened to him speak in a language that few of them could understand."[63] An Englishman tells of standing to hear Nehru on a terrifically hot day, in a "fiery furnace," while a strong wind "tears strips from the doors of the bamboo huts, blows the rubbish baskets over the sand with a noise like a rattlesnake, [and] hurls unripe mangoes at us from the trees." Even amid all this distraction and discomfort, "everyone leans forward, watching the Prime Minister's face. He looks strained as he begins to talk, the eyes heavily stained with shadow. . . . Conscientiously he avoids rhetoric and speaks not like the Prime Minister of the second largest population in the world but like a puzzled and burdened man."[64]

Nehru enacted his role convincingly and consistently because when he was most conscious of his audience he was most sincerely true to himself. His inner loneliness and his inability to form intimate associations combined to lead him to unusual candor in dealing with the public. All his writings and speeches were to a high degree autobiographical. He never tired of analyzing himself in public—perhaps because he needed an audience as an intermediary in order to explain himself to himself. Hence there is seldom any doubt about what he thought and felt. This is the point that emerged most clearly to the student of Nehru's philosophy: "With his pen he expressed his nature . . . in his basic writings or in casual letters, essays, or even talks."[65]

Nevertheless, the complexity of Nehru's mind presents challenges in the effort to depict him as he truly was. He was not self-contradictory as some have charged. But his consideration of any subject was infinitely various. Despite his habit of talking "man to man" to masses of the illiterate peasantry, he was studiously averse to simplification. After the final word had been spoken, there was always more to be said.

One of of his cardinal principles was that "the roots of the present lay in the past."[66] Yet he was no antiquarian. The "domination of the present" was his preoccupation; for, as he told an American audience, he felt himself standing on "the razor edge of the present," with the responsibility to bring all the wisdom and experience of the past to bear in estimating the probable developments of the future. Perhaps it suffices to say that he was historically minded, with a keen awareness that what happens today has largely been predetermined by past events, and that whatever is done today will have inescapable consequences for the future. It was a point of view that bred responsibility.

Another of his basic convictions was that man must work out his own problems in humanistic terms. "Any idea of a personal God," he wrote, "seems very odd to me."[67] He remained puzzled by Gandhi's emphasis upon the religious basis of nonviolence. For Nehru, nonviolence was not a conviction but a tactic. The British were too strong to be defeated by the Indians in war; what, therefore, remained to be tried as a means of securing independence? Until Gandhi proclaimed nonviolence, Nehru, like his compeers, did not have a promising answer. When nationwide passive noncooperation was explained to them, the solution appeared with wonderful clarity. Nehru embraced nonviolence gladly and fully *as a tactic*—good as long as it worked, and only because it worked, not at all from any belief that this was religiously the right way to deal with people.

There was, hence, no contradiction in his later advocacy of force in dealing with Pakistan over Kashmir, with Portugal over Goa, or with the Red Chinese armies that threatened Indian territory. Nehru was a thorough pragmatist—a Darwinian social behaviorist. His philosophy was to use whatever human means were available that seemed best suited to do whatever task came to hand. He did not confound his thinking by concern over whether in some inscrutable, unknowable manner this or that course of action might or might not be preferable in the view of some undefinable and unapproachable deity. Yet his skepticism was definitely affirmative, not negative. "God we may deny," he wrote, "but what hope is there for us if we deny man and reduce everything to futility?"[68] Again: "In spite of innumerable failings, man, throughout the ages, has sacrificed his life and all he held dear for an ideal, for truth, for faith, for country and honour . . . and, because of that, much may be forgiven to man, and it is impossible to lose hope for him."[69]

Of special consequence, in terms of the role Nehru came to play as a global referee between communism and the democracies, and in view of his long-sustained efforts to develop a "third force" that would be unattached to either side in the cold war, is the relationship of Nehru to communism. There is no doubt that he found it wonderfully attractive. In February 1927, he attended the "Congress of Oppressed Nationalities" in Brussels, and then went on for a hurried visit to Moscow. In both places he was tremendously impressed by the Marxist stress upon world brotherhood and justice for all. He thought that Russian foreign policy was "at least not hypocritical and not imperialistic."[70] In his view, "The practical achievements of the Soviet Union were also tremendously impressive."[71] Afterward, "A study of Marx and Lenin produced a powerful effect on my mind. . . . Much in the Marxist philosophical outlook I could accept without difficulty."[72] He wrote a book, *Soviet Russia,* which was uninterruptedly laudatory. Not even the brutal excesses worried him. "Nor can the revolution be said to have been a failure because the Bolsheviks ruthlessly exterminated their opponents and countered the white terror with the red."[73] His view of Lenin was that "by amazing power of will he hypnotized a nation and filled a disunited and demoralized people with energy and determination and the strength to endure and suffer for a cause."[74] In the view of his principal biographer, his "infatuation" with the Soviets lingered on for twenty years or so.[75]

As late as 1936, Nehru risked the loss of his personal leadership in the Congress party to emphasize his devotion to the Communists. In his presidential address in April of that year he said: "Fascism and imperialism thus stood out as the two faces of the now decaying capitalism. . . . Thus we see the world divided up into two vast groups today. . . . Inevitably we take our stand with the progressive forces of the world which are ranged against fascism and imperialism."[76] When World War II broke out, he viewed it not as a defense of democracy against totalitarian aggression but as "a prelude to vast change in the world, a revolution not only of the political map but of the social and economic structure."[77] He was convinced that Communists were right in charging that the democracy of the West was only a "shell to hide the fact that one class ruled over the others" and provided merely "a semblance of political equality but cloaked many social and economic inequalities."[78]

There is no doubt whatever that Nehru's sympathy with communism and with Soviet Russia influenced many of his later political stances— such as his dislike of NATO, his apologia for Russian intervention in Hungary, his fellowship with Asian Communists, and his bias against Syngman Rhee and the Republic of Korea. In view of Nehru's record of representing the United States critically and Russia favorably to the peoples of India and Asia, his attraction to communism was of enormous consequence.

But he did not ever become a doctrinaire Communist. He was too much the gentleman, too much the aristocrat. He understood himself well when he wrote that he liked much of what he saw in Russia, "but Communists often irritated me by their dictatorial ways, their aggressive and rather vulgar methods, their habit of denouncing everybody who did not agree with them."[79] When he was confronted by a practical choice between Communists and anti-Communists, as when he visited Chungking during World War II, he reacted naturally and strongly in favor of Chiang Kai-shek, "who embodies in himself the unity of China and her determination to be free," and Madame Chiang, "who has been a continuous source of inspiration to the nation."[80] Nehru was too much the individualist, too flexible in his view of situations, with too much integrity, ever to become subservient to the "party line." As he wrote in explanation of his impatience with the Communists of India, "Life is too complicated and, as far as we can understand it in our present state of knowledge, too illogical, for it to be confined within the four corners of a fixed doctrine." Then he added, "The real problems for me remain problems of individual and social life, of harmonious living, of a proper balancing of an individual's inner and outer life, of an adjustment of the relations between individuals and between groups, of a continuous becoming something better and higher, of social development, of the ceaseless adventure of man."[81]

The final word concerning Nehru's relation to communism is not easily determined. He was obviously too much the liberal, the rebel, and the romantic to be doctrinaire. He was, however, a lifelong revolutionist, hardened against Great Britain to the extent that he welcomed news of German victories in World War I and gladly went to jail rather than consent to even passive cooperation with the Allies in World War II. His temperament was definitely not totalitarian, yet he himself, in his anonymous self-portrait in 1936, warned that he had in him the makings of a dictator.

This picture of him is confirmed by a sketch his sister wrote in 1955: "It is said that power corrupts a man. It has not corrupted Jawahar. It has, however, had the effect of perhaps coarsening him to some extent. He was always inclined to be a little dictatorial—this must have been inherited from father—but nowadays he brooks no criticism and will not even suffer advice gladly."[82]

He was not repelled by the dictatorships he became familiar with in Russia, Yugoslavia, Egypt, and Red China. Yet he was far too English in his political understanding and far too Hindu in his identification with all manner of people ever to find it possible to fit himself into the Marxian mind. It is truer to think of him as he thought of himself: unaligned.[83]

In many ways Nehru mapped his own course and carried India with him. Much as he loved his father, he was so much in disagreement with him that his biographer concluded: "Rarely did they agree on the proper course of action, on objectives or on political philosophy, except for the broad goal of self-determination."[84] He virtually dominated the Congress party from the time of his first election as its president, succeeding his father in the post in 1929; yet he quarreled from time to time with its strongest members, denounced it for futility, and was outraged by some of its policies—notably when it decided to support the Allies in World War II. In his inaugural address to the Lucknow conference of the Congress party, in April 1936, Nehru commented about Gandhi: "We have differed from him in the past and we shall differ from him in the future about many things."[85] Gandhi in turn had to explain publicly that he and Nehru were not rivals, and he freely admitted that Nehru did not share his ideals.[86] The two admired one another deeply, and Gandhi was never in doubt that Nehru should be the chosen leader once independence was attained. Yet their differences were fundamental.

Gandhi's economic ideas were primitivistic, including a denial of modern industrialization and a belief that India could best serve its own interests by maintaining a strict economic isolationism. Nehru was firmly committed to rapid and large-scale industrialization for India;[87] and again and again he emphasized that India's welfare must rise or fall along with that of the rest of the world.[88] Gandhi was a firm believer in free enterprise, even to the extent of defending 10 percent profits. Nehru repeatedly emphasized that "socialism is for me not merely an economic doctrine which I favor; it is a vital creed which I hold with all my head and heart."[89] To avoid any misunderstanding, he affirmed: "I believe in the basic economic theory which underlies the social structure of Russia."[90] Then he explained why socialism was the vital core of his political philosophy: "What I seek is an elimination of the profit motive in society and its replacement by a spirit of social service, co-operation taking the place of competition, production for consumption instead of for profit."[91]

Gandhi was deeply, pervasively religious, while Nehru was humanistic and atheistic; Gandhi believed in nonviolence because it is morally right, while Nehru accepted it because it appeared in a given set of circumstances to be expedient. The list of distinctions could be extended considerably. Gandhi believed in celibacy; Nehru did not. Gandhi was a strict vegetarian; Nehru ate meat, albeit sparingly. Gandhi relied much upon intuition; Nehru believed strongly in the force and value of reason. Gandhi was suspicious of intellectuals; Nehru was essentially an intellectual. Gandhi placed the protection of cows at the very top of his list of priorities; Nehru outlawed "sacred cows" from New Delhi and would have eliminated them from India and from Hinduism if he could. Gandhi expected Indians to follow at his call but abjured organizational work; Nehru, sometimes rebelliously, was all his adult life an "organization man." In some respects Nehru and Gandhi worked at cross-purposes. Fundamentally, however, they complemented one another and together comprised the attitudes and skills that accomplished the independence of

India and the development of the Republic of India into an international power.[92]

The quality of Nehru's courage, sincerity, and self-denial equaled that of Gandhi. As a scion of wealth and the aristocracy, with great personal charm and abilities, he could easily have led a life of ease and luxury amid the plaudits of both the English and his own people. Deliberately he chose hardship, struggle, and imprisonment. Nine times between December 1921 and June 1945, he was sentenced to prison for his political activities, and he served a total of nine years in jail. For at least two decades he was consistently an object of scorn for the English, whom he vastly admired, and often he was attacked by his own peers in the independence movement. Yet not even the pleas of his own father nor the arguments and example of Gandhi could swerve him from his own chosen course. When India attained dominion status in 1947, Nehru was the only man considered for the post of prime minister—and he also took cabinet positions as minister of foreign affairs and of scientific research. On 26 January 1950, when the Republic of India was inaugurated, Nehru was sworn in as premier. He continued in this office until his death, on 27 May 1964.

Such was his influence that his successor, Lal Bahadur Shastri, was named simply because it was felt that he would continue Nehru's policies; and after Shastri's death the choice fell upon Indira Gandhi, Nehru's daughter, and after her, on Nehru's grandson. There may be continuing dispute concerning the merit of some of Nehru's basic policies, such as his devotion to socialism, his admiration for Soviet Russia, and his effective development of a "third force" in world affairs. But few would question the greatness of the man himself.

Divergent Ways: S. C. Bose and M. N. Roy

The role of communicative leadership in the shaping of India's independence took forms very different from the Sri Aurobindo-Gandhi-Nehru tradition in the activities and speeches of radicals who spurned the methods of nonviolence. Among them the most prominent were Subhas Chandra Bose and Manabendra Nath Roy.

Subhas Bose, who became an idol of Indian youth, advocated violence and insisted that freedom for India could only be won by war. Like Gandhi and Nehru, Bose was educated in England and passed the examinations for entrance into the British Civil Service. But in 1921, at the age of twenty-four, he resigned from the service and commenced a campaign advocating a revolutionary war. As a result he was arrested ten times and spent a total of some eight years in prison. He was friendly with Nehru and a sharp critic of Gandhi. In a book criticizing the Congress, published in 1938, Bose complained that "Gandhi's method is too lofty for this materialistic world and, as a political leader, he is too straightforward in his dealings with his opponents."[93] Through the twenties and thirties Bose traveled about in India speaking often to student groups, to whom he denounced Gandhi and his associates, saying that "it is not their lead we shall have to follow if we are to create a new India at once free, happy and great."[94] In 1939 Bose defeated Gandhi's candidate and won the presidency of the Congress party. Nehru supported him, but Gandhi's following was so large and so adamantly opposed to Bose that he resigned and founded his own party, the Forward Bloc. His appeal to the youth group was in part the spirit he displayed when he said, "There is nothing that lures me more than a life of adventure."[95]

When World War II broke out, Bose turned to Germany and Japan for help, saying that history did not record a single instance of a subject people winning national independence without outside help. He went to Germany in 1941 and then to Japan. With the help that they gladly extended, including the release to him of some forty thousand Indian prisoners of war, Bose formed the Indian National Army and a government that he named Azad Hind (Free India). At a military review of this army in Singapore on 5 July 1943, Bose said to the troops:

> George Washington of America could fight and win freedom, because he had his army. Garibaldi could liberate Italy, because he had his armed volunteers behind him. It is your privilege and honour to be the first to come forward and organize India's National Army. By doing so, you have removed the last obstacle in the path to freedom.[96]

Bose's troops won some battles with British contingents, but when the war ended his movement collapsed. Bose well understood that his program was opposed not only by the massive following of Gandhi but also by the Indian Communists. In a broadcast from Berlin in April 1942, he denied that he was an apologist for the Nazis and the Japanese, saying, "I need no credentials when I speak to my own people. My whole life is one long, persistent uncompromising struggle against British imperialism." When the Japanese bombed Indian cities, Bose spoke over the radio from behind the Japanese lines to urge that "Japan is our ally, our helper. Cooperate with the Japanese in order to eliminate British domination."[97]

Bose was indeed not a Fascist; he came close, like Nehru, to being a Communist. In his inaugural address to the Congress in 1938, he said that although he was not a member of the Communist party, he had been "in agreement with its general principles and policy from the very beginning." In a press release dated 18 December 1933 he denied being a Communist and forecast that "the next phase in world history will produce a synthesis between Communism and Fascism." He concluded: "It will be India's task to work out this synthesis." Like Gandhi and Nehru, Bose believed that national independence was not the whole goal—there must also be a vast improvement in the living conditions of the people.

Manabendra Nath Roy, who lived from 1887 to 1954, was in his youth a revolutionist, engaged in smuggling arms to terrorists in Bengal. Then he became a Communist, engaging actively in Communist movements in Mexico, Russia, China, and India. In 1931 he was sentenced to six years imprisonment, and upon his release he joined the Indian National Congress party. By this time he had renounced communism and directed his efforts most particularly to opposing Gandhi. Gandhi, he declared, was impeding independence for India by trying to convert politics to religion, and he was hindering modern progress by his campaign to replace manufacturing with the spinning wheel. Upon the outbreak of World War II, Roy joined with Gandhi in urging support for Great Britain in order that fascism might be eradicated. He declared himself confident that independence would be granted at the end of the war. He particularly scorned the claim of a superior spirituality for the Indian people, saying that

> intellectually it can hardly claim superiority to Western idealism, either modern or ancient. As regards transcendental fantasies, the Western mind has been no less fertile. The great sages of Athens, the seers of Alexandria, the saints of early Christianity, the monks of the Middle Ages—that is a record which can proudly meet any competition. On the question of moral doctrine, Christianity stands un-beaten on the solid ground of the Jewish, Socratic, and Stoic traditions. . . . The claim that the Indian people as a whole are morally less corrupt, emotionally purer, idealistically less worldly, in short, spiritually more elevated, than the bulk of Western society, is based upon a wanton disregard for reality.[98]

In books written during his last years, Roy turned from political activism to philosophy. Ghandism he renounced as a reactionary effort to maintain a static society, in which the people would acquiesce in their deprived status. He also renounced the class struggle theory of the Communists, and he came to consider that nationalism, as such, was not of great importance. "Radicalism," he claimed, "thinks in terms neither of nation nor of class; its concern is man; it conceives freedom as freedom of the individual."[99] In another book he concluded that "the Nation-State, in practice, makes no greater concession to the concept of individual freedom than the class-state of the Communists, and also of the Socialists. And no modern democratic state has as yet outgrown nationalist collectivism."[100] Far from idealizing independence, on 5 December 1954 he wrote that "if there ever was a Golden Age in the history of India, it was the latter half of the nineteenth century."[101] His chief allegiance was to liberal individualism based upon rationality. In summing up his philosophy, he stated that man did not appear on the earth out of nowhere. He rose out of the background of the physical universe, through the long process of biological evolution. The umbilical cord was never broken: man, with his mind, intelligence, will remains an integral part of the physical universe. The latter is a cosmos—a law-governed system. Therefore, man's being and becoming, his emotions, will, ideas are also determined; man is essentially rational. The reason in man is an echo of the harmony of the universe. . . . The innate rationality of man is the only guarantee of a harmonious order, which will also be a moral order, because morality is a rational function.[102]

Conclusion

This quotation from Roy may be an appropriate final word about the Indian independence movement, for in many respects it was a movement that transcended the struggle for nationalism. From Sri Aurobindo through Ghandi and Nehru to Bose and Roy, along with their many associates, the aim was always twofold: to win India's freedom, but also to improve the lot of mankind. This accords with what is perhaps the central strand of Indian religion and philosophy—the theme of universalism, of mankind's unity with all of nature and of an essential unity among all peoples of all nations. This is the dual message that the communicative leaders sought to convey. M. N. Roy's conclusion may serve as a memorial for them all.

India's passage to modernism and independent nationalism was characterized by the leadership of aristocrats and intellectuals and by their sharp differences of policies, methods, and philosophies. They also differed considerably in their personalities. These factors, combined with the long tradition in India of uninhibited verbal expressiveness and English tolerance for free discussion, led to acrimonious discussions and debates. The Indians hurled arguments not only at the English colonizers but also back and forth among themselves. More than anywhere else, the revolution that transformed India was a war of ideas and of words.

The discussions and the debates concerning goals as well as methods continue today, with little sign of abating. The typical Indian personality is paradoxical—intensely loyal to particular religious beliefs and devoted to culturally implanted traditions, but at the same time strongly and vociferously individualistic. The disunity explained in the opening pages of this chapter has not been eliminated. Princely states, of course, have been absorbed into the Republic. Caste distinctions have been outlawed. Political democracy has been attained. In many respects India's achievement of independent nationalism has been matched by its transformation to modernism. But few, either Indians or outside observers, would claim that the process is complete.

4

Quaid-I-Azam of Pakistan: Mohammed Ali Jinnah

The career of Ali Jinnah, the founder of Pakistan, involves a number of contradictory aspects: he was successively pro-English, pro-Indian, and pro-Pakistani; solitary yet central in a mass struggle; and self-centered, yet a symbol and spokesman for his people. He was an unusual man, more essential in the struggle to establish the new nation of Pakistan than Gandhi was in the founding of independent India, but antithetical to Gandhi in many ways.

The respect the English accord him is signalized by the fact that his portrait was hung in a place of high honor, over the entrance to the Great Hall and Library of London's historic Lincoln's Inn. Jinnah's biographer Stanley Wolpert believes that in his last decade, at least, he "may have been the shrewdest barrister in the British Empire." Yet so single-minded was he that "he burned out his life pressing a single suit"—a suit so important that "by winning his case he changed the map of South Asia and altered the course of world history."[1] In the opinion of H. V. Hodson, a historian of the final stages in the nationalist movement on the Indian subcontinent, "of all the personalities in the last act of the great drama of India's rebirth to independence . . . [Jinnah] was the most important."[2]

The most astute analyst of Jinnah's historical role, Sharif Al Mujahid, identifies the two crucial questions concerning him that must be evaluated: "(i) how and why he was hailed as the Quaid-I-Azam [the Great Leader] of Muslim India? and (ii) how did he manage to rouse and inspire the Muslim youth as no one else did, and to adroitly press their idealism, energy and enthusiasm in the cause of Pakistan?"[3]

To consider these questions adequately it is necessary first to get acquainted with the man himself—a leader of a different kind, confronted with a problem so difficult that it has not even now been wholly solved. What is the most suitable relationship between Hindus and Muslims in the Indian subcontinent? It was Jinnah's solution that was adopted but the question remains of how to make it work.

What Manner of Man

Mohammed Ali Jinnah changed his convictions and his policies several times during his life. But his personality, appearance, and manner remained remarkably stable. "An aristocrat by nature," "imperious and dictatorial by temperament,"[4] "he was cold, aloof and lonely."[5] He spent his life working closely with people, yet remained an intensely private man, isolated from intimacies. Small and slight in stature, he always dressed meticulously in the latest fashion, being so particular about his dress that he refused to wear a silk necktie more than once. From his highly polished shoes to the monocle that he wore to signal his distance from social contact, he looked like what he was: a man of rigidly correct behavior, without warmth of comradeship, utterly confident of his own judgment and dedicated to his mission of public service.

He was born in Karachi in 1876, probably on 20 October and not, as he claimed, on 25 December; the date is uncertain since Muslims paid little attention to birth dates. His father was a self-made, wealthy merchant of a haughty disposition. Ali was the firstborn in a family of seven children and remained his mother's favorite, egregiously spoiled by her and his sister Fatima. As a child he refused to study, even when his parents provided him with a tutor at home, but spent his time idly in the fields. When he was about eleven, his aunt took him from Karachi to Bombay for a visit, and Jinnah became so entranced with the city that never afterward could he consider Karachi to be his real home. By the time he was sixteen he determined, against the tearful pleas of his mother, to go to London for a taste of English life. His father, too, opposed such a plan, but Jinnah persisted and they finally gave their consent. His mother first married him to a fourteen-year-old local girl, so that he would not be lured into marriage while in England; and his father provided him with funds for three years of moderate expenses in London.

Through a British friend, a job as an accountant was secured for him near Threadneedle Street, in the heart of the City of London. "Far from home," he wrote, ". . . I did not know a soul, and the immensity of London as a city weighed heavily on my solitary life."[6] Even so, he fell in love with London and determined to become as English as he could. He quit his job (to the distress of his father) and began the study of law at Lincoln's Inn, which he was able to do only because at that time the entrance requirements were exceedingly lax. By the time he earned his law degree, both his mother and his child-bride had died, and his father refused to send him more money.

Jinnah returned to India but paused only briefly in Karachi before going to Bombay to live. From that time, Karachi, which became the capital of the nation he founded, saw him scarcely at all until his return there just before his death.

Jinnah died on 11 September 1948, just a few months after Gandhi was assassinated and less than a year after Pakistan became his foundling nation. At his death he was so wasted away by disease that he weighed only seventy pounds. His was a strangely alienated life. He was close only to his sister Fatima, who worshiped him. Yet his strength of will and his abilities made him one of the most influential individuals of his time.

What separated Jinnah most decisively from Gandhism was his fervent faith in constitutionalism. He was a lawyer by conviction and temperament. With little faith in people, his faith was strong in the necessity of law. He hated as much as Gandhi did the terrorism of those who sought to revolt against English rule, but he had no tolerance for Gandhi's theme of civil disobedience. Society without rule by law, he felt, would be intolerable. With a mind that was coldly logical, and with a strong attachment to English liberalism, he believed that the path to independence lay not through resistance but through persuasion. In his view, the case for Indian independence was like a suit in court—to be argued much as he argued cases before a judge or jury.

His opportunity to pursue the route to self-government through constitutional means came first in 1909, when the Muslims of Bombay chose him to represent them in the new Imperial Legislative Council established by the English Raj. Within a few years, Jinnah was recognized as a strong personality in public life in Bombay and, more importantly, in the Indian National Congress. Typical of his views and of his manner of stating them is a warning he issued in a debate in the Imperial Council in 1913—a warning addressed not to the English but to Indian radicals: "Let those men who still have these misguided ideas, let those men who still have these hallucinations, realize that by anarchism, by dastardly crimes, they cannot bring about good government: let them realize that these methods have not succeeded in any country of the world, and are not likely to succeed in India."[7]

Jinnah's faith in law was his guiding conviction. He was born into the Shi'ite sect of Islam, to which both his parents were devoted, but he lived as a skeptical humanist. "God and the Quran had no place in Jinnah's vision of the world."[8] Jinnah lived contemporaneously with Kemal Pasha Ataturk, who modernized and strengthened Turkey, and he was influenced by Kemal's renunciation of the Khilafat, which symbolized faith in global Muslim unity. Kemal's statement in a great speech in March 1924 was a credo that Jinnah found wholly acceptable:

To work within our national boundaries for the real happiness and welfare of the nation and the country by, above all, relying on our own strength in order to retain our existence. But not to lead the people to follow fictitious aims, of whatever nature, which would only bring them misfortune, and expect from the civilized world civilized human treatment, friendship based on mutuality.[9]

Despite Jinnah's faith in winning the struggle for nationalism through appeals to law and to "civilized human treatment," he came increasingly in his later years to emphasize the religious bond that unites Muslims. In one of his last speeches, he referred to the turmoil in the Middle East and said that "we are all passing through perilous times," and "it is only by putting up a united front that we can make our voice felt in the counsels of the world."[10] By no means, however, did he really feel part of a "united front" of all Muslims. Turkey and Afghanistan stood as barriers separating India from the Arabs, thus making it possible for Indian Muslims to pursue a way of their own. Jinnah was more nationalist than Muslim, more humanist than religious.

The conventional view of him is that he was inordinately self-centered, or at least self-guided. As a Pakistani professor of history summarized (though he did not endorse) the conclusions of most Western and Hindu critics of Jinnah,

He entered politics as an ardent nationalist but eventually abandoned his earlier creed. His dissociation from the Indian National Congress, of which he was a member until December 1920, came as a result of his inability to share the revolutionary views of the other Congress leaders, particularly Gandhi and Nehru. An aristocrat by nature, he was a misfit in the Congress which was a party of the masses. With the inauguration of the Gandhian era in Congress politics around the year 1920, he realized that he could never reach the top of the Party and did not wait long to resign his membership. Some years later, he came forward as the champion of the Muslim community. Despite the fact that his interest in Islam as a religion and a sociopolitical system was one of expediency rather than conviction he was able to "manipulate religious symbols" and play upon the religious feelings of his co-religionists. . . . Imperious and dictatorial by temperament, he neither asked for nor listened to the views of his colleagues. Inordinately ambitious, he only wanted power and glory which he was finally able to grasp as head of the State of Pakistan.[11]

The principal English historian of the period notes similar qualities but assesses them differently:

By nature, in his conduct of life, he was cold, aloof and lonely. . . . No intimates shared his secrets. No disciples watched his moods or tracked the straws in the wind of his thinking. . . . No collaborator of equal stature tempered his opinions or divided his responsibilities. He walked alone. . . .

Not even his political enemies ever accused Jinnah of corruption, or self-seeking. He could be bought by no one, and for no price. Nor was he in the least degree a weather-cock, swinging in the wind of popularity or changing his politics to suit the chances of the times. He was a steadfast idealist as well as a man of scrupulous honour. The fact to be explained is that in middle life he supplanted one ideal by another, and having embraced it clung to it with a fanatic's grasp to the end of his days.[12]

In Jinnah's loneliness he much resembled the younger William Pitt, who dominated British politics a century earlier. Unlike Pitt (who abandoned his most basic convictions to serve the purposes of King George III),[13] Jinnah recognized no master except his own inexorable mind. His convictions led him first to champion Hindu-Muslim unity as the necessary means of regaining Indian independence and then to demand Muslim independence from both English controls and Hindu dominance. The force of his pro-English and pro-law convictions led him to stand apart in 1920, when Gandhi's campaign for civil disobedience won the support of the Indian National Congress. Jinnah promptly resigned from the Congress, and Gandhi wrote him a letter pleading for his continuing support in the crusade to win "the new life that has opened before the country." Jinnah's reply indicates the passionate faith he held in the sanctity of law and the need to pursue the goal of independence by legal means:

If by "new life" you mean your methods and your programme, I am afraid I cannot accept them; for I am fully convinced that it must lead to disaster. But the actual new life that has opened up before the country is that we are faced with a Government that pays no heed to the grievances, feelings and sentiments of the people; that our own countrymen are divided; the Moderate party is still going wrong; that your methods have already caused split and division in almost every institution that you have approached hitherto, and in the public life of the country not only amongst Hindus and Muslims but between Hindus and Hindus and Muslims and Muslims and even between fathers and sons; people generally are desperate all over the country and your extreme programme has for the moment struck the imagination of the inexperienced youth and the ignorant and the illiterate. All this means complete disorganization and chaos. What the consequence of this may be I shudder to contemplate; but I for one am convinced that the present policy of the Government is the primary cause of it all and unless that cause is removed, the effects must continue. I have no voice or power to remove the cause; but at the same time I do not wish my countrymen to be dragged to the brink of a precipice in order to be shattered.[14]

In this renunciation of Gandhism, Jinnah by no means stood alone.

Nehru responded to Gandhi's civil disobediance campaign immediately following that crucial 1920 Congress meeting in words very similar to those used by Jinnah: "I will have nothing to do with this pseudo-religious approach to politics. I part company with the Congress and Gandhi. I do not believe in working up mob hysteria. Politics is a gentleman's game."[15] Nevertheless, neither Jinnah nor Nehru liked or trusted the other; they could not be allies, for their goals, their personalities, and their methods differed greatly.

The vital question was, if not Gandhism, what? To this question Jinnah had two answers: one governed the whole of his career from his entry into politics in 1906 until March 1940; the second he pursued with both emotional zeal and logical clarity from 1940 until his death. The first answer was that Muslim-Hindu cooperation was necessary to end British colonialism. The later answer was that Muslim separatism was essential in establishing Pakistan as a Muslim state. Both answers were based on a determination to obtain independence. The problem was, what did independence mean and how was it to be sought? These were the two questions, restated, that Mujahid, as quoted earlier, identified as being crucial.

For an assessment of Jinnah's leadership, the first consideration must be the latter part of the problem: What was his method? What was the nature of his political power? By what means was he effective? As a man who chose to stand alone, how could he win so large and so devoted a following? How did he compare with the other leaders? Gandhi, Nehru, and Jinnah were all strikingly different from one another. Yet one thing they shared—the power to communicate convincingly . Each used this power in his own way, but all of them achieved an overwhelmingly persuasive effect. Jinnah's power, like that of Gandhi and Nehru, came from no other source than this: his ability to persuade. Like them, he proved to have an irresistible personal force. What it was like was a conundrum that students of his career have found difficult to define.

Jinnah's Leadership through Communication

Jinnah had communicative handicaps to overcome that were as severe in their own way as was the extreme stage fright that afflicted the youthful Gandhi and Nehru. By temperament, Jinnah was introspective and solitary. He did not enjoy sociability, neither mingling with groups nor entering upon intimate friendships. His brief first marriage was merely a formality, and his second marriage was not happy. He did not get along well with people. Moreover, the only language that he spoke well was English. When he tried to speak to his audiences in his native Urdu, his vocabulary was inadequate and his pronunciation was awkward. Another problem was that his mind, while brilliantly perceptive, was not capacious. Neither in his schoolboy days nor in later life did he have the outreaching curiosity that leads to acquisition of broad knowledge. As he said of himself, his only interests were the law and politics. In law he specialized in probate cases rather than general practice, and in politics he was not a theorist but a pragmatist, seeking to solve immediate problems in a practical way. He made no great efforts to please his associates, and he was no panderer for public favor. In basic respects he did not appear to have the personality for persuasive public speaking. Nevertheless, he had tremendous force in compelling acceptance of his views.

> Although not oratorical, he was a cogent and convincing speaker . . . serious, grave, practical. Conviction, courage and sure knowledge informed his pronouncements. Indeed, almost proverbial was his flair for solid facts, cold logic, and coherent arguments which he marshalled and employed with unusual dexterity and amazing concentration of force— traits developed at the bar. . . . He spoke as if he was arguing a case in a court of law, and that with all the resources at his command. And his resources were not easily exhaustible. All of which made his public pronouncements impressive and appealing.[16]

Another listener found him a "polished debator [sic] . . . one of the most effective speakers in any assembly of men."[17] Yet another declared that "he is not the type who is very keen to play to the gallery" but added that "Jinnah was perhaps the best orator in the accepted British standards, with a dignified statesman's manners." This critic pointed out that "he spoke rarely," and concluded that "it was a pleasure to hear him when he was on his feet."[18] Hector Bolitho, a British biographer, says that "Jinnah was never to become excited by the charm of words: his prose, written or spoken, was bald and factual."[19] Jinnah himself insisted to those who tried to improve his speech drafts, "I don't care for beautiful language: I only wish to see my ideas come through."[20] And come through they did.

Until late in life Jinnah seldom spoke to general public audiences. His speaking was in courts of law, at the conventions of the Muslim League and of the Indian National Congress, and at the Bombay provincial conferences. In such meetings there was a homogeneity of feelings, even when divisive issues were discussed. The setting was right for debates, not for orations. In such meetings the keenness of Jinnah's logic kept him in the forefront of the leadership. When Gandhism spread across India, Jinnah withdrew and went for four years back to England, where he felt more at home. After he was drawn back to India again in the mid-thirties he undertook new methods and became in a sense a new personality. Up to that point, as Mujahid describes him, "he had concentrated on solid arguments and concrete cold facts; his appeal, couched in somewhat sophisticated, and from the popular viewpoint, even abstract terms, was limited." Then came the change;

> From 1937 onwards, he began to tap deftly and dexterously the springs of emotions and enthusiasm among the masses. He began to appear in the traditional Muslim dress in public—a thing which he had perhaps never done before. He began to address mass audiences and whistle-stop and roadside gatherings, and that in his unrehearsed, broken, anglicized, and accented Urdu—again something for which he had no preparation before; something extremely revolutionary for a man of Jinnah's tastes, temperament and training. And while still retaining his highly legal and parliamentary vocabulary for the council chamber and high-powered negotiations with the British and the Congress, he now began talking, with the enthusiasm of a new convert, the language of the masses. All this obviously added a new dimension to his leadership, its quality, depth and appeal. To the utter surprise of both his admirers and opponents, he now showed, though already in his sixties, remarkable qualities of mass leadership which, unless they had been latent in him all the while, could not have been so readily called forth at this ripe age, nor could have yielded such spectacular returns.[21]

For an understanding of the nature of Jinnah's appeal it is necessary to view the circumstances in which it emerged. For centuries the Hindus and Muslims had lived together in India, not really in comradeship, but with less divisiveness separating them than the other basic divisions of caste, of language, and of princeling states. In 1906 the communal feelings of India's Muslims led them to found the All-India Muslim League—which Jinnah did not join until 1916. What this league represented is well portrayed in the presidential address of Sir Ibrahim Rahimutulla in 1913. After noting that Muslims had come to feel their separation from the Hindu majority, he asked for "sincere co-operation in making an earnest effort to bridge over the difficulties which confront us in a spirit of considered compromise, so that instead of parting we shall all become solidly united again." Jinnah agreed. Moreover, Jinnah took it for granted, as the generality of Indians did, that British rule was irrevocable and that it was also good for India. He pleaded for restraint in presing for reforms, stating that "the foundation of British rule in India is laid on the bedrock of strength and righteousness, on its inherent sense of justice, and on fair play."[22]

In 1916, in the midst of World War I, when Jinnah joined the league and was elected its president, he was introduced by an elder statesman, Nabi-Ul-Lah, who reminded the members that "our King Emperor and his allies are fighting for the complete vindication of international right and justice," and that "in this gigantic task, the whole of the Empire, of which India forms a part, is absolutely of one mind and one resolution." He went on to say that changes to improve the lot of Indians were inevitable and

pleaded for "the sinking of all petty differences of races and creed" so that
the league could accomplish two objectives: protection of the political
rights of Muslims and cooperation with all other Indians for the attainment of autonomous home rule.[23]

Jinnah, who was praised by Nabi-Ul-Lah for his "clear gaze and ripe
judgment, his cool imperturbable temper, his sweet reasonableness, his
fearless courage and devotion to duty," then read his presidential address
in which he demonstrated a rarely used appeal to emotions.[24] In his
introduction he said,

> All that is great and inspiring to the common affairs of men, for which
> the noblest and most valiant of mankind have lived and wrought and
> suffered in all ages and all climes, is now moving India out of its depths.
> The whole country is awakening to the call of its destiny and is scanning
> the new horizons with eager hope.

He went on to discuss "two cardinal facts": first, British rule with its
"even-handed justice," which had brought to Indians "the thought and
ideals of the West, and thus led to the birth of a great and living movement
for the intellectual and moral regeneration of the people"; and, second,
"the existence of a powerful, unifying process—the most vital and inter-
esting result of Western education in the country—which is creating out of
the diverse mass of race and creed a new India, fast growing into unity of
thought, purpose and outlook." It should be easy, in a spirit of mutual
good will, to achieve agreement on home rule for India. But the problem
was that the hard-working and conscientious British civil administrators
were "naturally conservative" and had "a rooted horror of bold administrative changes." They meant well, he went on,

> but, as you know, pure, unalloyed reason is not the chief motive power in
> human things. In the affairs of our common secular existence, we have
> to deal not with angels, but with men, with passions, prejudices, per-
> sonal idiosyncrasies, innumerable crosscurrents of motive, of desire,
> hope, fear, and hate. The India problem has all such formidable com-
> plications in its texture.

He detailed the nature of the English prejudices—that peoples of the
Far East were unsuited for democracy, that they willingly accepted the
presumed efficiency of autocracy, that there was an inherent opposition of
interests between the upper and lower classes of India, and that for such
reasons the Indians were unfit to govern themselves. Nevertheless, he
insisted, "no cool-headed student of Indian affairs can lose sight of the
great obvious truism that, be the time near or distant, the Indian people
are bound to attain to their full stature as a self-governing nation. . . . It is

inevitable. Then why fight against it, why ignore it, why should there not rather be honest, straightforward efforts to clear the way of doubts, suspicions and senseless antagonisms?"

He admitted that in the past freedom had come only to people who fought for it. But "we are living in different times. Peace has its victories. We are fighting and can only fight constitutional battles." By such peaceful arguments, he concluded, Indians would "convince the British Empire that we are fit for the place of partner within the Empire."

The general feelings of India's Muslims were discussed during the 1917–18 session of the league, at which the chairman asserted the "steadfast loyalty" of Muslims to the British Crown and declared that "the energies of the best minds of the two great communities of India are concentrated on the problem of how to smooth away their differences and pave the way for greater harmony."[25] This precisely was the consistent and determined stance of Jinnah all through the decades until near the outbreak of World War II.

Meanwhile, as the years passed, he was tireless in his efforts both to arouse a sense of unity among the masses of India's Muslims and to restrain them from either revolutionary violence or participation in the Gandhian program of civil disobedience. When he was again elected president of the Muslim League, he claimed in his inaugural address on 15 October 1937 that

> within less than six months we have succeeded in organizing Muslims all over India as they never were at any time during the last century and a half. They have been galvanized and awakened in a manner which has astounded and staggered our opponents. . . . They are beginning to realize that they are a power.[26]

His main point in the speech was that the Congress party under the leadership of Gandhi and Nehru was bent upon depriving the Muslims of political representation; forcing upon the country the Hindi language, which would impose upon Muslim children the study of Hindu Sanskritic literature; and depriving Muslims all over India of freedom in observing their own religion. He concluded that

> it is no use masquerading under that name of nationalism. The Congress is a Hindu body mainly. . . . Muslims have made it clear more than once that . . . their future destiny and fate are dependent upon their securing definitely their political rights, their due share in the national life, the Government, and the administration of the country.

The nature of Jinnah's leadership by this time was clear—and so was its value. He had proved his ability to unify and to galvanize the Muslim masses. Henceforth, year after year, the Muslim League reelected him as its president. And in accepting this role, Jinnah emphasized what leadership meant to him. He sensed what the Muslims of India wanted, and he made himself the spokesman for their demands. As Mujahid explained Jinnah's position of unique centrality, "No man ever moulded the destiny of a nation except by making the sentiment of that nation his ally—by working with it, by shaping his measures and his policy to its successive developments."[27] In Mujahid's words, Jinnah "had the unique gift of constantly feeling the pulse of the people," and consequently he shaped "his policies and his programme in the light of his reading of their pulse."[28]

What this meant, primarily, is that Jinnah was a master of timing. He was always in the forefront of Muslim sentiment, taking care not to get ahead of it, and by no means lagging behind. What Mujahid failed to mention— apparently failed to realize—was the extent to which the sentiments of the Muslim community were not only articulated by Jinnah but were in fact defined, interpreted, guided, and aroused by him. He did not follow public opinion but formulated it—gave it form, clarified it, made it an effective force, and then rode upon its crest. Without his clear-headed, persistent, and effective leadership, there would have been no unified Muslim demand for an independent Muslim state. He indeed stayed "close to the people," but as their guide, not as their echo.

By no means was Jinnah a philosopher or a political theorist. He was not an original thinker. As a lawyer, he was devoted to precedents, to determining the established order and to maintaining it. Only slowly did he come to accept the notion that there should be a separate Muslim nation on the Indian subcontinent—an idea that was first proposed by Sir Muhammad Iqbal in 1930 and that subsequently was advocated by another Muslim League member, Choudhary Rahmat Ali. Jinnah's movement toward that goal was slow and cautious. At the 1936 league meeting he took the first discernible step, saying that "the Hindus and Muslims must be organized separately" so that "they will better understand each other." He warned the 1938 session that the time had not yet come for advocacy of a separate nation, telling them, "You have yet to develop a national self and a national individuality. It is a big task; and as I have told you, you are yet only on the fringe of it."[29]

When he crossed the great divide and exerted leadership of the movement to create Pakistan as a separate nation, he insisted that the right "to develop to the fullest our spiritual, cultural economic, social and political life in a way that we think best" was not his special ideal but the aim of "every Musalman." Quite explicitly, in a speech to students on 10 March 1941, he said, "I noticed that you were anxious" for the establishment of Pakistan. "In other parts of India I had noticed the same feeling. What I have done is to declare boldly what was stirring the heart of Muslim India."[30]

Naturally he did much more than simply represent the feelings of the Indian Muslims—he inspired and shaped them. Frank Moraes, a veteran Indian newsman, in an article published in the *Deccan Times* for 14 October 1948, claimed that Jinnah "willed a state into being." After noting that Winston Churchill "mesmerized England . . . by words," he said, "The Quaid-I-Azam did the same with Indian Muslims. The Congress was his target. And he mobilized his followers by words. No contemporary Islamic leader more surely understood the Muslim mass mind of India, nor knew better how intuitively to appeal to it, to cajole and rouse it. With Pakistan, Mr. Jinnah rang a bell which acted like a toxin." Professor Mujahid, taking his cue from Moraes, agreed that Jinnah's role was much like Churchill's:

> Indian Muslims came to discover in Jinnah such a man—one who was fully equipped, mentally, morally, and psychologically, to face and over-come the stupendous challenge that confronted the Indian Muslims. Besides, he had developed by then that instinctive sense of the nation's deepest emotions, wishes, aspirations, prejudices, which is generally considered a distinguishing trait of a great statesman. In the result, his enormous sensitivity to the moods and feelings of the masses, and his capacity to give them concrete political expression, conferred on him and his policies a kind of moral authority which a mere politician could never claim. And this, in part, explains the surging enthusiasm that he inspired among the masses.[31]

Thus, over a span of some three decades, the aloof, aristocratic, logical, and legalistic Mohammed Ali Jinnah, through a slow process of gradually expanding leadership, during which he spoke more and more frequently, first only to select audiences in formal settings, then increasingly to student groups in universities, and finally to massed audiences of urbanites and villagers out-of-doors, by this process evolved into a charismatic Great Leader whose words and gestures swayed the feelings of millions and thereby led them into separate nationhood.

Keith Callard, a British student of Pakistani affairs, described Jinnah as "by nature a commander and leader of men. . . . He organized the campaign for Pakistan as though he were a commander-in-chief issuing orders of the day to encourage the troops, and tactical directions to control the provincial commanders."[32] Obviously there was an element of truth in such an assessment. But Jinnah was describing himself well when he said, "My sole object is to serve the cause of the country as best I can."[33] And when the Muslim League offered to elect him president for life, he refused: "Let me come to you at the end of every year and seek your vote and your confidence. Let your President be on his good behaviour."[34] And when the Working Committee of the Muslim League sought to leave decisions to Jinnah, he retorted: "I want . . . every member to feel that he is free and . . . is not tied down or fettered by any step that we have taken which prevents him in any way from expressing his opinion or taking his final decision whatever it may be."[35] Both Jinnah's temperament and the high regard in which he was held pointed toward solitary decision making, but if he was not actually democratic he was legalistic and believed that everyone, including himself, must be governed by the will of the whole group. He could not abjure the role of Great Leader but he did avoid being a dictator.

But inspiring and organizing and leading the Indian Muslims was not the only, and perhaps not even the principal, challenge that Jinnah faced. Beyond this he had to persuade the British authorities that it was both feasible and ultimately necessary to divide India into two parts, so that the governmental power was surrendered not to the India that had long been ruled by the British Raj but to two separate and, indeed, sharply hostile nations: India and Pakistan. It was his success in this endeavor that led Hodson to account him the "most important . . . of all the personalities in the last great drama of India's rebirth to independence." And it was this that induced the Indian Muslims to proclaim him officially as their Great Leader—Quaid-I-Azam.

The Creation of Pakistan

Friday, 22 March 1940, was the historic date on which the goal of Pakistan for the Muslims was formally proclaimed. The site was Minto Park on the outskirts of Lahore. The occasion was the convening of the twenty-seventh session of the Muslim League. A huge hall had been erected, with a seating capacity of sixty thousand. Well before 2:30 P.M., the scheduled time for the opening of the meeting, the hall was packed, and an additional forty thousand crowded around the building, listening to loudspeakers. Jinnah arrived at 2:25 P.M. and was escorted to the platform. The *Times of India* reported that "everyone was waiting for the Presidential Address. Mr. Jinnah decided to speak extempore, and no one knew what to expect. . . .

"Mr. Jinnah's sallow face reflected the triumph of his reception. He spoke for nearly two hours, his voice now deep and trenchant, now light and ironic. Such was the dominance of his personality that, despite the improbability of more than a fraction of his audience understanding English, he held his hearers and played with palpable effect on their emotions. His words did not disappoint their expectations." He came quickly to his point:

I think it is a wise rule for everyone not to trust anybody too much. . . . I therefore appeal to you, in all the seriousness I can command to organize yourselves in such a way that you may depend on none except your own inherent strength. That is your only safeguard and the best safeguard. Depend upon yourselves. . . .

It has always been taken for granted mistakenly that the Musalmans are a minority, and of course we have got used to it for such a long time that these settled notions sometimes are difficult to remove. The Musalmans are not a minority. The Musalmans are a nation by any definition. . . .

Notwithstanding a thousand years of close contact, nationalities which are as divergent today as ever cannot at any time be expected to transform themselves into one nation merely by means of subjecting them to a democratic constitution and holding them forcibly together by unnatural and artificial methods of British Parliamentary Statutes. What the unitary Government of India for 150 years had failed to achieve cannot be realized by the imposition of a central federal government. . . .

The Problem of India is not of an inter-communal but manifestly of an international character, and it must be treated as such. . . .

It is extremely difficult to appreciate why our Hindu friends fail to understand the real nature of Islam and Hinduism. They are not religions in the strict sense of the word, but are, in fact different and distinct social orders. It is a dream that the Hindus and Muslims can ever evolve a common nationality. . . .

Muslim India cannot accept any Constitution which must necessarily result in a Hindu majority Government. Hindus and Muslims brought together under a democratic system forced upon the minorities can only mean Hindu Raj. . . .

Finally came his conclusion:

Anyhow, I have placed before you the task that lies ahead of us. Do you realize how big and stupendous it is? Do you realize that you cannot get freedom and independence by mere arguments? I should appeal to the intelligentsia. The intelligentsia in all countries in the world have been the pioneers of any movements for freedom. What does the Muslim intelligentsia propose to do? . . . I think that the masses are wide awake. They only want your guidance and lead. Come forward as servants of Islam, organize the people economically, socially, educationally and politically and I am sure that you will be a power that will be accepted by everybody.[36]

This was the culmination. Reaching this point had not been simple or easy. There were basic reasons for not partitioning the Indian subcontinent. Still, Jinnah insisted—successfully—that it must be done.

During the course of World War II the English government decided to find some suitable way to solve the India problem, and at war's end Prime

Minister Clement Attlee appointed Lord Mountbatten to work out a solution with the Indian leaders. He found them to be far apart in their policies and difficult to deal with. In a very simplified summary, Gandhi favored a united Indian government in which initial authority would be given to the Muslims (to satisfy their demands), with the knowledge that the large majority, composed of Hindus, would soon take control. Nehru rejected this idea as chimerical; his own solution was to grant a large degree of autonomy to the provinces, hoping that this would satisfy the Muslims. Jinnah was well aware that under either of these plans the Hindu majority would completely dominate the Muslims, who were outnumbered about four to one.

Mountbatten was unwilling to split India into two nations, as Jinnah demanded, well knowing that such a solution would be condemned by the Hindus and fearful that the plan could not work because Hindus and Muslims were intermixed all over India. Mountbatten conducted separate interviews with the leaders after his arrival in March 1947, trying to find common ground for establishing India as a self-governing dominion within the British Commonwealth.

Mountbatten found Jinnah to be "frigid, haughty and disdainful." He records an instance in which he argued that what Jinnah wanted would be politically disastrous, and Jinnah promptly said, "I see the point." "I'm glad you agree," Mountbatten exclaimed. "But I don't agree," said Jinnah.

What Mountbatten wanted was a short-term settlement that would make it possible for Great Britain to withdraw from India with dignity; what Jinnah wanted was a long-term arrangement—

> to seize from this moment of history, from these few months of opportunity, what might be a millenium of national identity for ninety million Indian Muslims. With such stakes a leader cannot afford magnanimity or compromises. . . . Mountbatten, ever ready to unbend, to change his mind, to stoop to conquer, found this hard to understand. He often felt he had worsted Jinnah in a political argument without yet gaining an inch of ground. . . . On the other hand, when the argument was on legal or constitutional points Jinnah was almost always right—as was to be expected of a highly successful leader before the Privy Council and the Indian High Courts.[37]

On the principal issue, whether or not there should be established a separate nation, Pakistan, Jinnah won—against the convictions of Mountbatten, Gandhi, and Nehru that this was unwise. He won partly by being correct in his view that Muslims would not relinquish the right to self-rule, partly by stubbornly taking a stand that none of the other three had counterarguments or force sufficient to overthrow.

Mountbatten, who kept careful notes of his separate meetings with the leaders, wrote concerning his talks with Jinnah on 9 and 10 April,

> I told him that I regarded it as a very great tragedy that he should be trying to force me to give up the idea of a united India. I painted a picture of the greatness that India could achieve. . . . Mr. Jinnah offered no counter arguments. He gave the impression that he was not listening. He was impossible to argue with.[38]

Jinnah's policy of "stonewalling" obstinacy in his talks with Mountbatten was very different from his customary mode of leadership either in his dealings with the political organizations of Muslims or the masses of the people. It has been pointed out that he made his own decisions without consultation with advisers. What needs also to be made clear is that he was not dictatorial and did not impose his will upon his followers. On the contrary, he consistently maintained that every Musalman should make up his own mind as to what to do and how to do it. As he had said long before, in his presidential address to the Calcutta session of the Muslim League in 1920:

> It is now for you to consider whether or not you approve of [the Gandhian noncooperation] principle, and approving of its principles whether or not you approve of its details. The operation of this scheme will strike at the individual in each of you, and, therefore, it rests with you alone to measure your strength and to weigh the pros and cons of the question before you arrive at a decision.[39]

It was this frame of mind—this recognition that individuals must be self-committed to programs that they understood and that they approved—that was Jinnah's principal source of strength as a leader. It was why he depended so thoroughly upon communication, upon explanation and persuasion, as the instrument of leadership. Mujahid elaborated the point:

> A cold-blooded logician, he believed in reason and argument rather than in sheer agitation and propaganda; not in hypnotizing the masses but in convincing them through sheer logic; nor, by the same token, in turning his followers into a herd of dumb driven cattle, following a leader blindly, hugging on to an "ideal" and a programme without consciously subscribing to them, and launching upon it without heed to consequences.[40]

This same trait, of respecting the right and indeed the need for individuals to make up their own minds and to pursue their own convictions, led Jinnah to respect even those whom he urgently opposed. For example, in a speech in Bombay on 19 February 1921, after his decisive repudiation of

Gandhism, he said that he still had "the greatest respect and reverence for Mr. Gandhi and the men who were working with him." He was aware, he said, "of what noble stuff they were made"; he was "convinced of their noble and sacrificing spirit"; and he was "even proud of them"—deeply as he was convinced that they were wrong.[41]

Neither did Jinnah ever claim that he had wisdom enough to know how to solve the basic problem of India—that it was sadly lacking in homogeneity. In his 1941 presidential address to the Muslim League he noted that Muslims in every part of the subcontinent were organizing to represent their own needs. He noted also that the Sikhs were a separate community, a nascent nation. He denied that either democracy, based on majority rule, or representative government, based on segmentalized political bodies, could possibly work. In his address to the league the following year he warned that "it must be realized that India was never a country or a nation. India's problem is international in their subcontinent; and differences—cultural, social, political and economic—are so fundamental that they cannot be covered up, concealed or confused, but must be handled by all as realists."[42] In his 1943 address he went further—further than he was later able to defend. "Our goal is clear," he said, "our demands are clear. What is it that we want? We want to establish independent States in those zones which are our homelands and where we are in the majority."[43]

This demand for not one but several Muslim nations Jinnah could not sustain. Neither could he ignore the simple fact that Muslims were not all concentrated in one area but, like the Hindus, were scattered and intermingled all through the subcontinent. What about the Muslims who would be left outside the Pakistan that he envisioned? What about the Hindus who would be in Pakistan? "The minorities," he granted,

> are entitled to get a definite assurance or to ask, "Where do we stand in the Pakistan that you visualize?" That is an issue of giving a definite and clear assurance to the minorities. We have done it. We have passed a resolution that the minorities must be protected and safeguarded to the fullest extent; and as I said before, any civilized Government will do it and ought to do it. So far as we are concerned, our own history and our prophet have given the clearest proof that the non-Muslims have been treated not only justly and fairly but generously.[44]

Beyond this Jinnah could not go. He had no other solution for Muslims in the south and east of India than to depend upon the fair-mindedness of the projected Hindu government. What he did demand was "the full sovereignty of Pakistan":

> Our formula gives the Hindus three-fourths of this Subcontinent, with a

population of nearly 250 millions. Hindustan will be a State bigger than any other State in the world, both in area and population, except China, and we shall have only one-fourth, and in this way we can both live according to our ideals, culture and the social constructon of the two major nations."[45]

In December 1947, with Pakistan established, the Council of the All-India Muslim League met in Karachi to consider the remaining vital question—What should be done about the Muslims who would remain under Hindu rule? To the 160 Muslim delegates from India (among the total of 450 in attendance) Jinnah could only say: "We cannot give directives to you. When you are strong and Pakistan is developed, the settlement will come."[46] The session was far from harmonious. One member, expressing the views of many, said that "Pakistan could hardly take pride in calling itself a 'Muslim State'. He found many un-Islamic things in the State from top to bottom. . . . The behaviour of the Ministers is not like that of Muslims. The poor cannot enter the houses of the Ministers; the needy and the lowly cannot see them. Only the courtiers can enter, those who possess large bungalows can enter. The name of Islam has been disgraced enough." After a three-hour intermission to allow tempers to cool, Jinnah answered the critic: "We are only a four-month old child. You know somebody would like to overthrow us. I know you would say we have not done such and such a thing, but we are only four months old."[47]

Jinnah was within nine months of his death and was already ravaged by the lung cancer that had developed after tuberculosis had plagued him for several years.[48] What lived after him is the devotion and gratitude of his people. In the words of Waheed-Uz-Zaman:

His main strength was based on his undisputed leadership of the Muslim masses. . . . He led them as no one had led them before and they in turn offered unconditional obedience as they had not offered to any one of the earlier leaders. . . . This whole-hearted dedication and not his alleged fascist methods and dictatorial demeanour was the basis of the authority he wielded over his people."[49]

Conclusion

There is no doubt that Mohammed Ali Jinnah was virtually single-handedly the creator of Pakistan. As Hodson concludes, "The irresistible demand for Indian independence and the British will to relinquish power in India soon after the end of the Second World War were the result of influences that had been at work long before. . . . Whereas the irresistible demand for Pakistan, and the solidarity of the Indian Muslims behind that demand, were creations of that decade alone and supremely the creations of one man."[50]

Mujahid believes that it was Jinnah who made the Muslim League viable (although he joined it a decade after its creation), for "of all the Muslim leaders he alone was capable of transforming the League into a nationalist coalition representing . . . the various segments in the society—the landed aristocracy and the landless peasants, the West-oriented elites and the ulama, the modernists and the traditionalists, loyalists and revolutionaries, the literates and the illiterates, the urbanites and the ruralites, the intelligentsia and the masses, men and women, the elders and the youth." And more than the Muslim League, Jinnah created Pakistan: "The idea was, of course, in the air; but before Jinnah entered the scene as its foremost advocate, it was something vague: it was considered a poet's dream, a political chimera, a student's fantasy. It was Jinnah who gave it a concrete shape: he gave it sinews and muscles, flesh and blood."[51]

Jinnah was not by any means always right. His lack of wisdom in demanding that Bengal be added to his new nation became apparent when, in 1971, East Pakistan was converted into another independent nation, Bangladesh. His belief that the Muslims he left behind in India could maintain themselves peacefully as a coherent minority was proved to be futile when savage warfare broke out after the division of the subcontinent, resulting in the slaughter of some six hundred thousand persons and the migration of nearly fifteen million more. His basic argument that the 23 percent of the Indian population who were Muslims could not endure rule by the huge Hindu majority took no account of the fact that in the newly created Pakistan some 40 percent of the population were Hindu or otherwise non-Islamic. His own recognition of the problems caused by partition he revealed in a speech delivered a mere two weeks before his death, on 27 August, 1948, when he confessed: "The blood-bath of last year and its aftermath—the mass migration of millions—presented a problem of unprecedented magnitude. To provide new moorings for this mass of drifting humanity strained our energies and resources to the breaking point. The immensity of the task very nearly overwhelmed us and we could only keep our heads above water."[52]

While the issue of independence was being discussed by spokesmen for Great Britain, the Hindus, and the Muslims, the multiplicity of problems afflicting the subcontinent appeared to be virtually insoluble. During the subsequent decades the new Indian and Pakistani governments have proved to be viable. On the principal problems, of poverty and of divisiveness, at least some substantial progress has been attained. The native peoples have proved to be better able to rule themselves than was generally expected by outside observers. For this their leaders deserve great credit, however much yet remains to be done.

5

The Emergence of Indonesian Independence

If Pakistan originated as an afterthought of its founder, Ali Jinnah, the Republic of Indonesia was even more an incidental byproduct of Japanese victories in the first part of the Pacific war, riding in on a wave of sentiments aroused by ardently patriotic oratory. To understand the nature of that oratory and the depth and intensity of the feelings that underlay it, both for the speakers and for their listeners, it is helpful to review the history of the islands.

For both the Indian and the Indonesian Muslims there was a deeply implanted feeling of cultural and religious identity. But essentially both were nudged into independent nationalism by larger forces that were pursuing broader and different objectives. Moreover, within their quite different circumstances, in both countries the progress toward independence was guided by centralized leadership, rather than simply reflecting popular demand.

The Indonesian Muslims, even more than those in India, had to be taught to feel a unifying bond of nationalism. Geography separated rather than united them. Clustered below the equator between the Philippines and Australia, some eight thousand or thirteen thousand islands (depending on how large an outcropping is considered an island) stretch across an expanse as wide as that from Russia's Ural Mountains to the Atlantic coast of France. Only about three hundred of them are inhabited. Never in their long history were they a single nation. Ironically, it was their colonizing power, the Netherlands, that taught these varied populations to think of the East Indies as an entity. Even into the opening decades of the twentieth century, there was no common urge for independence among the generality of the people. This was a goal that had to be envisioned and nurtured and afterward announced and then propagated by a very small band of intellectuals.

For such reasons, the revolution that established the Republic of Indonesia was designed and implemented by leadership that made extensive and skillful use of persuasive communication. As a result the revolution

was, strangely, both frenetic and passive. It resembed a geyser in which
the water is not particularly hot, but the surface bubbles and spouts
because of the rising gasses. The image of evanescent hot air seems
peculiarly appropriate when considered in relation to the founding father
of the revolution, Achmed Sukarno. Despite his other formidable qualities,
the most notable fact about Sukarno was that he was an orator—an
effervescent fountain of glowing words, magnified by exaggeration, hot
with feeling, and tending toward grandiloquence of style. As he said about
himself, he was a Romantic Revolutionist, loving crowds, loving excite-
ment, loving senuous pleasures; and he exuded charm. The wartime and
postwar developments in the Far East created circumstances that were
especially favorable to his type of leadership. His was the personality that
Indonesia most needed at the time, just as he needed the special circumstances that enabled him to succeed. The man, the time, and the place
were peculiarly suited to one another.

It should not be inferred that the transformation of Indonesia from
colony to nation occurred automatically or easily. By no means did the
Dutch allow the area to slip from their grasp willingly. The islands were by
far too rich a source of revenue and of other advantages to be parted with
except reluctantly. Outbreaks of fierce fighting continued for several years.
The principal revolutionary leaders—Mohammed Hatta, Sutan Sjahrir,
and Achmed Sukarno—all had to pay for their leadership with imprisonment and exile. Nevertheless, the transition from colony to nation, if not
harmonious, was accomplished—at a cost of prolonged bloodshed.

Every movement and every nation is reflective of its past and of its
environment. Why the revolution in Indonesia was so different as to be
virtually unique must be assessed in terms of its long history, of the nature
of Dutch rule during the three hundred years of their occupation, of the
geographical diversity and immensity of the islands' area, and also of the
policies and practices of the Japanese during their wartime rule. The
cumulative effect of these circumstances constituted both the challenge
and the opportunity for which Sukarno's leadership was well suited.

The Land and the People in Historical Perspective

Louis Fischer commenced his account of Indonesia with a poetic flour-
ish:

Between the Pacific and Indian oceans, between Asia and Australia lie
7,900 islands. Once they were the Dutch East Indies. Today they are
Indonesia. Three thousand of them are large, Java alone counting 57
million inhabitants. Some are no bigger than a peasant's farm. It is as

though the gods that made the continents had a great deal of material left over and cast it helter-skelter into the equatorial waters.[1]

The islands curl up around Singapore and Malaysia in the west and find an eastern anchorage in New Guinea. By no means are the inhabitants newcomers among the global communities of peoples. The bones of Java Man, *Pithecanthropus erectus,* discovered in 1891, prove that Indonesia was inhabited from an early stage in the evolution of humankind. Since the seas dotted with island steppingstones proved easy migration routes, successive waves of immigrants spread across the island chain: first Melanesians, then Negritoes, and next (around 3000 B.C.) the race from southern China that settled much of Southeast Asia. It is the languages of this group, called Austronesian, variants of the Malay lingua franca, that comprise the 170 spoken languages of the islands. In general character, they divide into two loose groups: the languages of the interior of Sumatra, Borneo, and Celebes, and the later languages of the coastal areas and of Java and Bali, which resemble the Malagassi of Madagascar and the Tagalog of the Philippines.[2]

Two different types of society developed early: urban along the coasts and agricultural in the interior, where the mountainsides have been terraced for rice culture from ancient times. A proverb still current declares that "religion comes from the seas, customs from the mountains." Hinduism, Buddhism, and Islam became prominent in succession. Trade with China and India has flourished from prehistoric times, and Indonesian spices and artifacts were imported by ancient Greece and Rome. The Temple of Borobudur, a massive stone structure decorated with some fourteen hundred bas-reliefs of buddhas and of Hindu gods, was built in the later eighth century A.D., just before the islands were inundated by the advent of Islam. "We object to the description of ourselves as underdeveloped!" Sukarno frequently insisted, noting that Java had a sophisticated civilization while England was still primitive.

As far back as history stretches, the islanders had been reasonably prosperous. Nature provided a favorable environment, including a hot temperature, abundant rainfall, and rich volcanic soil that is ideal for the growing of rice. Natural resources are abundant. Figures compiled before World War II show that Indonesia supplied 90 percent of the world's quinine, 86 percent of its pepper, 75 percent of its kapok, 37 percent of its rubber, 28 percent of its coco palm, 19 percent of its tea, 17 percent of its tin, and a variety of other products. Petroleum in recent years has been a major source of income. As is well known, it was the spices of the Indies that Columbus sought, and it was the East Indies that he thought he found. Vasco de Gama did find them, by sailing around the Horn of Africa. For Europe spices were more than tasty condiments; in the long millennia before refrigeration, spices were the chief preservatives of food, more valuable for practical living than gold or jewels. From the fifteenth century onward, the resources of Indonesia were exploited for European advantage, which in the view of the British historian J. S. Furnival is why Southeast Asia did not more quickly arise out of its torpor, as Europe did after the Middle Ages.[3] The area was exploited rather than developed.

The Dutch, the Portuguese, the Spaniards, and the English came into Southeast Asia in the seventeenth century with but one purpose. "The plunder of the east, for it did not deserve the name of commerce, was their direct object," wrote John Crawfurd, who served as British Resident in Java from 1811 to 1816. He also explained why the islanders chose Islam over Christianity: "The Christian religion, in the countries of the Archipelago, and in those around, is justly unpopular, because in every instance, it has been the instrument of political intrigue, or been propagated by violence, when the consequence of its introduction has been the inevitable loss of the most valuable political and civil rights."[4] The Netherlands ruled the islands not directly but through local satraps, regents, and tribal headmen whom they protected from rebellion by their military forces, and who enriched themselves while plundering the populace to supply the Dutch demands. Fischer neatly summarized the results: "The Indonesian people, thanks to Dutch oppression, Islamic sterility, and no leadership, succumbed to a cultural coma, political paralysis, and economic decline."[5]

During the Napoleonic Wars England seized the East Indies from Holland and ruled them, under the famous Thomas Stamford Raffles, who introduced humane reforms, until the Treaty of Vienna in 1815 restored them again to the Dutch. Raffles then went to Singapore, claiming it for England in 1819, and devoted the brief remainder of his life to making it a great free port to enhance trade between Asia and Europe. The Dutch promptly rescinded Raffles's reform measures, pressing the islanders for more and more revenue, which led to a war that lasted from 1825 to 1830. Guerrilla resistance to Dutch rule continued. Bali, for instance, did not yield to Dutch control until the twentieth century. In Fischer's words, "The entire period from the beginning of the Java War in 1825 to about 1877 can be viewed as a slow-burn Indonesian revolution."[6]

Dutch efforts at self-reform of their colonial practices were actuated by a novel, published in 1860 and written by a Dutch colonial official, Eduard D. Dekker, who resigned his post to write a fictionalized indictment of the sufferings imposed upon the Indies peasantry, much in the spirit of *Uncle Tom's Cabin*. The novel was widely read in Holland and stirred the conscience of the people. When in 1869 the Suez Canel was opened, encouraged by this fast route to the East, Dutch families in large numbers commenced emigrating to the East Indies. Spreading out through the islands, they carried with them their European standards of social aspirations and conduct—but only for themselves. They maintained a strict social distance between themselves and the Indonesians. In 1901 Queen Wilhelmina proclaimed what she called the "Ethical Policy" of liberalization. The Netherlands persisted, however, in economic policies that shifted immense revenue from the islands to the European rulers. But there were good aspects as well as bad. Dutch law, for example, was extended broadly to protect the villagers from the extortions of moneylenders and exploitive local headmen.

As happened all through Asia, Japan's victory over Russia in 1904–1905 aroused among leading Indonesians an exultant burst of self-confidence. For the first time, the idea was implanted that the area need not forever remain subject to European rule. Personal ambitions were stimulated. A major result was a demand for Westernized education. This was precisely what the Dutch were reluctant to provide. In 1900–1904, the total number of Indonesians enrolled in Western-type primary schools was only 2,987, in a population of some sixty million, with scarcely any in higher grades.

A small group of Javanese intellectuals, many of whom held minor posts in the civil service, in 1908 organized a society that they called Boedi Oetomo, or "high endeavor," designed to provide mutual aid and encouragement for higher education and self-improvement. This society had no tinge of nationalist sentiments. It excluded from membership all but the professional elites, and its sole aim was to win better opportunities for its members. Nevertheless, it was a beginning, a center for Indonesian aspirations. Four years later, stimulated by the success of the Boedi Oetomo, Muslim intellectuals organized the Sarekat Islam, or Muslim Association. At first its leaders disavowed any political aims. But at a meeting in March 1914, one of its founders, Raden Achmad, hotly declared, "The people have joined Sarekat Islam en masse because they seek their rights. . . . The people see their rights continually threatened. That is why there is a great cry for them to unite to defend themselves and to resist with more power those who rob them of their rights."[7] The leaders denied any religious test for membership and invited Christians and Hindus to join. As early as 1916 the membership, including teachers, civil service clerks, factory workers, and peasants, along with a few aristocrats, grew to 360,000. This was the beginning of the independence movement. "Indonesians were about to concern themselves with the lot of the masses and the future of their country."[8]

Not surprisingly, the movement quickly took on a Communist aspect. As Fischer points out, "The Indonesians, with few exceptions, had not yet entered the capitalist stage. . . . They had no capital, they were not in business. Not being capitalists the Indonesians easily lent themselves to anticapitalism."[9] An agitator named Tjokroaminoto, who quickly moved into central leadership of Sarekat Islam, became the first Indonesian leader to speak openly and vigorously in public against the Dutch authorities. The result was magnetic. "Whatever the subject of his speeches, they served to break the silence which until then had greeted the actions of the authorities," wrote the historian Tas. The effects were both immediate and far-reaching:

> Tjokroaminoto was in many respects a predecessor of Sukarno: indeed, his example had a major influence on Sukarno's political education. A skillful orator and, like so many agitators, propelled by artistic sentiment and desire for success, he was a man of the people in that he shared their customs and vices. A demagogue when circumstances demanded, he would readily disguise social phenomena in religious slogans or, if it better matched the mood of his audience proclaim himself an ultraradical.[10]

The Communist influence strengthened, and in its September 1918 session the Sarekat Islam adopted a resolution denouncing the "predominance of sinful capitalism."

In response, the Dutch in May 1918 formed the People's Council of Indonesia, with an appointed membership that was half-Indonesian, half-Dutch. The council had neither legislative nor executive functions but did meet twice a year to discuss problems and to offer advice to the governor general. Meanwhile, in 1920 the Sarekat Islam formally joined the Soviet Comintern. Stalin, in 1925, recognizing that the Indonesians lacked the will to pursue ideological Communist goals, advised the Sarekat Islam to launch a nationalist revolution. Armed fighting broke out in 1926, with disastrous results for the unprepared rebels. Some 13,000 were arrested, 4,500 were imprisoned, and another 1,308 were placed in concentration camps. The Indonesian Communists ceased to be a political force until after World War II.[11]

After this farcical 1926 revolt sputtered out, Indonesian nationalism faded. Some of the nationalists, both angered and frightened by the evidence of Communist control of the movement, shifted their allegiance to Muslim welfare and social organizations. Others believed that essential steps toward broadened political rights would be won through the People's Council. Ethnic and religious groups turned from fighting against the Dutch to quarreling with one another. Communists who survived the 1926 roundup were reorganized under the leadership of a shrewd organizer and persuasive orator, Tan Malaka, who stressed his independence from Soviet control. He might well have become the guiding spirit of the independence movement if the Communists had avoided the fiasco of the premature 1926 revolution. For the next two decades Tan Malaka remained embroiled in intrigues and plots, involving a "kaleidoscope of fortune-hunters which [he] paraded before the people—armed gangs, some in uniform, others not; officers seeking loot, glory, or promotion; fantastically inclined nationalists who collaborated with the Japanese; fanatics; Oriental racists; schemists and hysterics."[12] Finally, Tan Malaka was arrested by a local police official who had him summarily executed.

A different kind of movement, with different leadership, was inaugurated on 4 June 1927. The Nationalist Party of Indonesia, which did guide the movement successfully to independence, was organized by three men who were loosely allied but who had very different personalities. An American Foreign Service officer who spent some time in Indonesia while the new Republic was taking form described them as "Soekarno, the spellbinder, Sjahrir, the thinker, and Hatta, the realist."[13] All were Dutch-educated and Westernized. Sukarno was not only their spokesman but their leader. The founding of the United States of Indonesia was not his work alone, but his was the starring role.

The Saga of Indonesian Independence

The history of the Indonesian independence struggle has qualities of the "theater of the absurd," in which multiple characters intermingle in a disjointed plot, in which the dialogue and the action are not always clearly related, and in which there is no positive identification of the characters as good or bad, central or peripheral. The Dutch never established a bond of fellowship with the islanders. Coming to Indonesia from a very different kind of culture and very different kind of country, they remained much more distant from the people than the English did in India. As an Australian scholar saw it, "The tall blond invader strode among the small brown people like someone from another world."[14] Indonesians, meanwhile, with no sense or tradition of national unity and with a general level of welfare not below the living standards their ancestors had known, did not hate their foreign rulers, nor did they form friendships with them. The two peoples moved about among one another without coherence, according to a pattern that kept them interrelated but separate, like chess pieces during a game.

Realizing the crucial importance of communication, the Dutch sought to maintain a language barrier between the Indonesians and the outside world by using the Malay language for their administration and by discouraging the use or knowledge of the Dutch language by Indonesians. A French specialist-student of Indonesia concluded that "the real truth is that the Dutch *desired and still desire to establish their superiority on a basis of native ignorance. . . .* By opposing him [the Indonesian] with a language intended to mark the distance that sets him apart from the

European, the Dutch have striven and still strive, though vainly, to deprive their ward of contact with the outside world."[15]

Neither did the Dutch encourage Christian evangelism, being well content to leave the people apart in their own religion. Professor G. M. Kahin, a promoter of Indonesian studies, points out that the special character of Indonesian Islam made it a natural channel leading toward modernism, if not nationalism.

> The unique character of the Mohammedan religion professed by most of the 90 per cent of the Indonesian population of that faith [accounts for] the high degree of religious tolerance, lack of bigotry, and openness to new ideas that one finds in most of Indonesia. In Java, at least, this is partly due to the fact that Islam has usually been only a relatively thin frosting on top of thick cakes of Hindu-Buddhism and the older indigenous Javanese mysticism. But there and throughout most of the rest of Mohammedan Indonesia this also arises from the fact that—unlike the situation in the Near East—the Moslem religion has not been tied in with either the political or the socio-economic order or interpreted so as to maintin their *status quo.*[16]

With the schools largely closed to them, the Indonesians had few opportunities to learn of the world outside or to associate themselves with the surge of Asian modernism. R. A. Dartini, a Javanese aristocrat, wrote of her sadness because only a few members of the privileged class were able to find a way out of their tribal limitations. "The Hollanders laugh and make fun of our stupidity," she wrote, "but if we strive for enlightenment, then they assume a defiant attitude towards us." She illustrated what this meant socially. "My brothers speak in high Javanese to their superiors, who answer them in Dutch or in Malay. Those who speak Dutch to them are our personal friends. Several have asked my brothers to speak to them in the Dutch language, but they prefer not to do it, and Father also never does. The boys and Father know all too well why they must hold to the general usage."[17]

Almost the only way to win advancement was by going to the Netherlands to study, and this was difficult to do. A small group of Indonesian students, including Mohammad Hatta and Sutan Sjahrir, found inspiration in Holland from the call of Communists for independence of all subject peoples. They founded the Indonesian Association to urge mass action for nationalism. Returning home in 1923 they founded a journal, *Indonesia Merdeka,* and also a number of study groups for discussion of how independence was to be brought about. On this point there was a very great difference of opinion. Hatta and Sjahrir were convinced that the movement must be a small and tightly cohesive effort by intellectuals who understood the problems and how to deal with them. The goal they aimed toward was a parliamentary form of government that would be established by a gradual expansion of reforms.

Sukarno, on the contrary, had both a different goal and different methods. What he proposed was a combination of Islam and Marxist socialism that would be constructed on a base of village democracy. From ancient times, the villagers had sought for unanimous decision, *mufakat*, that emerged as the consensus after a problem was thoroughly discussed. What Sukarno wanted to avoid was "the tyranny of the majority." Instead of first debating and then voting, the local groups should feel out the various differences concerning how to deal with their problems and then should work out satisfactory compromises. All the localities should be united in a national federation that would pursue a similar method of conciliating and compromising differences until a consensus finally emerged. To Hatta and Sjahrir such a plan consisted of vague and impractical mysticism. Concealed within it, they felt, was a determination by Sukarno to exercise dictatorial rule, as the one who would define and declare the decision to be brought into effect.

There was an equally vital difference between their methods and Sukarno's. What he sought to create was a mass movement, aroused and directed by his own speeches. What they feared was that once people were aroused, they could not be controlled but would engage in senseless and ineffective outbursts of violence.

In 1929 Sukarno and several of his associates were arrested and brought to trial on a charge of treason. The prosecutors were constrained to limit their case to specific acts that were in violation of specific laws. Sukarno had a much wider latitude in his defense. In a long and rambling speech that was addressed less to the court than to Europeans, Sukarno quoted extensively from various European socialists to support his charge that the Dutch were not only exploiting Indonesia economically but were also denying civilization and the means of being civilized to the Indonesian people. For this reason, he contended, revolution (which the laws interpreted to be treason) was both justified and inevitable. As he said, "Whether or not we were given the rights, whether or not we were given the means or the strength—any individual, or community, or people, bar none, will ultimately respond in *a surge of energy* when the provocation of a bloodthirsty oppressor can no longer be borne!" This type of defense could not avert the verdict of guilt, and Sukarno was sentenced to two years of imprisonment.[18]

The concentration camp conditions that the leaders had to endure were so squalid and brutal that, as Sjahrir claimed, a majority of the prisoners became mentally ill. As for himself, "I have acquired a certain hardness . . . the human being of Tolstoi and even of Gandhi, whom I have long held before my eyes, has left me. In reality, man is stupid, vulgar, cruel and brutal."[19] Sukarno was separated from the others and held in exile on the island of Flores.

The outbreak of World War II and the occupation of Holland by the Germans in 1940 resulted in a vaguely worded proclamation by Queen Wilhelmina that after the war's end the circumstances in Indonesia would be reconsidered. Among the Indonesians there was considerable sympathy for the expansionist aims of Japan. The chief result, they felt, would be expulsion of the Europeans from Asia. After that, who could tell what might happen? As Sjahrir wrote:

> For the average Indonesian, the war was not really a world conflict between two great world forces. It was simply a struggle in which the Dutch colonial rulers finally would be punished by Providence for the evil, the arrogance, and the oppression they had brought to Indonesia. Among the masses, anti-Dutch feelings grew stronger and stronger. This was naturally reflected in the nationalist movement and in its leadership, part of which expressed sympathy for the Axis openly.[20]

Meanwhile, still another development in Sukarno's thinking was his attraction to the Marxist goals of brotherhood, just distribution of goods, and world peace that presumably would result from the withering away of nationalism. In 1926, Sukarno expressed his sorrow that his close comrades had rejected Marxism, thereby causing a split in the independence movement, which he called "the blackest page in our history." "It set our movement back by decades," he charged. Then he explained his own views:

> We are convinced that there are no important obstacles to Muslim-Marxist friendship. As we have explained, true Islam has some characteristics of Socialism. It is true that Socialism is not necessarily Marxism, and we know that this Islamic Socialism is different from Marxism—because Islamic Socialism is spiritual, while Marxist Socialism is based on materialism. But it is sufficient for our purposes to show that true Islam is Socialistic in character.
> Muslims should not forget that Marxism's materialist interpretation of history can often serve them as a guide when they are faced with difficult problems of economics and world politics.[21]

Dr. Hatta tried to dismiss the dispute over ideology by emphasizing the essential point that the big problem was to arouse and intensify the spirit of Indonesian nationalism. As he summed up:

> No, the idea of Indonesian unity has nothing to do with uniformity of political thinking. It poses the idea of a united and indivisible Indonesian people. The propaganda for unity must be concerned with the

education of the masses into Indonesian citizens; and the population groups of the various islands must be made to realize that they belong to one and the same nation, the *Indonesian* nation.[22]

Sutan Sjahrir, in a still different vein, argued that what Indonesia most needed was not nationalism but modernism—and that this had to come from learning the lessons exemplified by the West. As he wrote in his autobiography:

> For me the West signifies forceful, dynamic and active life . . . and I am convinced that only by utilization of this dynamism of the West can the East be released from its slavery and subjugation.
> The West is now teaching the East to regard life as a struggle and a striving, as an active movement to which the concept of tranquility must be subordinated. . . .
> We must extend and intensify life, and raise and improve the goals toward which we strive. This is what the West has taught us, and this is what I admire in the West despite its brutality and its coarseness. . . .
> Every vital young man and young woman in the East ought to look toward the West, for he or she can learn only from the West to regard himself or herself as a centre of vitality capable of changing and bettering the world.[23]

When Japan occupied the East Indies, it naturally aimed to pacify the population and to win its support. In furtherance of this aim, the Japanese offered leadership in the pacification program to Sukarno and Hatta. As the historian Tas viewed it, the decision by these two leaders to become spokesmen for Japan

> was certainly defensible. . . . It brought Sukarno and Hatta, for the first time, a position surrounded by official prestige, a factor of importance in a primitive society like that of Indonesia, and it also enabled them to travel the length and breadth of the country. Wherever they went, they were able to make propaganda speeches which, although subject to Japanese censorship, gave them the political prestige to which they were entitled. In those speeches they are obliged to emphasize cooperation with and service to Japan, and they were repeatedly forced to perform symbolic acts expressive of the willingness to serve. Sukarno in particular played his role with enthusiasm.[24]

Consequently, in May 1945 when the Japanese recognized the inevitability of their retreat from the islands, they prepared for establishment of a Republic of Indonesia—with Sukarno as its president. Sjahrir, with his Western orientation, strongly opposed accepting independence from Japan as a gift, arguing that to do so would bring down upon them the condemnation of the Western Allies. Hatta, however, supported Sukarno, and their combined weight overpowered the reluctance of the doubters. As Tas concludes, "Sukarno was the only man with a national reputation, whose name was known in every village, whose word evoked an echo throughout the territory, and whose actions had any significance."[25] Actual proclamation of the Republic was postponed until 17 August 1945.

The British navy protected Indonesia from the return of the Dutch administrators, and after an outbreak of severe fighting between British and Indonesian forces, the Allies decided they must accept the creation of the new nation. The main impediment to be overcome was the nature of Indonesian collaboration with Japan. This had always been resisted by Sjahrir, and, in a compromise solution, the government was changed from the presidential to the parliamentary form and Sjahrir was named prime minister. The Dutch rewon control over large areas, and fighting broke out between them and the Indonesian troops. The United Nations intervened, and several compromise plans were successively agreed upon. Finally, on 17 August 1960 the Republic of Indonesia came into being.

During all the fifteen years of political struggles for control, Sukarno served as president. In 1960 he asumed virtually complete control, with the title of "Great Leader of the Revolution." A People's Consultative Assembly, under his chairmanship, governed the nation, with the parliament and the cabinet reduced to mere advisory roles.[26] This government was unchallengeable but not peaceful, for it engaged in continuous warfare to bring all the Indies islands under its jurisdiction. In 1967 an army coup displaced Sukarno, and on 21 June 1970 he died, isolated and under house arrest. He was buried, with a stately funeral, at his birthplace of Blitar, far removed from the Hero's Cemetery in Jakarta. "The state burial brought enormous masses to the streets; it was a national event, a national memorial day—and no more than that."[27] Sukarno achieved much, but, again, at the end, his career was still reminiscent of the "theater of the absurd," theatrical but with its meaning obscure.

The Nature of Sukarno's Leadership

In simplest terms, what distinguished Sukarno and most truly characterized him is that he was an orator. He was not so much a leader who made speeches as a speaker whose mesmerizing eloquence brought him leadership—a dazzling personality whose prominence and whose significance were manifested through his persuasive platform power. As a political theorist, he sought to combine Islamic mysticism with Communist ideology, control mechanisms, and global ambitions, but he was unable to achieve real clarity or realistic effectiveness. As a nationalist, he was ambitious in his determination to extend the boundaries of the state to include the whole of the Dutch East Indies and to extend Indonesian influence outward over the Asian and indeed the global scene. As an administrator, he was inattentive and inefficient. As a leader who won and held authority through his personal persuasive communication, he was unmatched among his own people and merits high rank among the other orator-statesmen of the time. A review of the kind of message he delivered and of his method of delivering it will reveal his strength and his weaknesses and will show why he partially succeeded and why he fundamentally failed.

A chapter in Bruce Grant's book on Indonesia so well depicts the nature and the influence of Sukarno's oratory that it leaves little except further detail to be added.[28] The people, he says, came in time to expect little except inspiration from Sukarno's speeches. A schoolteacher expressed what was perhaps a general opinion when he said that President Sukarno was a good orator but had an empty head—for which quip he was punished with fifteen months imprisonment.

Still, the teacher was at least partly right. Vagueness was Sukarno's forte. When he was asked whether he expected to bring Communists into his cabinet, his reponse was ridicule of those who suffer from "Communist-phobia" as "soft in the head." He did not answer the question. When the people of West Irian complained that the government was not bringing them promised benefits, Sukarno replied with a typically rousing speech in which he said, "It turns out that the problem is: *there is not enough canned beer in West Irian!* Sisters and brothers in West Irian! . . . the Republic has never indeed promised schools, the Republic has promised and has brought independence, the Republic had promised and is bringing Clear Rays and Brightness."[29] Specificity and actuality were not Sukarno's trademarks. Directness and folksiness and at least the appearance of common-sense realism were—as when he explained that Indonesia would solve its economic problems because "if nations who live in a dry and barren desert can solve the problems of their economy, then why can't we?"[30] To his followers he was Bung, or "Brother," Sukarno— one of them, better in vision and in will power, surely much more eloquent, but more peasant than intellectual.

Louis Fischer, a journalist who wrote discerning biographies of both Gandhi and Sukarno, presents an insightful view of what their people demanded of their new leaders:

The new states of Asia and Africa were born in dreams and live on hope. Their people pine for a savior. They are hero-worshippers. They worship yet criticize. Imperfections in their idol make them bitter. He is a god who must produce miracles—or else. Asians are both impatient and impassive, and one can never know when impatience will take the upper hand. Everything depends on the leader's appeal to mass imagination.

This one-man eminence may turn his head or break it. It is a tremendous responsibility, a great opportunity, and in the final analysis an impossibility. No single individual can achieve what a poor, underdeveloped country expects of him. He inevitably disappoints. His pink charm grows tarnished.[31]

Of Sukarno, the people expected much—too much. Out of the scramble of islands, and out of a diverse and feuding people of many languages, differing customs, and no great sense of urgency about either unity or independence, he was expected to create a unified and productive nation. It was not a role that he sought to avoid. Even as a child on the playgrounds, he eagerly sought attention and applause. He was the one who climbed the tallest trees. His bravado won for him the nickname of *djago,* meaning "rooster." He loved to strut and to crow. And these were characteristics that he never outgrew. As Fischer pointed out, his love for power was primarily a love for personal display: "the possibility to stage-manage, rearrange, sway masses, express his personality, exert influence, display showmanship."[32] What he did not want was the drudgery of office, the routine, the study of details. He was above all the agitator, not the administrator.

After the Indonesians had an army of their own, Sukarno always appeared in public wearing a uniform, sometimes highly decorated with medals and ribbons, sometimes plain, but always a uniform. In 1962, when he was able to marshal the resources for it, he built in Jakarta a monstrous arena that seated one hundred thousand people. This was his kind of stage, huge and impressive and yet in a way intimate, for he stood not on a platform confronting his audience but out in the middle, surrounded by it.

On each 17 August, to celebrate the founding of the Republic, Sukarno made a speech that he described as "a dialogue . . . a two-way conversation between myself and the People, between my Ego and my Alter-Ego. A two-way conversation between Sukarno-the-man and Sukarno-the-people." He went on, continuing this self-analysis—as part of his speech, mind you—to his hundred thousand cheering auditors:

I become like a person possessed. Everything that is non-material in my body overflows! Thoughts overflow, feelings overflow, nerves overflow, emotions overflow. Everything that belongs to the spirit that is in my body is as though quivering and blazing and raging, and then for me it is as though fire is not hot enough, as though ocean is not deep enough, as though stars in the heaven are not high enough![33]

Despite this cascade of feelings, Sukarno typically commenced his speeches quietly and conversationally, and he tried to maintain this conversational mode along with his bursts of bombast. Since he repeated his speeches time and again in his tours of the islands, speaking in all the major cities and many smaller towns, the dates and the places make little difference. His speaking was all of a piece. He described himself as a Romantic Revolutionist and glorified in identifying himself with his Suffering People, as their Mouthpiece, as the Bearer of Messages to them, as well as their Supreme Commander. Typical of his mode is a passage he used many times:

> If, for example, at this moment, an angel were to descend from the heavens and say to me: "Hi, Sukarno, I shall grant you a miracle, to give the Indonesian people a just and prosperous society as a gift, as a present," then I would reply: "I don't want to be granted such a miracle, I want the just and prosperous society to be the result of the struggle of the Indonesian people!"[34]

His speaking in this vein was interminable, and perhaps it had to be. As the studies by such experts as Feith, Tas, and Kahin document in detail, the politics attending both the founding and the conduct of the new government was a battlefield of contention for places and for power. Sukarno stood above his rivals, on a high peak, but his position was far from unassailable. As Fischer rightly said: "Sukarno's power seemed real. Yet it rested on intangibles like oratory, appearance, and past—on his public appeal. At least a few rivals would have been glad to replace him, and many were ready to support them. Sukarno, therefore, had to perform a complicated balancing act, and his skill at it was a sight to see and study."[35]

Fischer also notes that "often, he takes a point of some complicated matter of principle or policy and produces a masterful summary." In sum, he went on, "as an orator . . . Sukarno is among the masters, and his speeches have provided a continuing reality in Indonesian politics; they represent his hold over the Indonesian people, and they represent his capacity, sometimes exhibited under strain, for playing with ideas and concepts."[36]

Sukarno's ability to marshal arguments when he chose to do so is illustrated by a speech he made in 1926, pleading for the Muslim population to work with, not against, the few and generally foreign or foreign-influenced Marxists:

> The nationalists who are reluctant to seek contact with Marxists and work together with them show great ignorance of history and of the way the world's political system has evolved. They do not realize that the Marxist movement in Indonesia and Asia generally has the same origins as their own movement. They forget that the objectives of their own movement are often similar to those of the Marxist movement in their

country. They forget that to oppose those of their own countrymen who are Marxists is to reject comrades in the same struggle and to add to the number of their enemies. They forget or do not understand the significance of their fellow fighters in other Asian countries, such as the late Dr. Sun Yat-sen, that great nationalist leader who happily and wholeheartedly cooperated with the Marxists, even though he realized that a Marxist organization of society was still impracticable in China because the necessary conditions did not exist.[37]

What he himself stood for, as he explained in his speech of inauguration when the Republic was reorganized as the United States of Indonesia, was "Eastern democracy . . . Indonesian democracy . . . a democracy with leadership."[38] Having in mind the traditional village councils in which consensus emerged after discussion and meditation, Sukarno declared that "democracy is jointly formulating truth."[39] His real idea was that democracy should be "guided" or directed by a leader who understood what the people wanted. In 1951 he frankly avowed that what the people wanted, in his view, was dictatorship.[40] He did not accept the Western democratic principle that "fifty per cent plus one are always right."[41] Far truer, in his view, is the principle that "democracy is the unity of God with his servant."[42] Twice Sukarno made a pilgrimage to Mecca, and his "public references show a tendency to connect his political activities with the will of God."[43]

Sukarno was never in favor of political parties, which in his view divided the people and substituted dissension for consensus. Yet political parties did develop, for in Indonesia there were many divergent groups. In a speech on 28 October 1956 Sukarno complained about this "disease":

> Let us be frank about it, brothers and sisters. We made a very great mistake in 1945 when we urged the establishment of parties, parties, parties. . . . Do you know, brothers and sisters, what my dream is as I speak to you now? . . . My dream is that the leaders of the parties would meet, would consult together with one another, and then come together to the decision of "Let us now join together and bury all parties".

Two days later, to a convention of teachers, he continued the theme: "I do not want to become a dictator, brothers and sisters. . . . That is against my spirit. I am really a democrat. But my democracy is not liberal democracy. . . . What I would like to see in this Indonesia of ours is guided democracy, democracy with leadership, but still democracy."[44]

In the long view of history, Sukarno may well be remembered in terms phrased by his longtime associate and sometime rival, Mohammed Hatta, who in 1960 wrote of him: "It cannot be denied that Sukarno is a patriot who seeks to achieve a just and prosperous Indonesia as quickly as possible. Due to his nature and aptitude, however, he sees only the broad lines of his conceptions, without bothering about details which may be decisive in their implementation."[45]

Conclusion

Indonesian independence was won against heavy odds under the central leadership of a galvanic leader whose eloquence reached across the many barriers that divided the people, and whose inspiration penetrated the spirits of a people who, until aroused, had no special urge to seek independent and unified nationalism. It could be said of Sukarno, as also of Jinnah, that he "spoke his nation into being." There were other factors. There always are. But without the incitement and persuasion of Sukarno, Indonesia would almost surely now be decisively divided into many parts and would probably not be free. For this reason the movement to establish and stabilize the Republic of Indonesia provides a laboratory for study of the effects of leadership that is sustained and exerted through persuasive communication.

A nation is more than boundaries. It necessarily comprises also a depth of commonality of feelings, of aspirations, and at least substantial agreement on methods for its governing. In none of these respects might it be said that full and complete nationalism has come to Indonesia even yet. There is about the island peoples an air of expectation and anticipation. "The best is yet to be." The geography, the history, and the linguistic and ethnic diversities are bars against the fulfillment of the aim by which Sukarno and his comrades, Hatta and Sjahrir, were inspired.

Another reason for the partial, rather than complete, attainment of Indonesia's nationalistic goal lies in the relationship between it and the West. This is also a factor in the developmental processes of other new nations in the Orient, and particularly in Southeast Asia. These new and as yet not wholly developed nations depend upon and desire help from the industrialized West.

But the need to be helped, and the fact of being helped, pose psychological handicaps. For self-confident self-respect, people need to give as well as to receive, and for this the West needs to become a fuller partner not only in giving but in taking. There needs to be a much stronger sense in the West of what the East has to offer. Sjahrir was speaking for many in his hemisphere when he said that he and his people need the dynamism and vitality of the West. But he was also right in wanting to avoid what he called its brutality and coarseness. In other terms, the West stresses striving for oneself, in a quest for both temporal and heavenly individual advantages. The East, meanwhile, is being wooed away from familyism and clannishness but still has lessons to teach about social responsibility and the virtues of interdependence. One of the greatest boons the West can offer to the East is to ask from it the recipe for brotherhood.

This, amid his vagueness and bluster, was a central part of what Sukarno was trying to say. This is the burden of his repetitive 17 August speeches on the theme: "The Social Consciousness of Man Prays for Our Victory."

> Therefore, all you people of Indonesia, [he would say] keep your heads high! Do not retreat, do not stop, put your feet firmly on the ground! If there are times that you feel confused, if there are times that you almost despair, if there are times that you do not quite understand the course of our Revolution, which indeed sometimes resembles a vessel at sea tossed in a raging storm—return to the source of our Message of the Sufferings of the People, which is congruent with the Social Conscience of Man.

This seems somehow to be vaguely good, like Sukarno's speeches in general. Both he and the troubled development of Indonesian nationalism may best be understood in terms of the dimensions in which cultures may usefully be analyzed. As the preceding chapters have illustrated, they vary in terms of *power-distance,* or how social inequality is institutionalized; of *uncertainty avoidance,* or how different cultures show tolerance or intolerance for ambiguity and lack of precision; of *individualism,* or the balance of personal autonomy and collectivism; and of *masculinity,* or the degree of emphasis upon self-assertiveness versus the sense of interdependence.[46]

The shaping of Indonesian nationalism and modernization has varied from Western experience and values, in large part reflecting the differences between Asian and Western cultures. Sukarno's leaderhip exemplifies the fact that both expectations and possibilities during this transitional period in Indonesia were vastly different from what are taken for granted in the West. And the analysis of the rise of Filipino independence in the chapter to follow will show that these cultural differences will again be influential. It is in terms such as these that the communicative effectiveness of Asian leadership must be assessed.

6

The Philippines: A Three-Pronged Revolution

The process of nation making in the Philippines has followed a different course from that in any other Asian country. It commenced earlier, it passed through diversionary stages, and in some unfortunate ways it is still not wholly complete. In significant respects the rebellion of Filipinos has been three-pronged—against Spain, against the United States, and against themselves. Over the span of a generation, the steps toward independence were nurtured by the colonizing power. For this reason the process was weakest at its roots. It demonstrates that there was point in Sjahrir's insistence that he did not want independence to be "given" to Indonesia; to be real it had to be won.

In any event, the making of the Filipino nation proceeded very differently from the nation-building developments in Japan, China, India, Pakistan, and Indonesia. The circumstances were different, and different kinds of leaders emerged to deal with them.

Leadership is always needed everywhere, but in the Philippines it has proved to be especially important. The islanders historically have been essentially community-minded. Localism has mattered more than nationalism. Personal loyalties have been given more to local leaders than to broadly inclusive national issues and policies. This has made communication with the national audience a problem difficult for Filipino leaders to solve. The bond between leaders and their close and immediate following has always been strong. But barriers that divide groups severely handicap national unity.

The problem is not one of multiplied political, racial, or religious divisions. Neither is it geographical; there is much less diversity of geographical divisions in the Philippines than in Indonesia. The central problem is largely social. Aside from the Communists, there have generally been only two major political parties in the islands. But party members feel their attachment chiefly to their local leaders, who serve as their middlemen, their defenders, their benefactors, and their spokesmen in their relations with the national party organization. This localization of sentiment

159

strengthens community leadership but tends to make national leadership more titular than vital. Local party units rally behind, support, and vote for the national leader of their party but do so rather superficially, without feeling a depth of attachment. The distant leader with whom their contact is secondhand, through the medium of their local chieftain, is little more than an abstraction. Consequently, the majority support for national candidates or for the government may in times of crisis prove to be fickle or undependable.

Filipino society consists of layered relationships that are partly a matter of traditional class distinctions, more vitally a result of uneven distribution of wealth, power, and privileges. Together these factors have created a special kind of mind-set. The village people expect to be led and guided. When they move into the cities this habit of mind to some degree persists. It is cemented by self-interest.

The ties that bind local leaders to their local followers have long been in significant degree based on patronage. Officeholders at all levels, from administrators to clerks, school teachers, and even manual laborers, are largely appointed by the top-ranking politician. In return for the largess he is able to dispense, the party members support him. He is the fountain from which flow their rewards; to him their loyalty is given. Because of such factors it is difficult for national leaders to have a charismatic appeal on a broad scale. They must address themselves less to the mass of the people than to the designated spokesmen for local groups. And just as their breadth of appeal is limited, so is the faith and confidence that the people feel in the head of their party. Consequently, both political leaders and the individual voters have learned to scan with canny skepticism whatever is proposed and to watch alertly for unexpected changes in promised programs. For such reasons democracy—when defined as equality of rights, of privileges, and of responsibilities—has not yet matured in the Philippines. In this sense at least, the process of its nation making remains incomplete.

The Roots of Nationalism

Nationalism has proved to be one of those terms that scholars simply cannot define—and actually it does not need definition. Perhaps it suffices to say that a nation consists of people who feel themselves to be a nation. Obviously nationalism does not depend upon a single language, or a single religion, or a single race. It does not depend upon common economic needs or shared territorial aspirations or agrement on a unitary sense of mission. Shared myths and legends and traditions and memories surely help, but such cultural binders often have small regard for political boundaries. National songs and flags and rituals and laws emphasize the fact of nationality but could scarcely create it. Somehow the Filipinos came to feel themselves a nation, not as coherently as the Japanese and the Koreans, not as zealously as the Indians or the Pakistanis, but with less regional divisiveness than the Indonesians and more inclusively than the Chinese. Their feeling of common identity, nevertheless, along with their localism, has deep roots. Whatever their differences, they are Filipinos, one and all.

The 7,100 or so islands that make up the group have a total land area of some 115,600 square miles—about the size of the state of Arizona. They are far less widely scattered than are the East Indies, and actually form a rather close group. Most of the area and most of the population are in eleven islands. Two of them, Luzon in the north and Mindanao in the south, contain about two-thirds of the area. The fact that the islands are relatively close together at least offers the chance for greater unity than Indonesia has been able to achieve. There are abundant sheltered waterways that draw the Filipinos to the seas for food and transport. But there is no broad east-west channel among the islands suitable for large-scale ship operations, which has the advantage that the islands have not tended to separate into north-south entities, nor is it easy for foreign power to cut them asunder.

The islands were peopled by many Malay tribes speaking scores of dialects, of which Tagalog, Ilocano, and Visayan are the most widespread. Some Muslim influence penetrated the islands from the sultanates of the East Indies. The decisive Spanish settlement came during the sixteenth century. The Spanish invaded the islands with the sword in one hand, the cross in the other. They easily established supremacy and then set about converting the people to Catholicism, while subjecting them to ruthless local administrations that built roads and plantations with enforced labor. They also systematically transferred ownership of land and resources to the foreign civil and ecclesiastical officials. The Spaniards introduced from Central America such crops as tobacco, pineapple, cacao beans, and eggplant, but agriculture was largely neglected in favor of trade, conducted in a famed fleet of galleons. This trade attracted an influx of Chinese merchants and moneylenders. The Spaniards settled in the cities and, except for their missionaries, had little direct contact with the Filipino people. Local government was through a system of barrios. Spanish friars, through churches built in all the barrios, helped to ensure obedience to His Catholic Majesty in Madrid. Coastal areas were firmly governed, but from the mountains there were periodic raids by the unconquered Igorots and Moros, directed against the Spaniards, the Chinese, and the Filipinos who were under direct Spanish control. These various factors combined to cause disunity and enhance dissension.

Schools were established and taught by priests whose principal aim was to inculcate and enforce the precepts of their Catholic religion. As Dr. Raphael Palma wrote, describing his school days: "The young man of yesterday was trained to conform absolutely to established dogmas and precepts. He was not taught to assert and to talk; much less to discuss with his parents and teachers."[1] Submissiveness was taught, not inbred. To become independent-minded, they had to be retaught.

The beginning of militant nationalism developed among intellectuals who sought to repudiate the Spanish view that Filipinos "are fit only to tend carabaos, to pray, and to follow blindly the instructions of the friars."[2] If the revolt against Spain began late, after some three hundred years of colonial rule, one reason is that the priestly influence entrenched in every barrio was by no means all bad. As a Filipino scholar wrote, "There are two Spains· one great, generous . . . and another 'black' Spain."[3] Another wrote of qualities that were a mixture of good and bad in the typical priest:

> He must be treated with a just measure of understanding; unlike the English district officer in India and the Dutch plantation overseer in Java, he did not, indeed he could not, raise the color bar between himself and the Filipinos; he was a missionary who must seek them out, he was a priest who must care for their souls; . . . he had taken vows from which there was no holiday or retirement. Above all, he was lonely, a Spaniard two oceans away from Spain, a man forbidden to have a woman, a clerk of some culture deprived of conversation and of books. . . .
> [But also] he was the most dangerous of men, one combining great power with a sense of mission, a self-justified ruler and governor of souls and bodies. . . . What was this man to think of liberalism, progress, nationalism, freedom, and independence?[4]

While priests enforced discipline and taught obedience, the secular rule was frankly exploitive, designed to squeeze out of the islands as much wealth as possible for the colonizing power. In sum, "Tributes were paid by the Filipinos in exchange for being ruled ruthlessly and exploited by the new masters."[5] It was in protest against this system that leaders emerged who captured the imagination and aroused the spirit of the suppressed population.

Still another thread in the fabric of Filipino nationalism must be identified. In a sense, the seeds of nationalism were planted not by Filipinos but by Spaniards, and not in the Philippines but in Spain. In 1812, while Spain was subject to Napoleon's rule, a new constitution established a legislative assembly, the Cortes, in which all the colonies as well as Spain itself were represented. With two representatives in this body, the Filipinos attempted to win reforms. "The battle, then, would not be between Spain and The Philippines; that is an over-simplification. In simple justice it must be said that Spain herself was an older and a larger battlefield for the same ideas, and Spaniards had fought and would fight Spaniards much longer and with greater devotion and ferocity for these ideas than ever Filipinos would fight Spaniards."[6] It was only when the reformist efforts had clearly failed that a new force, a demand for independence, was brought to bear.

This was accomplished by a novelist and poet, Jose Rizal, brought up in a wealthy family, educated by private tutors, whose mind was further shaped by several years of fashionable travel in Europe. As Rizal confesses through the words of his principal character, Ibarra, in his novel *Noli,* "I was not brought up among the people, and perhaps I do not know what they need. I spent my childhood in the Jesuit school and grew up in Europe. My opinions were formed by books, and I know only what has been exposed; I know nothing of the things that remain hidden, that have not been written about."[7]

Wealthy though Rizal's family was, in his European travels he spent all that he had and was reluctant to write home for more. He was lonely, friendless, and only twenty-five years old. He was working on a melodramatic novel, entitled *Noli Me Tangere,* while he lived in a cheap apartment in Berlin, existing on bread and butter and coffee. Finally, when the novel was finished, he could find no publisher except a nonprofit printing house that brought out two thousand copies for which it charged the author three hundred pesos. This was the book that "changed the course of Philippine—and Spanish—history. It was the greatest work in Philippine literature—creating in Filipinos the sense of being one nation—the indispensable foundation for progress and eventual independence."[8] Not only in the Philippines but also in Europe the book quickly became enormously popular.

Rizal returned home and on 3 July 1892 founded an organization called La Ligua Filipina, pledged "to unite the whole archipelago into one compact, vigorous and homogeneous body."[9] For this Rizal was arrested and deported to a remote southern island. On 7 July a group of Rizal's associates organized a secret society, which they named Katipunan, "the idea of the plebian Andres Bonifacio, who became and remained to the last its spiritual leader."[10] A flag was designed, with the sun at its center, which became the official flag of the newly organizing revolutionary forces. This was the background for proclamation of the revolution by Emilio Aguinaldo on 31 October 1896, when he addressed a crowd in the plaza of the town of Imus, saying: "Filipino people! The hour has arrived to shed blood for the conquest of our liberty. Flock around and follow the flag of the Revolution—it stands for Liberty, Equality and Fraternity."[11] This was the climactic step of declaring independence and calling for revolution. But it could not have been taken without preparation, and during this preparatory stage others than Aguinaldo took the lead.

The spark of national identity had been lighted by Rizal and Bonifacio. The inflammable material was the sense of outrage, slowly but strongly developed, among the exploited mass of the Filipino people. But the spark was not so placed as to ignite the mass. Rizal did not believe in revolution, nor was he anti-Spanish. Through his novel he made his own sentiments clear. He has his hero Ibarra exclaim: "Never! I will never lead the multitude to get by force what is deemed improper by the Government, no! And if I see the mob arming themselves, I will side with the Government and fight them, for I cannot recognize that multitude as the people."

The enemy against which Rizal poured his wrath was not the Spaniards per se, but the rich (Spanish or Filipino), as he emphasized in a speech he wrote for his elderly reformist character Pablo: "Did you say he is rich? The rich do not think of anything else save to augment their wealth; they are blinded by pride and pomp, and because they are ordinarily safe, especially if they have influential friends, none of them bothers to think of the suffering poor. I know all this because I was once a rich man."[12]

Bonifacio, with an eloquence matching that of Rizal, issued an impassioned appeal, in Tagalog, translated as "What Every Filipino Should Know," in which he contrasted an idealized past with the harshness of Spanish rule:

> The Filipinos, who in early times were governed by our true countrymen, before the coming of the Spaniards, were living in great abundance and prosperity. They were at peace with the inhabitants of the neighboring countries. . . . The Spaniards came and offered us friendship. The self-governing people, because they were ably convinced that we shall be guided toward a better condition and led to a path of knowledge, were crumpled by the honey words of deceit.
>
> Now nothing can be considered stable in our lives; our peace is now always disturbed by the moans and lamentations, by the sighs and grief of innumerable orphans, widows and parents of the countrymen who were wronged by the Spanish usurpers; now we are being deluged by the streaming tears of a mother whose son was put to death, by the wails of tender children orphaned by cruelty and whose every tear that falls is like molten lead that sears the painful wound of our suffering hearts; now we are more and more being bound with the chains of slavery, chains that are shameful to every man of honor. What, then, must we do? . . . Reason tells us to be united in sentiments, in thoughts and in purpose, in order that we may have the strength to find the means of combatting the prevailing evils of our country.[13]

What should be done, beyond feeling united, was not yet decided. The Katipunan society denounced the middle class for doing nothing but talk. "All of you are learned, and where there are learned men everything is brought to naught by discussions."[14]

Rizal, not knowing himself what to do in the Philippines, and alarmed by increasingly militant talk, took ship for Cuba, to serve in the Spanish army as a surgeon. But the Spaniards, blaming him for arousing the spirit of discontent, removed him from the ship, returned him to his homeland, and on 30 December 1896 had him executed by a firing squad.

The spark of discontent was ready to be fanned into flaming revolt. One who fanned it with incitive oratory was Lopez Jaena, a friend and close associate of Rizal. He as born on 18 December 1856 into a poor family but was enabled to study through the generosity of a rich uncle. He undertook to become a medical doctor but was too lazy to do the necessary preparatory work. In 1891 he settled in Barcelona as a journalist, advocating reforms. He was better known as an orator, possessed of almost mesmeric eloquence. How he spoke may be illustrated with brief extracts from a speech he delivered to a large audience in Barcelona on 25 February 1889. It describes what he and Rizal stood for and also their belief that the Spaniards would respond to proper appeals. Jaena started his speech gently:

> In taking the liberty of addressing you, I do not forget, because I do not want to forget, that I stand on a platform on which men eminent for their learning and admired for their eloquence had shone, as I do not ignore either that I have before me an enlightened and learned audience. For these reasons I feel humble and uneasy, overwhelmed by chaotic sensations, without the knack, without the adroitness to fulfill the obligation of honor that brings me to this place.

He proceeded for an hour with felicitous and wholly unchallenging descriptions of the Philippines. Then, abruptly, his tone changed:

> The friars, gentlemen, are the omnipotent factor of ruin, backwardness, and miseries of these islands of Oceania. In their hands are the vales of knowledge, science and morals, but they teach fanaticism, they imbue idiocy, they corrupt the people as they teach. . . .
>
> And why? Because the religious orders, gentlemen, as prescribed in their statutes, do not recognize any other homeland but their convents, no other ruler but their prior, no other law but their own constitution, their motto being intransigence; and they are opposed to the advancement of the countries on which they prey.[15]

These were strong words but still stopped well short of revolution. Like Rizal and Bonifacio, Jaena was not prepared to plunge into revolution and did not really know what to do. A new type of leader was needed and soon appeared.

Aguinaldo's Dual Revolution

Emilio Aguinaldo, who waged revolutionary war first against Spain and then against the United States, to become father of the Republic of the Philippines, was born into a moderately wealthy family at Kawit, a town on the eastern shore of Manila Bay, on 2 March 1869. He was a sickly child and grew to be a puny boy, beset with illnesses so that, as he said, "from childhood, my life has always been fraught with hardships and sadness."[16] His father, after serving several terms as mayor of Kawit, died at the age of forty-eight, and nine-year-old Emilio felt heavy family responsibilities. He withdrew from school at the age of thirteen, to start a small trading company, in order to pay off debts left after his father's death. The family had some small real estate holdings, but even so life was hard. "The government authorities made life worse. The islands drew the dishonest like a magnet, and it became impossible to pass through life as a peasant without making heavy contributions to the pockets of corrupt officials as well as to the bottomless coffers of the colonial government."[17]

When Aguinaldo was seventeen, his mother, in order to prevent his being inducted into the Spanish army, had him appointed barrio captain of Kawit. Eight years later he was elected mayor of the town, and in that same year he joined the Katipunan society. That was the beginning, as he recalled in his autobiography, *Memoirs of the Revolution,* of his friendship with Andres Bonifacio. The following year, 1896, was a notable time for Aguinaldo. He was married in January, and his first son was born in October. Just a few weeks earlier, on 31 August, Aguinaldo addressed a mass meeting in Kawit of a thousand civilians who advocated a new revolutionary government. The next day Aguinaldo assembled some two thousand men armed mostly with sticks and bolos and with them attacked a Spanish army post and forced it to surrender. The next day a column of Spanish reinforcements approached, and Aguinaldo called for volunteers to repel them. Only five hundred men responded. As Aguinaldo reported in his *Memoirs:* "We had nine guns only. Our men carried wooden stakes and nipa sheaves which looked like guns at a distance. Others had bolos and daggers." The battle continued for two days. The first day the Spanish drove the rebels from the field; the second day the rebels drove the Spaniards into the thick mud of rice paddies and waded among them with their sticks and bolos. When it was over, "we had two cartloads of tattered dead bodies," Aguinaldo wrote, "70 remington guns and other equipment. When I examined General Aguirre's sword, I found these words inscribed: *Made in Toledo, Spain, 1869.* This was the year when I was born. The coincidence made me happy. From that time on I brought this sword in all my battles.:[18]

That was astounding success, and it continued. For several more days other engagements were fought. As an observer noted, Aguinaldo stood among his men with the new Filipino flag in one hand and a revolver in the other, calling on them to advance. Bonifacio was also leading insurgents in a series of small fights that lasted for just one week before he was forced to withdraw. The Spanish forces numbered more than nine thousand, but they were widely dispersed. The governor general reported that "I have hardly at my disposal enough forces to nullify such efforts in so vast a territory, for the rebels have more than enough men with which to organize expeditions to points which they believe convenient."[19]

On 31 October, Aguinaldo, well realizing that words are more potent than bullets, issued in quick succession two manifestos to the Filipino people. The first of them was brief and incitive: "Filipinos! Open your eyes! Let the innocent blood of your brothers, victims of Spanish hatred, leave in your hearts a lasting impression. Let this, our innocent blood, and the countless tyrannies of our enemies, serve from now on as the insurmountable barrier between Spain and The Philippines."

The second was longer, combining arguments justifying the rebellion with plans for setting up local governmental units.[20]

In December a naval force from Spain brought reinforcements, which were greeted by the Spanish president of the Manila Casino with words that stirred a fighting spirit in the newly arrived troops but also strengthened the determination of the rebels. "You arrive in time," the speaker shouted to the troops; "the cannibals of the forest are still there; the wild beast hides in his lair; the hour has come to finish with the savages; wild beasts should be exterminated; weeds should be exterminated."[21]

The fighting, however, continued to go badly for the Spaniards, and on 22 March 1897 a rebel convention met at Tejeros estate in Kawit to proclaim the new government of the Republic of the Philippines. The day was Aguinaldo's birthday. He was absent but elected president. Bonifacio (who was there and who claimed and was refused the right to preside) was further humiliated be being denied first the presidency and then the vice-presidency. In a rage, Bonifacio left the meeting to organize a rival government that he would head. Aguinaldo's soldiers captured him, and on 10 May 1897 Bonifacio was executed on the charge of treason. For a few months the fighting was virtually ended by the rainy season. Then, with a new general leading a revamped Spanish army, an agreement called the Pact of Biaknaboto was reached. It restored Spanish rule, and Aguinaldo and eighteen of his principal aides were exiled to Hong Kong with an indemnity of four hundred thousand pesos. This money Aguinaldo placed in a bank, telling his followers that it was to be held in trust for the renewal of the revolution.

With the United States at war against Spain, an American agent was sent to Hong Kong to propose that Aguinaldo join with the Americans to defeat the Spanish in the Philippines. Aguinaldo went to Singapore, where Consul General Pratt handed him a telegram from Admiral Dewey that read: "Send Aguinaldo at once." Pratt further assured Aguinaldo that the United States "would at least recognize the independence of The Philippines under the protection of the U.S. Navy." Aguinaldo's reply was: "If I can secure arms, I promise you that my people will rise as one man against the Spaniards." On 7 May, after Admiral Dewey's victory in Manila Bay, a small vessel, *McCulloch,* arrived to pick up Aguinaldo and his associates to return them to Manila. Aguinaldo withdrew the pesos from the bank and paid the American consul for arms, which were to be delivered in the Philippines.

In Manila Aguinaldo was received by Admiral Dewey, who, according to Aguinaldo's notes, assured him that "the United States had come to The Philippines to free the Filipinos from the yoke of Spain." When Aguinaldo asked for a written statement, Dewey shook his head, saying that "the word of honor of Americans was more positive, more irrevocable, than a written agreement." Aguinaldo promptly went ashore and led Filipino troops against the Spaniards, driving them back into the mountains. He then issued a triumphant proclamation, declaring that "the Americans, not from any mercenary motives, but for the sake of humanity and the lamentations of so many persecuted people, have considered it opportune to extend their protecting mantle to our beloved country."[22]

On 12 June the Filipinos held an impressively large meeting in Manila, at which was read their Declaration of Independence. Admiral Dewey did not attend, remarking that he was too busy. By 30 June Filipino troops held nearly every province in Luzon and also held some nine thousand Spanish troops as prisoners. On 4 July, when several troopships were landing American soldiers, Aguinaldo met with General Thomas M. Anderson, who assured him that the United States had "entire sympathy and most friendly sentiments for the native people" and that never in its history had America imposed colonial dependency on any territory. More American troops arrived and were ordered to take positions held by the Filipinos. Aguinaldo sought assurances from the American commanders but was told that he had no need for concern.

On 15 September Aguinaldo convened a constitutional convention, which he proved unable to control. The constitution that was adopted named him as president but deprived the presidency of powers. The right to vote was restricted to the propertied class. At the conclusion of the convention, Aguinaldo proudly asserted that "the Republic we established was the first crystallization of democracy in all the east."

Meanwhile, ever-increasing American forces were established in strategic positions. On 4 February 1898, four Filipinos who approached an American guard post were shot. Aguinaldo sent a message to the American command asking for a neutral zone to prevent more accidental shootings but was told that "the fighting having begun must go on to the grim end." Aguinaldo noted in his journal: "We had no honourable course but to resist and sell our lives dearly."[23]

Thus the first revolution, against Spain, merged into the second, against the United States. Aguinaldo's misgivings about American intentions were intensified in June 1898, when he read an article that appeared in the 5 May issue of the London *Times,* saying that the United States would either annex the Philippines or sell them to England or another power. Aguinaldo wrote a letter to President McKinley, stating his disbelief that "so sensible a public man as you would venture to make an assertion so contrary to public sense." McKinley did not answer the letter, but he did enter in his records a handwritten note which reads: "While we are conducting war and until its conclusion we must keep all we get; when the war is over we must keep what we want."[24] As an American historian notes, on the day after Aguinaldo proclaimed establishment of the "little Filipino Republic, gay with banners and glad with music," President McKinley sent word to the American delegates to the Paris Peace Conference between the United States and Spain, which "signed its death warrant."[25]

General Aguinaldo's second war for independence, that against the United States, lasted for three years. His untrained, eighty-thousand-man ragtag army, without artillery and with rifles enough for only half of the soldiers, was finally defeated by the sixteen thousand well-armed and well-trained Americans. Aguinaldo himself was captured by a ruse when four American soldiers disguised as Filipino peasants slipped into his field headquarters on 23 March 1901. When he signed an oath of allegiance to the United States, the American military commander, General Arthur MacArthur, ordered his release and return to private life. On 19 April 1901 Aguinaldo issued a farewell proclamation to his people, bringing the Republic to an end: "Enough of blood, enough of tears and desolation. . . . By acknowledging and accepting the sovereignty of the United States throughout the entire archipelago, as I do now without any reservation whatsoever, I believe that I am serving thee, my beloved country. May happiness be thine."[26] Thirty-four years later, at the age of sixty-six, he sought to return to leadership, announcing his candidacy for the presidency of the new Commonwealth government. Launching his campaign, he spoke to a huge throng in Manila from a platform over which was flown a flag preserved from his days of battle. With an effort to recapture the martial spirit of that earlier time, he said:

Here, dear countrymen, you have this sacred banner, mute witness of our efforts to redeem our country from slavery. It is fortunate that it has been possible to preserve it for three decades. It was carried in victory by our liberating throngs. Watch it closely and you will observe holes and tears not caused by age but by the bullets of enemies. The smoke of gunpowder blurred its colors. It reminds us of the lives of our brethren sacrificed and blood generously poured for the redemption of our country. This flag reminds of the tears that dimmed the eyes of thousands of wives, mothers and daughters of those compatriots who "fell in the night without seeing the dawn."[27]

These were brave words spoken by a brave man, but they did not represent the spirit of the time. Aguinaldo was decisively defeated, and later, after the grant of independence, he tried vainly once more for the presidency. When I visited him in 1956 he was eight-seven years of age, still slender, still erect, still alert—and still refusing, as he always had, to speak English. He had ceased to fight, but he did not surrender. Eight years later, very peacefully, at the age of ninety-five, he died. He never forgot and never forgave what he felt was the breaking of promises made to him while he fought as an ally of the Americans to help wrest the islands from Spanish control. He was buried on the grounds of his Kawit home from which he had proclaimed the birth of the first republic in Asia. Many Filipinos remember him as the man who envisioned and strove to win the independence that they achieved a generation later. Others reject him as a relic of a primitivistic past before the era of Westernized modernization.

Commonwealth Politics

The First Philippines Commission, which arrived in Manila on 4 March 1899, was assigned the charge of recommending what American policies should be. The members found considerable turmoil and wide difference of opinion on what the Filipinos wanted. A spokesman for the propertied class testified that "The archipelago as a whole is composed of three classes of individuals: the rich and intelligent element; the poorer element of the country—the element that is willing to devote itself to work—and an element that may be called intermediate, made up of clerks and writers, who have a habit of stirring up the town."[28]

This was the impression that prevailed and that formed the foundation for the American Philippine policy. Dean C. Worcester, a member of the commission, who had special authority as author of a two-volume work on the islands, summed up what guided the plans for a semicolonial rule:

The great mass of the people here are ignorant. They have a very vague idea either of independence or liberty as such. I think it is more or less a matter of indifference to them what their government is so long as it is not oppressive. . . .

The second class, the highly educated class, the wealthy class, are clearly desirous of peace here . . . because they wish to continue in their business and make more money. . . .

The middle class is the class that is opposed to us . . . those who declare that the Filipinos are today fitted for self-government.[29]

This analysis of the islanders was probably basically correct. In any event, correct or not, it became the basis not only for the American political design but also guided the policies of the major Filipino leaders. The rich wanted only stability; the poor wanted jobs; only the middle-class intellectuals had genuine concern about what the government would be like.

Elihu Root, who was appointed U.S. secretary of war in mid-1899, was requested by President McKinley to draw up plans for governing the islands. With a conviction that most Filipinos were "but little advanced from pure savagery," he concluded that self-government would not be appropriate. To a campaign audience in 1900 Root argued that "the immutable laws of justice and humanity require that people shall have government, that the weak shall be protected, that cruelty and lust shall be restrained, whether there be consent or not."[30] To implement this principle, President McKinley appointed a commission headed by William Howard Taft. Taft's many virtues did not include open-mindedness. He found the Filipino people, in his observation, to be "ignorant, superstitious, and credulous to a remarkable degree," and what must at all costs be avoided was a turning of government over to a clamorous "coterie of Tagalog politicians." Instead, what Taft set out to do was to restore order, ensure stability, encourage American investment, and educate the people for eventual self-rule. Taft's immediate aim was to attract to his support the wealthy class, which welcomed American rule, and to silence or restrain agitators who were advocating either independence or as much self-rule as could be obtained. These were dangerous opportunists, Taft wrote to Secretary Root, for the Filipino people

are easily influenced by speeches from a small class of educated mestizos, who have acquired a good deal of superficial knowledge of the general principles of free government, who are able to mouth sentences supposed to embody constitutional law, and who like to give the appearance of profound analytical knowledge of the science of government.[31]

With Taft's approval, a group of Filipinos headed by Pardo de Tavera, a well-to-do physician and landholder of Spanish descent, who was educated in Europe and who believed that what the islands needed was not independence but modernization, organized the Federalista party, which advocated annexation by the United States and statehood for the Philippines. To General Arthur MacArthur, who was military governor, Tavera wrote:

> After peace is established all our efforts will be directed to Americanizing ourselves; to cause a knowledge of the English language to be extended and generalized in The Philippines, in order that through its agency the American spirit may take possession of us and that we may so adopt its principles, its political customs and its peculiar civilization that our redemption may be complete and radical.[32]

This political party Taft welcomed, but when another group sought sanction for creation of a Democratistas party that would urge early autonomy and eventual independence, Taft denied their request, saying it would mean "gathering into one movement all the lawless, restless, lazy, and evil members of society."[33] In 1905, after the Federalista party changed its advocacy from statehood to independence, President Theodore Roosevelt decided on the ameliorative step of establishing an elective National Assembly, to be chosen in 1907 by a carefully selected 3 percent of the population. Minimal though this step was, it provided a new opportunity for some Filipinos to emerge into national leadership.

The first to win real prominence was Manuel Quezon, a young lawyer, governor of a province, and a protégé of Pardo de Tavera. As a candidate for the Assembly, Quezon's speeches were cautiously guarded. "The Americans," he told the audiences, "came here to give us liberty and independence if we wish it after we have proved ourselves capable." Quezon had fought with Aguinaldo against the Americans well enough to rise in rank from second lieutenant to major. He refused to run for an Assembly seat as a member of a party but insisted on his independence: "I like to talk if I have something to say, and I talk regardless of the consequence of my words. I aim to raise hell inside the halls of the Assembly, which I could not do if I belonged to the Nationalista party, for then I would be compelled to measure my words—so I ran as an independent."[34]

Quezon's campaign impressed not only the small group of Filipino voters but also the Americans who were running the country. William C. Forbes, one of the officials, assured Taft that Quezon "has, I think, the most brilliant mind of any Filipino that I know . . . and makes speeches in Spanish and Tagalog that simply sway everybody within hearing. He does not use extravagant phrases, keeps carefully within facts, depends on sound reasoning for the merit of his arguments, and has really been, without exception, the most useful man to the government that we have had since I have been in the islands."[35]

After Quezon won his Assembly seat, he was appointed by the commission to be the first resident commissioner from the Philippines to sit in the U.S. House of Representatives—without a vote, as an observer. There he made the kind of speeches that were expected of him—faithful to Filipino interests as he saw them, but moderate and supportive of American rule. "We are living in the world of today," he told the Congress, "and we want to see our country prosper and develop." He cited the fact that American businessmen were coming to dominate the Philippine economy and said, "We are not opposed to any capital coming into and properly developing the islands." He went on, however, to warn against the ill effects of American control over business and trade. "We have learned that . . . the American people . . . have not yet succeeded in throwing off the heavy yoke of great corporate capital. What, then, can the Filipinos hope for in the undoubtedly forthcoming struggle between them and these powerful corporations in The Philippines . . . considering the fact that the Filipinos have no control of their government, which is in the hands of alien people?"[36] In Washington, Quezon moved easily in social circles, had high prestige as an intellectual and reasonable Asiatic, and was popular with officials and with the press. His speeches in the House of Representatives made few ripples and had little effect but were listened to with respect.

By Claro M. Recto, a member of the Philippine Assembly who knew him well, he was assessed as a thoroughgoing opportunist who shifted his tactics as circumstances changed and who was unhampered by any political philosophy. In presenting this estimate, Recto was more admiring than condemnatory. As he said in a speech in Manila on Quezon's seventy-fifth birthday, 19 August 1935, "In any particular political situation Quezon did what was politically useful and convenient." He explained what this meant:

It is about time that we scrap the legend that Quezon was a sincere and a frank, brutally frank, politician. It was the silliest, shallowest judgment ever passed upon the great man. It does him an injustice because it charges him with naivete, the worst insult to a brilliant and skillful player in the game of power politics. Quezon was a successful politician precisely because he was a master of political intrigue. He knew how to build strong and loyal friendships even among political opponents, but he also knew how to excite envy, distrust, ambition, jealousy, even among his own loyal followers. . . .

He was lavish and calculating in his exercise of the rights of patronage and allocation of public works funds. But he never overstepped the bounds of these legitimate forms of political warfare. He was zealous in maintaining the purity of the electoral processes. This was the heart of democracy, and Quezon guarded it even against his own party and his own immediate political interests.[37]

As a rather cynical realist, Quezon estimated his role in Filipino-American relations accurately and pursued his career with the realities as his guide. To be an effective leader he knew that he must court broad Filipino support by advocating independence and by staunchly representing Filipino interests. He knew also that to have effect he must never forget that the United States held absolute power over the islands, beyond any possibility of successful revolution. During the presidencies of Taft and Wilson, both of whom paid lip service to "eventual" Filipino independence, Quezon's speeches and actions were pro-American. When Presidents Harding, Coolidge, and Hoover were silent about independence and supportive of exploitive economic practices, his criticism of American rule was harsh. In 1923 Quezon broke his relationship with Governor General Leonard Wood, partly to regain ground he had lost with his Filipino following and partly in protest against the American view that the islands had become an indispensable military asset that could not be abandoned. Quezon announced dramatically that he preferred a Filipino government run like hell to an American rule run like heaven and declared that his slogan was "immediate, absolute, and complete independence."

After the Pearl Harbor attack, Quezon gave unstinting support to the United States. On 26 October 1943, he wrote a careful exposition to President Franklin D. Roosevelt of what he felt to be his lifelong views. After noting that the Japanese were attempting to win the Filipino people to an oriental way of life, and reminding Roosevelt that he was, as he always had been, an advocate of Philippine independence, he concluded:

> My advice and counsel to the Filipino people is that they should preserve and perpetuate their Occidental way of life which they can do only through continued association and cooperation with America and the Western world. Geographically, we Filipinos are Orientals, and will forever be so. Spiritually, that is to say, because of our culture and Christian civilization, we are with the West. The great destiny of the Filipino people, as I conceive it, is to play the role as the connecting link between Orient and Occident.[38]

Second only to Quezon among Filipino leaders during the Commonwealth period was his friend, schoolmate, and sometime rival, Sergio Osmeña. Osmeña did not bear arms during the dual revolutions against Spain and the United States, but he built a good record as editor of a newspaper that supported the rebels. Like Quezon, Osmeña was elected governor of a province and along with Quezon was elected to the first Philippine Assembly. When it was organized, Osmeña was elected Speaker, which gave him social rank second only to that of the American governor. His firm declaration, however, that his policy was "the Philippines for Filipinos" brought severe attacks against him, not only from the

Americans but also from the wealthy Filipinos who feared injury to their favored position.

Of largely Chinese ancestry, Osmeña was not a member of the Hispanicized upper class. He studied law and history in the United States but never became proficient in the English language. He seldom traveled outside the Philippines and had only a small circle of intimates. Nevertheless, he was a masterful political strategist who knew and observed the rules of the game, used patronage skillfully, and was both astute and ruthless in his alliances. Quezon used to say of him that it was "useless to try to defeat Osmeña; he is in alliance with God."[39] Osmeña lived to the age of eighty-one, but his political influence was strong only between his twenty-ninth and forty-fourth years. His last thirty-nine years were spent in subordinate or ritualistic offices, honorific but without power.

Osmeña's principal political alliance was with Manuel Roxas, who, like Osmeña, came from the central islands, south of Luzon. Roxas was a heavy-featured, fat-cheeked peasant type, with an unruly black mass of hair tumbling over his forehead. He lacked the finesse of Osmeña and the charm of Quezon, but he was powered by ambition, determination, robust vigor, and a spirit that surmounted failures and disappointments. A lawyer by profession, Roxas was an eloquent speaker who spoke to the people as one of them—plain, simple, without intellectual pretensions, practical-minded, and doggedly determined to maintain their rights. Like Quezon and Osmeña, he won election to the Assembly after serving as governor of a province. He built his own independent political following through an organization he named Bagong Katipunan, taking the name of the revolutionary Katipunan society founded by Bonifacio. In addition to demanding independence, as virtually all politicians did, Roxas also developed a Gandhi-like economic doctrine. "We shall struggle for economic self-sufficiency," he told his followers. "We shall break the chains of our economic bondage by buying from abroad only those commodities which we cannot produce. We shall encourage the restoration of our household industries. We shall patronize our countrymen who are engaged in business and condemn those who exploit their customers."[40]

In 1922 Roxas succeeded Osmeña as Speaker of the Assembly. Eleven years later, after breaking with Quezon, he was deposed. In a scene of raucous disorder, on 20 July 1933, the galleries of the Assembly were packed with Roxas's followers, while a three-hour debate on the floor concerning his status was beset by shouts and protests. Roxas made an effort to calm the protesters by calling up to them, "My friends who are in the gallery, any pain that I would feel because of any action that the House may take . . . has been erased by your sympathy." After the vote of expulsion, galleryites carried Roxas from the chamber, and outside, on the steps of the hall, he made impromptu what he regarded as his greatest speech—but it was not recorded. During the Japanese occupation of the Philippines, Roxas urged them not to grant independence to a puppet republic, telling them that this would not bring them any popular support. When the Japanese nevertheless did establish a republic and named Jose Laurel as its president, Roxas urged him not to play the role of hero by inciting an uprising against Japan, since this would cause the death of thousands of innocent people. Roxas agreed with Laurel that expediency demanded a declaration of war against the United States; it could do no harm and would save the people from Japanese oppression. After the liberation of the Philippines, General Douglas MacArthur cleared Roxas of charges of collaboration with the enemy and indicated his support for Roxas's candidacy for the presidency of the new American-proclaimed Republic.

All through the Commonwealth period Filipino political leaders were confronted by an impossible situation. They had to demand independence. They had to recognize that it was a goal impossible to achieve. And they had to cooperate with the American authorities in order to retain any influence or to accomplish any good for the Filipino people. Naturally, in taking such contradictory positions, they did not look good, even to themselves, and they were subject to severe denunciation by their critics. What Roxas said of Quezon in 1933 might with some justice be said also of Roxas, of Osmeña, and of Laurel, for in their political roles they were much alike: "He will advocate liberty or independence to gain or maintain himself in power, but if to gain power he has to turn his back on the age-old longings of his people, he is ready to sacrifice their liberty to serve himself."[41] Their motives were better than this suggests. But political advocacy, under those conditions, was a tiger they could not gracefully ride.

Independence—and After

The preceding chapters have ended with the achievement of independence, or in Japan and in China, with the formation of a new type of government. The Filipino struggle for the fulfillment of the national aspiration does not conclude so decisively. In all the Asian countries problems continued—and in many of them multiplied—after the people got a government of their own. Even so, in the Philippines, the inauguration of the new Republic on 4 July 1946 was much less of a climax than was independence for the other Asian nations, and it was not a real conclusion of the process of nation making. The date chosen for the transfer of power was significant. It was not a natal day of Filipino nationalism, either August 17 or October 31, but the American day of freedom. The real formative period for the Philippines still lay ahead.

The population continues to be divided into three groups: the wealthy, whose main concern is to protect and increase their wealth; the poor, whose main concern is to survive and hope for better times; and the middle-class intellectuals, who are politically contentious because a consensus on what the society should be like has not yet crystallized. Personalities continue to be more influential than issues and policies. In the formative period, there were Rizal and Bonifacio and Aguinaldo; then Quezon and Osmeña and Roxas; and after 1946, Roxas in a new role, Magsaysay, Marcos, and Aquino, continuing the leadership task of guiding the people into a coherency of feelings and of actions. Through all this time there have been many more whose claim to leadership was urgently supported. For, as was noted at the beginning of this chapter, in the Philippines, locally supported leaders (increasingly with national aspirations) are numerous. To a high degree the politics of the islands are personalized. This makes for instability.

The tutelage period of preparation for independence has been variously characterized as either too slow or too fast, too protective of American interests or too optimistic concerning Filipino abilities. On the general calendar of developments there is general agreement.

1901–1913. The Philippines Commission sought to implant a Westernized educational and administrative system and to substitute American for Spanish influence.

1913–1921. Under Governor General Burton Henderson the civil service was largely turned over to Filipinos.

1921–1929. Under Governor General Leonard Wood governmental, fiscal, and economic affairs were brought to greater efficiency under far stricter American management.

1929–1935. Under the stress of the Great Depression and spurred by Filipino agitation, the U.S. Congress adopted legislation preparing the way for Philippine independence.

1935–1946. With independence delayed by the Japanese advances in the Pacific, plans for installation of the Philippine government proceeded with inadequate preparation because all resources were devoted to winning the war.

To Manuel Quezon the problems did not seem complex. "If we are prepared to defend our country," he said, "we are free from foreign molestation; if we are just to our people, we will be free from internal rebellion. That is the whole problem—the club in one hand and the bread in the other."[42] This analysis ignored relations with the United States, which were such that independence had to be considerably modified by interdependence. For one thing, the American military bases in the Philippines—army, navy, and air force—were, and still are, too vital to defense of American, allied, and Filipino security to be endangered, let alone abandoned. For another, the economic ties between the United States and the Philippines were, as now, so deeply implanted that they had to be preserved for the benefit of both countries. And for yet another, there was no real consensus in the Philippines favoring the breaking of solid ties with the United States—nothing akin to the feelings of animosity toward Spain a generation earlier.

Quezon died in August 1944, as the war was ending. After the liberation of the Philippines, General Douglas MacArthur championed Manuel Roxas for the presidency of the soon-to-be republic. Osmeña, weak and ill, and disheartened by MacArthur's avowed support for Roxas, nevertheless sought the presidency. In an election flawed by corruption, and disrupted by the wartime destruction and dissension, Roxas won 54 percent of the 2.5 million votes. His inaugural address, delivered on the steps of the bomb-damaged legislative building, was somber:

> Look about you, my fellow-citizens. The tragic evidence of recent history stares at us from the broken ruins of our cities and the wasting acres of our soil. Unemployment is increasing. . . . There is hunger among us. . . . Plagues and rats and locusts gnaw at our food supplies. . . . Housing for most of our urban citizens is shocking in its inadequacies and squalor. . . . Our communications are destroyed. . . . Schools have been burned and . . . our educational system is in large measure a shambles.

Then, after claiming that Filipino resistance to the Japanese occupation was a "standard by which all heroism may be measured," he found in it "a proof and product of the passion for democracy and freedom which America has taught us during 48 years." Despite problems with some parts of the American rule, he declared that

> we have never had cause to waver in our confidence or faith in America. We have clasped to our bosom her system of government, her language, her institutions, her historical traditions. We have made them ours. . . .
> Yet we have today in our own land a few among us who would have us believe that we are in danger of an imperialistic invasion from the very nation which is granting us our sovereignty. . . . No, my mind will not stoop to so low a conceit as that.

He referred then to the disorders created by some seventy' thousand

Hukbalahaps—Communists and displaced peasants—armed with weapons left over from the war, and warned them not to try to replace with armed power the government elected by votes of the people. He promised that the injustices they had suffered would be rectified—"But first, arms must be surrendered."[43]

These three themes—that the Philippine economy was in a shambles, that the new government was molded on the American pattern, and that the security of the new nation was threatened by internal rebellion—continued to be emphasized throughout the Roxas presidency. In speech after speech he continued to stress the need for American support. Typical is a passage from his speech to Filipino war veterans on 5 February 1947:

> I have no foolish fear that Americans will seize, steal, or rob our natural resources and exploit or enslave us. . . . I invite them here, with every inducement I know. I am sure that when they have helped us to develop our land, to rebuild and repair our damaged facilities, and to expand our economy, they will also have trained many of our people to take over, to take command, to continue the work they have started.[44]

Roxas's successor, Elpidio Quirino, presided over four years of corruption, deteriorating economic conditions, and an expansion of the Huk (Hukbalahap) rebellion to a degree that threatened overthrow of the government. On American advice he appointed Ramon Magsaysay as his minister of defense, charged to rebuild the military and to subdue the uprising. "As soon as he took office, we started feeling the punch of a new, vigorous, inspired leadership which made its effect felt in every aspect of our fight against the Huks," reported a field commander of the Filipino army.[45] Magsaysay's program was reformist, recognizing the justice of the peasantry's complaints and seeking to improve their living conditions. Reflecting what Aguinaldo had told his followers, Magsaysay warned the armed forces under his command: "When your bullets are exhausted, the hungry man will get his gun and fight again."[46]

In 1953 Magsaysay was elected president. He was forty-six years old, had had only seven years of government service, and had grown up in an underdeveloped agricultural area, in a family with neither wealth nor position. He was, until the advent of Corazon Aquino, the only major leader of twentieth-century Filipinos who was not a lawyer and who had never been elected to any high office. His education had been scanty, and he was a poor student with little to recommend him except his attractive appearance and pleasing personality. After his election, he mused to friends, "Here I am about to assume the presidency, and I don't know what to do." Then he added, "I will just do what I think is right. I will let my conscience be my guide."[47]

Like his predecessors, Magsaysay leaned upon Americans for advice and depended on American support. Unlike them, he conducted an administration that was honest and forthright. It was far more vigorous than the others but scarcely more efficient—primarily because Magsaysay had never learned to delegate authority and to operate through a bureaucracy, but tried to oversee governmental processes personally. His most spectacular action was establishment of direct communication from the countryside to his own office by providing free telegraph service to anyone who wished to address a complaint or a suggestion to him. For the first time the barrio people—the farmers, the local leaders, and the local appointed officials—were brought into direct contact with their president. One effect was to create a national wave of renewed confidence in government. Another effect was to strengthen yet further the personalization of Filipino politics, with attention centered more on personalities than on issues.

Magsaysay's attention to details and his openness to messages and visits from all manner of individuals led him to confess, "It's true they wear me down sometimes," and "Often I get rattled. . . . and confused . . . sometimes I cannot attend to big things of state."[48] To those who criticized him for spending too much time talking to unimportant individuals, his retort was: "To whom do they want these people to turn for help, to the Communists?" Magsaysay's popularity was such that he would assuredly have been elected to a second term—but how much he might have accomplished by way of enabling the Philippines to attain a full measure of independence and of economic and political stability is unknown, for on 17 March 1957 a small airplane in which he was riding crashed into a mountainside and he was killed.

A few months earlier, on 31 October, I spent several hours with him while he consulted with a succession of visitors in his office, then rode beside him in his car when he went out in the afternoon to make two definitive speeches on the relationship between the Philippines and the United Statets. The first speech, in the Ilocano language, was at the site of a newly opened irrigation project that had been built with American aid funds, and in it he told the assembled peasant-farmers of the great debt that they owed to "our good friends" the Americans. The second speech was made in the hometown of the aged revolutionary president Emilio Aguinaldo, and Aguinaldo sat beside him on the platform. The speech was in English, for the audience, living close to Manila, all used this language. Magsaysay paid tribute to the patriotism that had impelled Aguinaldo to wage war against the Spaniards and the Americans; then he pointed out that world conditions had changed, so that now what was most needed was to support the American defense against Communist imperialism.

The two speeches together defined the status of the Republic of the Philippines: sovereign and proud but not wholly independent. In a sense, it was an epitome of the new world that transocean communication has brought into being, in which interdependence has become increasingly the ideal if not yet quite the fact. After him came Marcos and then Aquino, and the struggle continues to establish nationalism on a basis firm enough to transcend dependence on foreign protection and to reconcile the internal conflicts of interest among the wealthy, the educated elites, and the poor.

Conclusion

Leadership and communication with the people were important in establishing the Republic of the Philippines, as they have been also in the remainder of Asia. In the Philippines the problem of divisiveness has been as severe as in Indonesia, and its leadership has lacked centrality. Localism, in support of local needs and aspirations, resulted in attachment to local leaders. In an unfortunate degree the Filipino people do not even yet constitute so much a national audience as a cluster of diverse audiences. The greatest challenge that President Aquino confronts is to forge a true national unity.

Especially since the attainment of independence, Communist insurrection has been an unsolved problem. It is rooted not in ideology but in the long-existing division of the people into distinct classes—the wealthy, the poor, and the middle-class intellectuals—whose members have little feeling of commonality. Still another basic problem that is not yet solved is the establishment of a truly Filipino industrial and commercial base, on which could be built sufficient wealth to provide adequately for the general needs. The transition from American to Filipino rule did not include a transition from American economic dominance to all-encompassing native ownership and management. The reasons are complex. Aside from the evident need for development of greater technological and managerial competence, there is perhaps even more basically a failure to attain unification of feelings and of effort.

Only now is a new generation coming into leadership. The long period of Commonwealth dependence on the United States created attitudes of assertiveness without responsibility, and of stress upon independence concurrent with attempts to profit as much as possible from the status of dependence. A new national psychology takes time to develop. Hampered as it is by an economic system that has yet to deal realistically with the poverty of the masses and by the disorderliness of the Hukbalahap rebellion, such growth is difficult. But it appears to be under way. A new attitude of self-confidence and responsible assertiveness is forming. To be effective it needs more material resources, a leadership sophisticated in dealing with domestic and international problems, and increased national unity. The way of the future is not yet wholly clear.

7

Reshaping Southeast Asia: Personalized Politics

Continental Southeast Asia stretches from Vietnam and Malaysia to Burma, and from Bangladesh and Nepal to the island offshoots of Singapore and Sri Lanka. During the colonial period, France ruled over Indochina, and England extended its control from India into Burma. In between was independent Siam, now Thailand. Leaders who mostly were educated in the West developed new visions of guiding their people out of both colonialism and outmoded traditionalism into modernism and nationalism. Although lacking military power, they were able to establish independence in the "brave new world of persuasive and mediated messages."[1]

In doing so, they opened a Pandora's box of divisive yearnings. As was pointed out in 1968 by Singapore's foreign minister:

● Anti-colonial nationalism in the post-independent era has degenerated into a divisive ideology, breeding with a significant consistency all over Asia sub-nationalisms based on race, language, religion, and tribes. Peoples who were once united are going in for political archaeology. They are rummaging among ancient myths, doubtful legends and historical records to find reasons why they are entitled to be distinct and separate from the rest of the national community.[2]

This tendency causes them, as a student of the area concludes, to be "not yet nations in being but only in hope."[3] The disintegrative effects of this centrifugal tendency have been heightened by the cold war, which in Southeast Asia has tended to verge into hot conflict between Communist and anti-Communist groups.

● The group feeling that characterizes a nation—the sentiment of "us against them"—arises from a tangled complex of history, language, race, and religion. Southeast Asia is peopled largely by offshoots of the Malay race. The dominant religions of Buddhism and Islam show small regard for boundary lines. The educated minorities tend to look outward for their education, modern cultural values, and economic opportunities: the Cambodians, for example, incline toward France; the Burmese, toward England. What, then, were the centripetal forces that led to creation of the new nations?

• Nationalism is historically a relatively new concept, even in Europe. In Asia, including Southeast Asia, the imposition of an alien colonization that in Eastern terms was rude, unfeeling, and destructive of ancient values, shocked the native population into the realization that loyalty to family, clan, social class, religion, tribe, and village was not enough to serve its needs for welfare, for protection, and for communal pride. Colonial boundaries either came in native thinking to represent national boundaries or to suggest other compartmentalization that pointed to other groupings. In a genuine sense, nationalism was a lesson learned from the Western intruders.[4]

• The idea of national independence began not as a group concept but as the vision of a small number of leaders, mostly Western-educated. Peoples who had dwelt for centuries in closed and isolated communities were aroused by issues that were given propulsive power as slogans, inducing them to pursue promises and programs offered by persuasive individuals. Politics tended to be highly personalized, much like the pattern in the Philippines. Leadership is a factor rooted and honored in Asian traditions, and the masses were prepared to follow where a charismatic leader led. Willard A. Hanna, in his study of "Southeast Asia's Charismatic Statesmen," identified a dozen or a score of special men who

> managed to stand out for prolonged periods in the full heat of the midday political sun. They are men of extraordinary personal attainment and versatility, quite self-assured in at least two languages, two cultures, and two world blocks, acting and reacting sometimes within one frame of reference, sometimes within another. What each of them thinks, says, or does gives the cue to what some two million to one hundred million people are going to think, say, or do.

Drawing from his extensive experiences in the area, he concluded that "politics is people, the politics of underdeveloped areas is people of overdeveloped politics, and Southeast Asian politicians, as people, are extra special specimens."[5]

What has made them "extra special specimens" of agitators, demagogues, or patriotic orator-statesmen (depending in part on who does the judging and what standards are used) derives partly from historic traditions and partly from post–World War II circumstances. Another factor that distinguishes many of Asia's new leaders is their cultural marginality, the combination within their personalities and their value systems of Eastern traditional conservatism and Western activism. As the various nation-building processes in Southeast Asia are examined, these two factors will be evident and vital: the clashing forces of the old and the new, and the dynamic influence of peculiarly Asian (modern Asian) personalities.

In some of these countries persuasive communication was a major instrument of leadership—in others, not. It is instructive to consider the degree, and the ways, in which it was influential along with reasons why, in some circumstances, it had much less effect. In either case, the answer lies both in personalities and in the general context.

Factors Affecting Leadership

Civilizations have generally tended to develop in river valleys and to be separated from one another by mountains. This is notably true of Southeast Asia. The high Himalayas mark the northern border. Within the region mountain ranges tend to run north and south, with long rivers—the Salween, the Menam, the Mekong, and the Irrawaddy—running roughly parallel courses. The valleys bordering the rivers are broad, with deep alluvial soil. Heavy monsoon rains provide ample water for rice culture and also cause periodic disastrous flooding. Heavy forests girding the mountains help to contain the population within separated plains and valleys. Warm weather makes living relatively easy and helps ensure sufficient food. Across all the area is a general commonality of conditions, along with the terrain-dictated compartmentalization.

During prehistoric times and on into the first millenium of the Christian era, an Austro-Asian stock (the Mons) migrated from their mountainous homelands down into the favorable agricultural lands of Burma, and a related group (the Khmers) moved on into Cambodia. Descended from primitive Chinese stock, the Shan or Thai people settled in what became Siam and then Thailand. Into the eastern coastal and peninsular areas came a Chinese migratory tide that pushed its way southward to meet and to mingle with the Polynesian-Malay population. Although ethnically diverse, the various peoples shared similar religious views, compounded of ancestor worship, animism, and magico-cosmological rituals. Subsequently, waves of Hinduism, Buddhism, Islam, Confucianism, and Christianity brought overlays of new value systems that were partly competitive and partly became an amalgam along with the primitivistic earlier faiths. It is this "merging of foreign and indigenous elements" that makes the subcontinent "distinctively Southeast Asian."[6]

A basic factor in the Southeast Asian character is religion. Hinayana Buddhism is the faith of Burma, Thailand, and Cambodia (Kampuchea). It incorporates animism, or the view that a spiritual force exists in all animate creation. The Buddhist beliefs stress karma, or the view that individuals are responsible for all the virtues and vices, the ills and the benefits, that affect them, since all arise from the inherent nature of the individuals; and reincarnation, or the view that individual life proceeds in a chain of being from one life to another, guided upward toward greater perfection or downward into deterioration by the karma of the individual. A strong sense of responsibility for one's own destiny is one result of such beliefs. Another is the view that some individuals are vastly better than others, having "ascended" to a higher level, and thus are to be respected and accepted as guides. Both of these views have considerable political effects.[7]

●As a general principle, it may be said that a function of Southeast Asian leadership has been to rationalize a new identity that represents both the local isolation of valley-dwelling groups and their sense of universalism that is a result of their religion. To do so the leaders defined common advantages that had to be supported by common loyalties, and they made their messages vital and viable by means of persuasive communication. The nation building that they guided required a shift from personal values, which were determined by physical necessities and by long-standing traditions, to the new stance of accepting and supporting nationwide communal values. These new values had to be interpreted in terms of the "rules of the game" of politics, which dictate what may be, what should be, and what must be done or avoided. The aim of the leaders was to guide the people from small-group (family and clan) self-seeking to cooperative service for the good of the whole. In order to do so they had to create self-doubt or a sense of personal inadequacy regarding faith in traditionalism, and to replace it with such transcendent loyalties as religion and patriotism or with the new ideology of communism.

Historically, in the last century, ancient kingdoms or tribal divisions were reshaped by colonialism. This pattern, during the Pacific phase of World War II, was broken by the Japanese conquest and occupation. Then a new nationalistic organization was brought about by leaders who adhered generally to a common pattern of appealing to unifying features from the past, to immediate needs of the present, and to shared hopes for the future. In view of the prevalence of religious conviction throughout the subcontinent,●"its leaders are more like priests than politicians."[8] This characteristic has proved to be a source of both strength and weakness. It has endued leaders with greater power than they might have had on purely secular terms, but it has also limited the range of changes that they might bring into effect. Thus it has at once enhanced their authority and limited what they can accomplish with it.

Such religious-political characteristics are not favorable to what the West conceives as "democracy." Equality of rights is a concept that is, at least in spiritual terms, Asian as well as Western. But the Western notion that human values are best attained and preserved by partisan divisions that contend against one another for majority support of particular policies and programs does not fit into the age-old Asian emphasis on homogeneity. Does the general welfare demand that there be opposition within the society and freedom to exert it? The question is posed in practical terms by Rupert Emerson, a longtime student of Southeast Asia:

> Is it really desirable, where there are predominantly illiterate populations with very little acquaintance with the world at large, and particularly with the modern world into which one assumes they want to move, that government should operate on the basis of consultation with the people? Or is it reasonable to assume that decisions should be taken by the relatively few on top who know better where they want to go and how to get there? And perhaps a more fundamental question: is there reason to assume that the mass of the population in these countries really cares about the exercise of democratic rights?[9]

Such questions are rendered the more reasonable, as Emerson goes on to argue, because the new leaders in Southeast Asia tend to be also the old leaders. This is to say, the aristocrats who predominated in the traditional society produced the sons who acquired Western education and now hold status as the natural spokesmen for the people. It is this that enables "the old governing class to be also the new governing class."[10] As one result, the changes that came with nationalism were less drastic than those in other parts of Asia.

Nevertheless, change there has been, far greater in some countries (Singapore, for example) than in others (such as Cambodia). Illiteracy is being whittled away, much more in some of the nations than in others. And there are indeed divisive issues—deeply divisive, particularly between communism and its opponents and between educational, industrial and commercial modernism and proponents of something like the vanishing traditional status quo. It is these contrarieties that defy simple analysis. The old East that was does not contain, though in basic respects it limits and shapes, the new East that is and is becoming.[11]

Leadership and Nationalism: Difficult Challenges

Leaders necessarily advocate midpoint policies and programs that are rooted in their own methods and ideas but that are drawn one way and another by their various constituencies. In Southeast Asia, where democracy has not yet been established as the political norm (and where in some parts it is not yet so much as a major goal), it is nevertheless true that the needs and aspirations of the people do have considerable influence. How the necessary adjustments have been made varies from country to country, as leaders have confronted different kinds of opportunities and have been constrained by different types of limitations. For an understanding of how persuasive communication, skillfully employed, helps to shape the course of events, it is instructive to note where it has failed, or has been largely absent, as well as to note other places in which it has had much greater effect. To do so entails an examination of circumstances in each of the Southeast Asian nations, including those in which leaders have not used persuasive communication for the arousal of public support.

THAILAND

Thailand is a suitable starting point for such analysis, for three reasons. One is that it occupies the midpoint of the subcontinent, separating the former English and French colonies. Another is that it did not have to win independence, for its separate identity had been maintained for many centuries. This lack of a revolutionary crisis probably accounts for the third factor of significance, namely, that Thailand did not produce new leaders who needed persuasive advocacy in order to win support for new measures. Why, then, is it worthy of consideration in a study of leadership through communicative effectiveness? The reason was well stated by Conan Doyle when he had Sherlock Holmes observe that what is significant is that the dog did not bark. Why, in Thailand, persuasive politics did not develop is surely an important question.

The country was known as Ayuthia until 1871, then as Siam, until in 1939 it assumed its current name of Muang Thai, the "Land of the Free," or Thailand, as it is known in the West. Interest in the country was generated in 1944 by the opening of the popular musical comedy, *The King and I.* King Monkut was well-educated and international-minded, and he greatly expanded Siam's trade with the West. The real modernization of the country was greatly advanced by his son and successor, King Chulalongkorn, who abolished slavery and forced labor, ended the humiliating requirement of prostration before the throne, reformed taxation, introduced free trade, and expanded roads, schools, and systems of communication. His reformist spirit is manifested in his declaration that "all children from my own to the poorest should have an equal chance of education." For these reforms he did not have to appeal to or arouse public support. The power of the throne, along with the self-interested cooperation of the entrenched aristocratic bureaucracy, was all that he needed.

A special characteristic of the Thai people is their traditional individualism. They display little of the social discipline that is typical of most Asian societies. Thais are not inclined either to "keep in line" or to "be on time." Perhaps this is why they have not, until recently, had a standing army and why foreigners were hired for court guard duty. Alone among Southeastern Asian peoples, the Thais avoided being colonized by European powers.⁰A major reason was Thai verbal ingenuity. As John Embree, a specialist in Thai history, explains: "What saved it was the diplomatic skill of the Thais—a kind of delay and doubletalk which doubtless irritated more than one foreign diplomat but which succeeded in preventing them from ever joining forces to carve up the country."[12] The "buffer zone" location of Thailand between English and French interests made it particularly vulnerable to being dismembered (as Poland has been). But when foreign powers made demands on the Thais, they would smile, shrug, and say, "Well, I'll see," while weeks and months passed without affairs coming to a crisis.•Among Thais, Embree concluded, deception and lying to avoid direct confrontation is not only acceptable but is admirable. It represents a quality of calm control that they call *choei*. Landon, another Thai specialist, agrees that the practice of deception and avoidance is typical, and he also agrees that the term *choei* is complimentary. He interprets it as implying "coolness of attitude toward work, responsibility or trouble."[13] Whatever else it implies, this attitude surely is more acceptive of imposed reforms than a basis for revolutionary zeal.

In 1932 the absolutist monarchy was converted by constitutional reforms, and Thailand's first general election was held in 1934. During the next decades Thai politics was dominated by three men: a law professor named Pridi Banomyong and two army colonels, Thya Phahol and Pibul Songgram. During the Japanese occupation, after the outbreak of the Pacific phase of World War II, Japan granted Thailand control over British colonial areas in Burma and Malaysia, which was relinquished at the war's end. A succession of political struggles was ended in 1958, when the army commander Thanarat Sarit seized power. Through all of this, as was observed by historian Nicholas Tarling, "the nature of Thai politics had not changed. There had been no Western intervention to change it. There was no pressure from within. No invasion, no struggle against colonialism stimulated popular participation in politics."[14] The cold war, which deeply affected much of the world, had small influence within Thailand. In the Thai tradition, crises and changes at the top level of government flowed quietly around the people without greatly affecting them. Notable as an exception among the peoples of Southeast Asia, the Thais remained coolly untroubled. During the Vietnam War, the Thai leaders used their traditional *choei* diplomacy to play off Peking's Communists against American diplomats, thereby maintaining the neutrality of their nation.

৶ Modernism is developing more slowly in Thailand than in most of the remainder of the region. But its independent nationalism and its own traditional way of life remain strong. The circumstances offer small opportunity and even less inducement for an emergence of leadership that might derive from the skillful use of persuasive communication. Where contending issues are unimportant, there is no need for animated public discussion.

BURMA

Burma historically was not united until the British annexed the area during the mid–nineteenth century, in a succession of stages. Traditionally, under its monarchy, the country was ruled chiefly by village hereditary headmen and, after 1825, by appointed officials who governed clusters of villages. Under British administration, the major taxpayers who were appointed district governors had neither much local support nor local prestige. In 1907 a broad system of bureaucracy was established. This departure from the personalized leadership that had been traditional made it "hard for the mass of the people to comprehend or appreciate the government's activities."[15]

Disunity was emphasized by such governmental practices. Lower Burma was developed agriculturally by the British, with the result that its population greatly increased and so did the indebtedness of newly settled farmers under a commercial system dominated by foreigners. Upper Burma was developed later, and its petroleum and tungsten deposits were owned and marketed by foreign capitalists. Along with the British, Indian bankers and moneylenders and Chinese merchants and traders dominated the society, with the Burmese providing the labor. The sons of Burmese aristocrats who attended schools and (after 1920) a university in Rangoon mostly majored in liberal arts, since technical and administrative posts were not available to them. This resulted in growth of an intellectual group of elites that promulgated nationalist ideas to the discontented masses. The Buddhist priesthood, or *Sangha,* was highly regarded by the people, and it was largely through the priests that the ideas of independence and nationalism were implanted among the villagers.

In 1930–31 a Buddhist demagogue named Saya San attempted to arouse a rebellion against British rule through appeal to the presumed "golden age" of the Burmese past. The effort was quickly subdued, but the enticing idea of independence was solidly introduced among the populace. The educated elites had adopted Western ideas through the influence of Christian missionary schools, but they sought a middle way by establishing the Young Men's Buddhist Association, modeled on the YMCA., and a series of Buddhist-managed schools. Development of the Congress party in India, and the British declaration in 1917 of accelerated self-government in India, had encouraged nationalist sentiment in Burma. In 1917 the Burmese Legislative Council, which had been largely an appointive body since its creation in 1897, became elective.

The Burmese intellectuals confronted a dilemma: they wanted the advances being made in India, but they also wanted separation from India. In 1921 the Gandhist boycott movement spread to Burma, and Burmese leaders had to deal with the problem of favoring it while at the same time emphasizing the non-Indian nature of Burmese political goals. In 1921, a charlatan named U Ottama returned from India and built through the Buddhist organization a mass movement that stressed independent non-cooperation directed against British rule. Under his leadership considerable turbulence continued for several years. Meanwhile, other Burmese intellectuals favored participation in the Westernized industrial development and created a non-Buddhist "Burma for the Burmans League," which demanded separation from the administration of India and prohibition of Indian immigration.

After the suppression of the Saya San–led rebellion in 1931, several Burmese politicians, led by a lawyer named Ba Maw, organized the All-Burma Youth League. It quickly came under domination of university student rebels, particularly the brilliant Aung San (who was to be assassinated in 1947 on orders of U Saw), who called themselves *Thakins,* a Burmese honorific title, to identify them as nationalists. They represented a confused medley of Western ideas, including communism and other sentiments borrowed from Sun Yat-sen, Ireland's Sinn Feiners, and European and American socialists.

The Japanese occupation in 1942 led to the expulsion of Indians from Burma and the establishment of a pseudo-Burmese government that was headed by Ba Maw. After the war's end, Prime Minister Clement Attlee agreed to independence for Burma, which was proclaimed on 4 January 1948. The new government, headed by U Nu, was assailed by disorders. Upper Burma resisted domination by Lower Burma; Communists and anti-Communists contended for influence. Refugee Chinese nationalists poured into Burma after the 1949 victory of Mao Tse-tung, and were turned back by the government from fear that Chinese Communists might enter the country in pursuit of them. U Nu's government pursued a policy of "nonalignment" between the Soviet Union and the United States. Severe economic distress that resulted from the wartime diversion of Burmese resources to Japan's needs, and from the postwar turbulence, was rectified in part by the new demands for Burmese rice and other products that resulted from the Korean and Vietnamese wars.

U Nu had won the premiership with Communist support and also because of his charismatic oratory, his Buddhist organization, and popular revulsion against the army influence. But he proved unable to overcome the severe disunity of the population. To satisfy his Buddhist supporters, U Nu proclaimed Buddhism the state religion, which aroused the wrath of other religious groups; and his efforts to satisfy regional rivalries by making Burma a federal union caused more dissent than agreement. In

March 1962 an army coup was accomplished by leaders who opposed Western industrialism and favored a self-contained socialist economy.

The development of nationalist sentiment in Burma was difficult because of the regional, religious, ethnic, and tribal divisiveness that had persisted from early historic times. Professor Kyaw Thet of Rangoon University points out that ethnic and cultural diversity results in "problems of political integration that have always existed and never have been adequately solved in Burma."[16] Particularly intractable is the antagonism between the hill people of Upper Burma and the rice farmers of Lower Burma. The effort to define federalism in a way that is acceptable to the major divisions resulted in a Burmese constitution that gives the right of secession to some of the constituent states but not to others and provides differing methods of elections and differing degrees of autonomy for the states. The government tries to counter such divisive factors by stressing that dissimilarities do not mean disunity. Each year on Union Day (in May) representatives of ethnic groups are transported to Rangoon at government expense to perform their traditional dances in their ethnic costumes. During the year, on days that are special in different localities, government officials travel to the major states, dressed in the local ethnic costumes, to stress recognition of their different identities. The presidency has been rotated among the three major ethnic groups. Different elementary school systems are maintained, taught in one or another of the three major languages. In all such ways cultural pluralism is not only recognized but encouraged.

Simultaneously, efforts to create "unity out of diversity" consist of such measures as a requirement that in the Parliament only Burmese may be spoken; location of all major advanced educational, research, and publication facilities in Rangoon; and a Mass Education movement that trains teachers and sends them out to remote areas to teach the Burmese language and promulgate Burmese culture. The Buddhist religion also serves as a nationalistic influence, as Buddhist missionaries go out into the remote hill communities and free transportation is provided to bring people from all parts of Burma to Rangoon for major Buddhist celebrations. General Ne Win, who became premier on 31 October 1958, tried cautiously to increase unity while protecting diversity. This remains the principal challenge confronting Burma's government. As J. S. Furnival, perhaps the chief among Western experts on Burma, concludes in his 1958 monograph, "the main function of government is to create unity in a disintegrated social order."[17]

Amid its distresses, Burma has at least had stable leadership. During most of its first three decades, Burma had only two chief executives. As Lea Williams summarized the circumstances: "Admittedly, the first, U Nu, allowed events to overtake and engulf him while the second, Ne Win, has been the victim of his own political and economic dreams; but stability of sorts has been promoted by the relative absence of coups and erratic power shifts."[18] This leadership has been generally communistic, in agreement with the view of U Ba Swe, an early nationalist, who declared (in parallel with Indonesia's Sukarno) that "Marxist theory is not antagonistic to Buddhist philosophy. The two are, frankly speaking, not merely similar: in fact they are identical."[19] The rejection of private enterprise, the policy of expelling Indian and Chinese entrepreneurs, and the distancing of Burma from Western democracies combine, in Dick Wilson's informed opinion, to consolidate army control. For all of these reasons "Burma's prospects are far from bright."[20]

General Ne Win, whose long tenure shaped the nature of independent Burma, was an uninspiring speaker and made few public appearances. More and more he came to govern less by persuasion than by authoritarian force, while claiming that Burmese circumstances made strong centralized leadership necessary. "It is regrettable to note," he said on several occasions, "that at the present time such cardinal virtues as mutual trust, magnanimity, and the spirit of cooperation are almost nonexistent."[21] Burmese leaders have not as yet managed to infuse the populace with a spirit of patriotism strong enough to create the unity that any nation needs.

Ba Maw, in his *Memoirs of a Revolution,* probably spoke for many Asians when he wrote: "We are in a position now to take a complete view of colonialism or imperialism, to see the brutal truth that colonialism was historically right and progressive . . . to pull us out of the ruts in which we had lost our way."[22] Then he added, "And their leaving also was a historical necessity; and the Burmese revolt against them also was such a necessity." Many Asians and Westerners would agree, in parallel terms, that dictatorship or "guided democracy" may have been a historical necessity for ruling the newly independent nations with high illiteracy and small experience in dealing with national and world problems. But as education advances, the transition to genuine democracy is becoming another historical necessity, and until it is achieved the problems that limit well-being continue to increase and will expand. The casting off of colonialism propelled Burma and much of Asia into another "brutal rut"—out of which it has become their need to climb.

CAMBODIA (KAMPUCHEA)

Under Indian influence, in the sixth and again in the fifteenth centuries, Cambodian culture produced magnificent monasteries, palaces, and monuments at Angkor Wat and other locations that fully rival the European cathedrals in magnificence. Seldom was the area at peace, because its borders lacked geographical definition, and because restless migratory peoples of Thai origin swept back and forth. In the late sixteenth century the Spaniards, based in Manila, entered Cambodia to bring the Khmers the "blessings of Christian civilization and Western trade." In 1595 Spain managed to place a puppet king on the throne at Phnom Penh, but four years later, after a bloody massacre of Spaniards and their puppets, Cambodia was brought back under Siamese rule.

In the mid–nineteenth century, after Britain's success in the Opium War against China, French forces seized control of the broad area of Indochina, including Vietnam, Laos, and Cambodia. In 1897 France consolidated all these countries into an Indochinese Union. Under French rule the life of the villagers remained virtually unchanged. No high school was established in the Cambodian area until 1935, and Cambodians were restrained from attending schools in France. Buddhism remained the predominant religion and a Cambodian king was retained on the throne, not in power but for religious symbolism. M. F. Hertz, in his *Short History of Cambodia* (1958), credited the French with "keeping Cambodia alive as a nation," and it is doubtless true that Cambodian nationalism drew its substance largely from the coherence imposed on the people during the French colonial rule.

The first Khmer-language newspaper was founded in 1936 by a nationalist intellectual, Son Ngoc Thanh, who aimed at a readership of young semieducated urbanites and the Buddhist monks. Nationalism was difficult to nourish, for the people were uneducated, administrative colonial control was not very intrusive in their lives since it was centered outside the country in Saigon, and Cambodian economic activities (restricted mostly to rubber production) were dominated by France through Vietnam. A weak westernizing influence was the drafting of some few Cambodians into the French army. One result was that a Cambodian youth named Khim Tit, who was a corporal in the French army in 1918, became the Cambodian prime minister in 1958.

Another westernizing influence was the European need for rice, especially during and after World War I. Increased pressure for greater productivity of the rice paddies resulted in the combination of farmlands, the introduction of new technologies, and the education of small numbers of Cambodians to serve as managers and traders of the expanded agricultural production. This in turn led to more reading about Western history, so that gradually more people came to learn of and be inspired by the American and French revolutions. The ideas of European socialists and, after 1920, of Russian Communists also penetrated into the limited intellectual circle.

Native roots of Cambodian nationalism are at best obscure. Around 1850 Europeans discovered the ruins of Angkor Wat and out of sheer ignorance fabricated a theory of a once-great civilization that was mysterious in its nature and that mysteriously faded away. King Norodom, who came to the Cambodian throne in 1862, claimed that his ancestry derived from the ancient rulers of Angkor Wat. With French support, King Norodom guided Cambodia away from Siamese domination. He ruled ritualistically, and sumptuously, under French control for forty years. Several more kings in succession showed much more devotion to dancing girls and champagne than to the chores of government. In 1939, upon the outbreak of World War II, the French selected for the throne an eighteen-year-old youth with royal blood named Norodom Sihanouk.

Prince Sihanouk had been educated in French schools in Phnom Penh and then in Saigon, where he was preparing for (but never attained) *le baccalauréate de rhétorique*. His family was neither rich nor prominent. He was quick in his studies, active in sports, and outstanding in neither. Sihanouk's coronation was delayed, and he actually became king on 26 April 1941, after the fall of France. Then King Sihanouk disappeared within the walls of the complex of royal palaces, where he lived luxuriously, voluptuously, and virtually anonymously. His only "emergence" was after the failure of a febrile French attempt to stage an anti-Japanese coup. Then, by Japanese decision, he announced that Cambodia was independent.

After the defeat of Japan, King Sihanouk proclaimed himself head of a new revolutionary government. He renounced the throne and named himself Prince Comrade, as head of the newly organized Cambodian Naitonalist Community. Luckily for him and for Cambodia, France was too embroiled in Vietnam to care much about its Cambodian problems. Comrade Sihanouk was granted a ten-year respite from French attack, during which time he developed his amazing amalgam of political views—demagogically attacking the French, the Communists, the Chinese, the Russians, the Americans, the royalists, the intellectuals, and, above all, the Thais and the Vietnamese.

Sihanouk's only real rival for nationalist leadership was the man who had founded the first Cambodian newspaper, Son Ngoc Thanh. After the outbreak of the Pacific war, Son Thanh joined the Japanese army and rose to the rank of captain. On 1 June 1945, when the Japanese recognized Cambodian independence as their own defeat loomed, they brought Son Ngoc Thanh back to serve as foreign minister. After Japan's surrender, Son Thanh led a palace coup to make himself prime minister. When it failed, the French arrested him and exiled him to France. Sihanouk, now enthroned again as king, brought him back to Phnom Penh, where the public greeted him as the heroic father of their country's independence. He reopened his newspaper and used it to attack both the French and Sihanouk, for which reason he was driven from the city back into the hill country, where he organized guerilla forces. One of his associates, Dap

Chhuon, promoted himself from corporal in the Cambodian army to general of guerrilla jungle fighters. Dap Chhuon soon deserted Son Ngoc Thanh to join Sihanouk, then deserted Sihanouk. This has continued to be the story of Cambodian politics: shifting alliances, with personal ambitions more notable than patriotic service.

Sihanouk himself went through a bewildering series of changes. In 1947 he proclaimed a democratic constitution and sponsored election of a Constituent Assembly. When he deemed its conduct irresponsible, he dismissed it and called for election of a new parliament in 1951. In mid-1952 he suspended the constitution, and shortly declared martial law, arrested his political opponents, and then left for France, to plead for recognition of Cambodia's independence. This failing, he spent the next three years going from one capital to another—Washington, Bangkok, Paris, Tokyo, Peking, Manila, Bandung, and many more—always conducting a vigorous propaganda campaign on behalf of support for Cambodian independence. To the French, who were hopelessly mired in their war to retain Vietnam, he argued that the only alternatives for Cambodia were himself or communism. The French saw the point, and on 8 November 1953 King Sihanouk returned to Phnom Penh to rule an entirely independent nation. Then on 2 March 1955, he abruptly renounced the throne. Going to India to talk with Nehru he gave his reasons—in a report in which he referred to himself in the third person: "He had to build up a really democratic government and put an end to oppression of the people by a privileged few . . . as a monarch he would have been prisoner of a rigid system that would have prevented him from acting efficiently. . . . he gave up his throne to serve the people better."[23]

With the title of head of state, Sihanouk founded the Sankgum party, which ruled the country from its own headquarters, apart from the government bureaucracy. Through this apparatus he controlled the nation without the inconveniences of formal governmental procedures. He also traveled—interminably—to Warsaw, Madrid, Vienna, Prague, Moscow, Djakarta, Cairo, Belgrade, New Delhi, Rangoon, Washington, Outer Mongolia, and, again and again, to Peking, everywhere delivering stirring messages of the great progress he was bringing to Cambodia. The country indeed assumed a new appearance, with new schools, clinics, roads, bridges, and public buildings. As the Vietnam War continued, Sihanouk took up virtually permanent residence in Peking, (by then renamed Beijing), still occasionally declaring Cambodia a "third world" neutralist nation, unaligned with either the Communist or the anti-Communist bloc.

Among all the nationalist leaders in Southeast Asia, Sihanouk was surely the least definable, a man with assuredly great qualities, who seemingly did not know what to do with them; yet in his erratic course he in fact guided Cambodia into independence, if not into full self-realization.

He did this less by persuasive communication with the Cambodian people, who exert little weight on government, than by his propaganda abroad and his appeals for understanding and support addressed to foreign governments. What he achieved manifests the usefulness of the Thai ambiguous mode of communication, *choei*. Like much else in Southeast Asia, this mode transcends national boundaries.

LAOS

Laos is akin to Thailand and Vietnam racially and linguistically. The linguistic map of Southeast Asia is fully as confused as its racial combinations; but the major source of both the racial stock and the dialects of Laos was southern China. Geographically and culturally, Laos was more closely related to Thailand than to Vietnam. It was ruled loosely by a king, with princes serving as governors of provinces. Under French colonial rule which was extended over Laos in 1893, this arrangement was little changed. The French had small interest in Laos except to mine and export its tin. Western education was available only to a few princes and members of some wealthy aristocratic families. Laotians were neither trained nor utilized by the French in their colonial administration.

What is now Laos was divided in 1707 into two hostile states, Vientiane and Luang Prabang. Before the end of that century, Luang Prabang was incorporated into Burma and Vientiane, into Siam. The French reunited the two divisons and incorporated them into French Indochina. In August 1947, in agreement with France, the name "Laos" was restored and the autonomous nation emerged within the French Union. After several changes of government, while the United States and both Soviet and Chinese Communists sought to attain influence, and while palace intrigues made it difficult to discern whose influence at any given time was strongest, a coup was accomplished by an adventurous young captain named Kong Lê, who managed to seize control of the country with the force of 750 paratroopers that he commanded. With the education accorded a military officer, Captain Kong Lê, became distressed by the corruption and inefficiency of the royal court, in which one member and another formed alliances within and outside the country while boasting of "progress," which amounted to little more than a few superficial construction programs. Hanna, who found some few biographical facts about him, concluded that Kong Lê was "in fact typical of the decent, responsible, intelligent, far-above-average little man of Southeast Asia to whom the Communist formula sometimes offers hope in an all but hopeless dilemma." After the success of his coup, he "proved himself an aimless organizer but a stirring orator." Under his inspiration, "students, priests and incidental riffraff roared revolutionary slogans."[24] Russians hurried to fly in military supplies for him, and the United States countered by assisting an anti-Communist general, Phoumi Novasan, with sufficient effect that Captain Kong Lê was driven across the border to North Vietnam's Plaine des Jarres. Here he was greeted as a hero and supplied with arms and other military materiel by the Vietnamese and by Russia.

In a conference held at Geneva during May–June 1962, it was agreed that Laos should be "neutralized." The United States withdrew its 750 military advisers, and the Communists withdrew an undisclosed number of their "technicians." A coalition government was installed, under supervision of a commission made up of an Indian, a Pole, and a Canadian. Laos remains not really a nation, but a conglomeration of isolated valley communities with little feeling of national unity. Captain Kong Lê remained in Vietnam, to become a general in the northern army. Laos has not been fortunate in the quality of its leadership, and there has been little effort to unify the people through any sustained program of persuasive communication. Its true nationalism is yet to be attained. A suitable summation is that offered by Stuart Simmonds, of the London School of Oriental and African Studies:

> The events of 1945–61 suggest that there has been little political evolution in Laos, if by that is meant the progressive development of forms of government able to manage the changing problems of state and society. . . . It is plain that there is a future for Laos as a unified non-aligned state only if her leaders still their quarrels and co-operate in an attempt to balance and control potentially destructive foreign influences during the lengthy process of nation-building.[25]

SRI LANKA

Ceylon, the island of Serendip from which evolved the happy term *serendipity,* emerged into independence quietly and easily, in such genial accord with its colonizing power that the leaders of its independence movement could not conceive of "a better and safer friend for Ceylon than Britain."[26] The Ceylonese National Congress did not join in the agitation sponsored by the Indian National Congress under the inspiration of Gandhi. Quite to the contrary, "there were no mass demonstrations and excessses as in India, nor did the Ceylon nationalists enourage violence in their fight for independence."[27] An amiable transfer of authority from Great Britain made Ceylon a member of the British Commonwealth on 4 February 1948. Twenty-four years later, when the Sri Lanka Freedom party, in close alliance with Soviet-led Communists, won power with an impressive majority, the ties with Great Britain were severed and the Republic of Sri Lanka was proclaimed on 22 May 1972. The reasons for this change had at least as much to do with internal differences as with foreign influence.

The two major racial-religious groups in Ceylon are the Sinhalese, who comprise the large majority of the population and among whom the Goyagama form of Buddhism prevails, and the Tamils, who are descended from Hindu immigrants (many centuries ago) from India. They speak different languages and have little sense of common community.

In 1912 the English established a Legislative Council in Ceylon, with the Western-educated 4 percent of the population permitted to vote for the eleven elected members of the total of twenty-one members. In 1921 the council was revised, so that the Tamil membership was reduced from equality to just three, while the Sinhalese held thirteen council seats. In 1931 the British enlarged the council to include fifty elected members and twelve who were chosen by the administration. For the first time in Asia, the vote was granted to all adult males, and Sir Sidney Webb, then colonial secretary, redefined the regulation to include women as well. Since the rule was "one person, one vote," the Sinhalese Goyama Buddhists attained control. After the 1936 election, the Tamils had not even one member on the Board of Ministers.

The United National party, formed in 1948, brought together virtually all the Ceylonese except the Tamils and the growing numbers of Communists. This party ruled Ceylon until 1956, at which time a highly skilled politician, S. W. R. D. Bandaranaike, won the premiership with a coalition of "almost all the other parties" except the Tamils.[28]

Bandaranaike's success was founded on his strong grass-roots organization, which was Buddhist-based. The Buddhist influence was strengthened by celebration of the twenty-five hundredth anniversary of Gautama's attainment of nirvana. Another factor was Bandaranaike's support for making Sinhalese the national language, to displace English. Still another was economic distress of the majority of the population, coupled with resentment against the better-educated and more industrious Tamils, who held a disproportionate number of professional and commercial positions. The Bandaranaike administration was unstable because it incorporated the political extremes of both Left and Right. He himself was in favor of socialism for the domestic economy and nonalignment in international relations. Accordingly, he abrogated Ceylon's defense alliance with Great Britain and also socialized the transportation and port facilities. These actions, along with his advocacy of the Sinhalese language, led to country-wide disruption, in the midst of which he was assassinated in 1959. His widow, Sirimavo Bandaranaike, who succeeded him in office, became the first woman head of government in modern history. She expanded socialistic controls and strengthened ties with the Communist bloc. She was defeated in 1965 but regained power in an impressive electoral sweep in 1972. Promptly she changed the name of the nation to Sri Lanka. Among other changes, she brought the schools under Buddhist control, made

Sinhalese the national language, placed the press and public assemblies under strict censorship, outlawed opposition political parties, and installed martial law.

In Sri Lanka the strange course of events included an easy transition from colonialism to independence, followed by increasing violence and dissension within the country. B. H. Farmer, in his study of Ceylonese politics, identifies a number of reasons for the growing internal disorder. For one, "Ceylon has lacked leaders with the vision of Gandhi and the intellectual grasp of a Nehru." Another is "economic frustrations" that arise from population growth, decline in per capita income, and growing unemployment. As a third reason he cites the ease with which independence was won, without any struggle that might have united the people. And finally, he wonders if universal suffrage without political experience or maturity might not breed irresponsibility.[29] Another study, by Bryce Ryan, concluded that the rural dwellers are keenly alert to their own interests but lack a grasp of national issues.[30]

In sum, these and other students of Sri Lankan affairs generally agree that the island nation has not as yet had the kind of leadership that builds strength through communication with the general population. In this respect, the circumstances of Sri Lanka are a reminder of the difficulties that beset Laos, though not to the same extent. Not only is leadership indispensable but so is the persuasive communication that knits together a coherent and stable nationalist sentiment. In some countries this conclusion is supported by the success of movements, in others by their failures or weaknesses.

MALAYA (MALAYSIA) AND SINGAPORE

As the Pacific war neared its close, Indonesians slipped into the Malay Peninsula to talk with local leaders about a postwar federation. One whom they sought to influence was Dato Onn bib Ja'afar, member of a prominent Johore family. Meanwhile at Kedah, in northern Malaya, young Malay and Indonesian socialists were trying to win to their cause a youthful prince named Tunku Abdul Rahman. Both of these efforts failed. Both Onn and Rahman were primarily interested in attaining more welfare for the Malay people. During the next decades both played leading roles.

The British in October 1945 converted the Straits Settlements into the Malayan Union, with Singapore maintained as a separate Crown Colony. Singapore had been ruled by Great Britain since 1819 and was a prosperous free-trade port with a predominantly Chinese population. In 1885 England had undertaken to protect the Sultan of Johore against Thai attacks, and in 1909 had negotiated a settlement of the boundary dispute between the Straits Settlements and Thailand.

At war's end the British were confronted in the Malay Peninsula by an extensive Communist guerrilla army that had fought against the Japanese in the jungles all during the war years.[31] Communists were also active in the cities, under protection of the British policy of free speech and free association. To counter them, in April 1946 Dato Onn bib Ja'afar organized the first genuinely Malayan political party, the United Malays National Organization. In 1954 the communists organized the Malayan Democratic Union and commenced a series of general strikes, which led the British to proclaim a state of emergency that sharply restricted political activity. Onn sought to broaden his party by including sizable numbers of Chinese. Since this was unacceptable to the Malays, Onn lost leadership of the party to Tunku Abdul Rahman. Rahman, like Onn, favored inclusive cooperation among Malaya's Malays, Chinese, and Indians. As an aristocrat with conciliatory manners, he was more successful. Rahman sought also to work with the Communists in the common cause of nationalism. But when he met with the leader of the Communist guerrillas, a Chinese named Chan Peng, on 28 December 1955, Chan told him that his men would fight to the death rather than give up their arms. Rahman returned to his headquarters, saying, "Chan Peng really taught me what Communism was. I had never really understood and appreciated the full meaning. When I was briefed on Communism by the British experts, I always felt that they were interested in making a bad case against the Communists. But in that room Chan Peng taught me that Malaya and Communism can never co-exist."[32]

Within a week Rahman went to London to discuss what proved to be a question easily settled. Agreement was readily reached on home rule for Malaya for some two years, after which the Federation of Malaya would be recognized. As the Singapore *Straits Times* editorialized: "There has been nothing quite like it in the entire history of colonies and dependencies." On 31 August 1957, Tunku Abdul Rahman proudly read to an inaugural throng the Malayan Declaration of Independence, and became the prime minister of independent Malaya.

The island-city of Singapore, much the richest and most literate Malay state, agreed to incorporation in the federation under agreements that carefully guarded Singapore's virtual independence and also safeguarded Malaya from dominance by the wealthy and well-educated Singapore Chinese. The mayor of Singapore, Lee Kuan Yew, a socialist economist, became prime minister of the world's only truly independent city-state, the Republic of Singapore, when, in a spirit of mutual accord, Singapore seceded from the federation on 9 August 1965.

The wholly peaceful and in general mutually satisfactory settlement that resulted in the creation of these two independent nations was rendered easy and natural by the quality and character of the two leaders, Rahman and Lee, along with British recognition that its time of colonial governance in Asia had come to an end. The culmination was a triumph for good will and human rationality. It was nation building of a different character than in other parts of Asia. It represented leadership largely aloof from the people, rather than the building of support through persuasive communication.

THE VIETNAM EXCEPTION

Among the continental Southeast Asian nations Vietnam is exceptional for several reasons, the most notable being its long and costly postliberation war that was partly civil, partly international. Why this happened in Vietnam and not, for example, in Thailand, or Burma, or Laos, was partly because of the nature of Vietnamese nationalist leadership and partly the result of big power foreign policies that were hastily improvised with little regard for coherence or rationality. The leader around whom the conflict centered was Ho Chi Minh; and the issue that animated foreign policymaking was whether or not Vietnam would be allowed to establish a Communist government. What eventuated was a war of vicious ferocity; but the outcome was finally determined less by force of arms than by persuasion. This was the chief lesson the Vietnam conflict taught.

The Vietnamese have an ancient proverb that attests that just as the length of a road is known only from traveling on it a long time, so are the qualities of a man known only by living with him a long time. Appearances are deceptive. A road is not measured, realistically, in miles but in how speedily, how comfortably, how efficiently, it can be traversed in all kinds of weather and conditions. A man has so many contrarities of character, temperament, mood, and behavior that he is not to be known by brief or casual acquaintance. These messages that the proverb seeks to convey were not heeded by the foreign shapers of Vietnamese policies. Neither the Vietnamese people nor their enigmatic leader were known well enough by the Western democracies as World War II ended. What was needed was better audience analysis.

France had ruled Indochina, including Vietnam, Laos, and Cambodia, for less than a century. Annam, Tonkin, and Cochin China, known collectively as Viet Nam, dated from the founding of the kingdom of Aulac in 280 B.C. A hundred years later it was conquered by a vassal of China's Chin dynasty and for a thousand years was annexed to the region in south China that was called Nam Viet. In 1802 an exiled king of Cochin China asked for French help to regain his throne, and with that aid he made himself also emperor of Annam. In 1862–63 France secured treaties by which the general area came under its protection, and in 1884 China was forced to recognize the provinces of Annam and Tonkin as French protectorates. An Indian historian of the area concluded that French rule "certainly brought some benefits" but "only two per cent of the population received elementary education. There were only one university and thirty-one hospitals, yet eighty-three prisons. The poverty of the people in the country was extreme. "[33] Anti-French sentiment was strong as the twentieth century advanced. This was the crux of the Vietnamese problem.

In northern Vietnam an ambitious youth concerning whom remarkably little is known, named Nguyen That Thanh, went to Paris and, in 1920, helped to found the French Communist party. Then he returned to his homeland, changing his name to Nguyen Ai Quoc, meaning Nguyen the Patriot. There he joined with discontented young intellectuals who organized the Revolutionary Party of the Young Viet Nam in 1925 and the Nationalist Party of the Viet Nam in 1927. In 1930 Nguyen Ai Quoc headed a group that established the Vietnamese Communist party.

When World War II broke out, Nguyen led guerrilla forces that took refuge in the forests and mountains along the China border. During these war years he entered into relations with the American Office of Strategic Services, which parachuted agents into Tonkin to join him and supplied him with arms intended for use against the Japanese. Actually these guerrillas generally avoided conflict and instead stored the weapons for a later time. In 1943 Nguyen Ai Quoc once more changed his name, this time to Ho Chi Minh, meaning "He who Enlightens." So much did he deemphasize his communism during these years that after weeks of working with him, the American major in command of the OSS agents asked him curiously, "Mr. Ho, are you a Communist?" Ho replied, "Yes, I am. But we can still be friends, can't we?"[34]

Ho Chi Minh was far from being the only nationalist leader in Vietnam. Historically there had always been distinct differences between Tonkin and Annam in the north and Cochin China in the south. As antagonism toward France sharpened and as nationalist sentiments in Vietnam were heightened and encouraged by the changed circumstances in Japan and China, numerous groups were organized separately throughout Vietnam, headed by leaders with personal ambitions and aims. These rebel groups were able to gain strength after the surrender of France to Germany in the spring of 1940. Japan also took advantage of the weakness of the French to seize control over the areas south of the Chinese border; and after the Pearl Harbor attack precipitated Japan into war with the Western Allies, Japan pressed the French harder to yield to it virtual control over most of Vietnam. In 1945, as the defeat of Japan impended, Chinese armies moved into northern Vietnam and a British force occupied the south, around Saigon. In the summer of 1945 a French force began to take over the task of disarming and, afterward, of repatriating the defeated Japanese. But the French paid little attention to the Vietnamese people.

During the Japanese occupation, Ho Chi Minh brought together the chief divergent groups into a coalition called the Viet Minh. On 2 September 1945, at Hanoi, Ho Chi Minh read a declaration of independence and proclaimed the Democratic Republic of Vietnam. The French government invited him to Paris where a series of talks were held to work out cooperative relations between France and this newly independent government of Vietnam. The swift succession of French governments prevented the reaching of firm agreements and finally, after some eight months of negotiations, the French launched a devastating naval attack against Hanoi on 19 December 1946 and drove Ho Chi Minh and his following back into the hill country. The success of Mao Tse-tung in taking control of all China in September 1949 initiated a period of increased Chinese support for the Vietnamese Communists. Both sides prepared for war.

Meanwhile France maintained that it was not attempting to resume colonial rule but wanted instead to work out relations with an independent and non-Communist Vietnam. In furtherance of this policy, France recognized a regime it organized under the name of the Associated States of Vietnam, with Emperor Bao Dai proclaimed by the French as its chief of state. In 1950 France suffered its first major field defeats by the forces of Ho Chi Minh and his military commander, General Giap. Four years later Dien Bien Phu, defended by the principal French force in Vietnam, was captured. Then France's Western Allies intervened. The United States initiated an active program to prevent Communist control over Vietnam in the fall of 1951, when it began secret military staff talks with the British, French, Australians, and New Zealanders to form a joint defense plan for Southeast Asia. These efforts were renewed in 1954, in a series of bilateral discussions between the United States and these other participants. Then in 1954 a conference was convened in Geneva to consider what should be done about both Korea and Vietnam. The problem in Vietnam led to an agreement by the Allied Powers to recognize a temporary north-south division of the country along the 17th parallel.

This division, splitting Annam in two, provided a roughly equivalent area (sixty to sixty-six thousand square miles) and population (ten to twelve millions) to each part of Vietnam. Each part had a major city (Hanoi and Saigon) that had long been an administrative center. Each also had a major river bordered by richly productive rice paddies. The major difference was that the north had a leader, Ho Chi Minh, who had long been a representative of the people; whereas the south had a foreign-designated leader, Ngo Dinh Diem, who was selected by the French because he presumably would have American support.[35]

Diem was a member of the Mandarin class, was a devout Roman Catholic, and had few connections with the people of Vietnam. Between 1950 and 1953 he lived with the Maryknoll Fathers at Lakewood, New Jersey, and in 1953–54 he lived part of the time in Paris and part of the time in the Benedictine Monastery in Bruges, Belgium. He had little affinity with the people he was chosen to lead, nor did he make any special efforts to communicate with them. Wesley R. Fischel, one of the principal authorities on the Vietnam developments, concluded of Diem's leadership that

> the regime's propaganda has been awkward and dull. Few Vietnamese students overseas—indeed, few exiles in general—have been won over to the government's cause by its bumbling approach. And it has failed to keep the support of those who actually returned to take part in the "national revolution" that Diem was thought to be leading.
>
> [Moreover] It has failed to win over large elements of the fence-sitting nationalists, who, disheartened by years of civil strife, looked hopefully to Diem for leadership.
>
> His approach to these people has been consistently clumsy and vacillating, with the result that they became disillusioned and went back to the sidewalk cafes and gossipy criticism that had long been their habit.[36]

There is no doubt that Ho Chi Minh's communication with the people was far more successsful. For one thing, he adhered to the general Communist system of requiring attendance at weekly (or more frequent) discussion meetings. A veteran observer of the process, Theodore White, described how the Viet Minh had used it throughout World War II:

> Within the mountain redoubt the Communist leaders call meetings— meetings for youth, meetings for women, meetings for students, meetings for tillers. In the primitive uplands the Communist leaders have much to teach. . . . They give names and ascribe causes to all nameless aches and grievances of the peasants—it is the landlord, or the Japanese, or the white man or imperialism that makes them hungry. . . . Ambitious young intellectuals sneak out of cities and schools to find careers in the hill governments; sturdy young peasants graduate out of the paddies to join them in leadership.[37]

Joseph Alsop, a journalist who was strongly anti-Communist in his reporting from Vietnam, nevertheless testified to the success of the Viet Minh's communication with the people during the struggles against France in 1954:

> At first it was difficult for me, as it is for any Westerner, to conceive of a Communist government's genuinely "serving the people." I could hardly imagine a Communist government that was also a popular government and almost a democratic government. But this is just the sort of government the palm-hut state actually was while the struggle with the French continued. The Viet Minh could not possibly have carried on the

resistance for one year, let alone nine years, without the people's strong, united support.[38]

The observations of Alsop, an American, were largely confirmed by those of F. Spencer Chapman, a Briton, who spent four of the war years with Communist guerrilla forces in the Malay jungles. Chapman's narrative of his experiences indicates both the extent and the limitations of democratic participation in the day-by-day local operations of the Communist patrols. Each morning, he records, the "top command" presented to each patrol a written statement of what its assignment would be. This was read to each patrol group, which thereupon "discussed how it was to be carried out. If a man criticized a leader's decision in private, he was liable to be severely punished, but in public he could say whatever he liked, and any disagreement with a superior could be taken to higher authority. The control of section commanders was thus very much undermined, and the men tended to go into committee about every decision instead of getting on with the job . . . then they went into a huddle and discussed the matter in loud voices and at great length."[39] This, of course, was in circumstances of severe personal hardship and danger, from which desertion was easy and in which the maintenance of authoritarian discipline was difficult. Nonetheless, it was a pattern that involved the whole group in the process of decision making.

The Vietnam War finally ended in 1973. Ho Chi Minh did not live to see this victory by his Viet Minh—or, as it had come to be generally known by that time, the Viet Cong. An independent nation, the Democratic People's Republic of Vietnam, extended its control over the entire country. For the accomplishment of this goal, there had been some three decades of bitter and generally savagely cruel fighting, with vast destruction of property and loss of lives. Following the victory of the north, the southern Vietnamese who had been allegiant to the United States and other anti-Communist allies, were treated so harshly that many tried to escape. The northern authorities, ignoring the example of Ho Chi Minh's career, have sought to control the south by repressive force rather than trying to win the loyalty of its people by concessions and persuasion. Centralism prevailed over democracy.

But even in the exceptional and brutal situation in Vietnam, the attainment of modern nationalism was directly dependent upon leadership that drew its strength primarily from persuasive communication with the people. Ho Chi Minh was not an orator. But he did employ the same two processes that won victory in China for Mao Tse-tung. One was conciliatory and comradely communication systematically and inclusively maintained at the grass-roots level with all the people. And along with it he exercised ruthless force against all who opposed his programs or even complained about them. It could not be said that he ruled through persuasion, let alone by consent. But he ruled with persuasion as a principal and indispensable corollary force.

Conclusion

Continental Southeast Asia is so diverse a region that few conclusions may be reached with confidence concerning the nature of its transition from colonialism to nationalism. As in the rest of Asia, the goal of national independence was conceived by leaders well in advance of popular demand. How well, how generally, and with what effects they exercised their leadership role through persuasive communication varied greatly from country to country. So did the nature of the audience that mattered most in the attainment of independence. In Malaya and Singapore, for instance, the most crucial communication by leaders was with the English government. This was also true in Ceylon (later Sri Lanka), but there the internal problem of hostile disunity demanded a kind of domestic communication that has not as yet been produced. In Burma, by a curious bifurcation, the emergent leaders found it necessary to encourage and support disunity while concurrently trying to develop a sense of national communion. In Laos the development of national sentiment was comparatively desultory and incomplete. In Cambodia Prince Sihanouk customarily addressed his persuasive campaign primarily to foreigners.

In those Southeast Asian countries where independence was only partially attained, or where disunity remains more marked than unity, the record shows either a lack of leaders with communicative skills or that leaders who had predominant influence were themselves disunited and working at cross-purposes. In either case—whether measured by success or by failure—the crucial role of effective communication by leaders who are skilled in its use is manifest. Amid all the diversity of Southeast Asia, this is one central thread. Either persuasive communication worked, or the lack of it proved to be damaging.

8

The Korean Dilemma: One People, Two States

In Korea the use of persuasive communication as a foundation for leadership was unusually difficult, both because of the nature of the domestic audience and because of the nature of foreign interference. The quality of Korean leadership, measured against the difficulties it had to overcome, was unusually high. The methods used by the major leaders were more largely dictated by circumstances than a matter of their own choice. The leadership responsibility for recommending the best solutions that were available, and for winning popular support for them, was curbed and distorted by the severity of both internal and external conditions. Assessment of what the leaders did and of how they did it demands consideration of the historical circumstances. As is always true, meaning depends upon context. In Korea, historical circumstances made participatory democracy difficult to attain. When the peninsular nation was divided by foreign power after World War II, Russian and American aims took precedence over the people's own will. These were basic factors with which Korean leaders had to deal.

Korean nationalism claims a history of at least two thousand years, with another two thousand years of legendary prehistory dating back to the supposed founding of Korea by the demigod Tan-gun. In 1876 it was forced partway out of the isolationism that caused it to be known as the "Hermit Kingdom" by a treaty imposed upon it by Japan. In 1882 the United States also secured treaty relations, through the intervention of China, and in quick succession Korea agreed to treaties also with England, France, Russia, and Germany. Within a generation, Korea's primitivistic agrarian society, governed autocratically by a monarchal-aristocratic structure, turned toward modernism.

The society at the time was cruel and unjust, yet the educated minority shared deeply the Chinese and Japanese view that their Confucian system was genuine civilization, contrasted with the barbarism of the outside world. Typical was the view expressed in 1896 in a book written by Sin Kison, the minister of education:

Europe and America are far removed from China, the center of civilization. It would not be too far from the truth to think of Europeans and Americans as more like animals than human beings. Their languages resemble the chirpings of birds more than human languages, so that one finds it hard to understand them. Their religion, called Christianity, is a paganism so full of vulgarities, fallacies, and superstitions that it is not worth our attention.[1]

Why these views changed is the subject of a novel, *Tears of Blood,* written by Yi In-Jik. In it he says,

> The nobility is to blame for the tragic fate of the nation. Noblemen did everything they pleased to us. Noblemen killed many of us of low birth, wrested wealth from us if we were rich, made our wives their concubines if our wives were pretty. How could a man of low birth like myself have served his country well when he was completely at the mercy of noblemen for his life, his wealth, and his wife? How could he have exercised his rights in a society where noblemen threatened to chop off his knees or elbows, or condemn him to exile for the slightest wrongdoing?[2]

Another view of the country under its monarchal rule, that was presented by an American George Kennan, was important because it influenced President Theodore Roosevelt to favor turning the country over to Japanese rule. Kennan wrote,

> The activities and operations of the existing Korean government may be briefly summarized as follows: it takes from the people, directly and indirectly, everything they earn over and above a bare subsistence and gives them in return practically nothing. It affords no adequate protection to life or property; it provides no educational facilities that deserve notice; it builds no roads; it does not improve its harbors; it does not light its coasts; it pays no attention whatever to street cleaning or sanitation; it takes no measures to prevent or check epidemics; it does not attempt to foster trade or industry; it encourages the lowest forms of superstition; and it corrupts or demoralizes its subjects by setting them examples of untruthfulness, dishonesty, treachery, cruelty, and a cynical brutality in dealing with human rights that is almost without parallel in modern times.[3]

This was the old Korea, although Kennan's account was far from being complete. In the villages there often was laughing and singing. Not for nothing was Korea known as The Land of Morning Calm. There was much in its way of life to breed contentment. There was also the beauty of the countryside. And there were stirrings of new ideas. Leaders emerged who were determined to change conditions and who knew that to do so they had to arouse, educate, and guide the people. This is what made the new Korea.

From Hermit Kingdom to Colony

Protests against unjust social conditions began to appear in books published in the eighteenth century. Yi Ik (1681–1763) set forth a broad-ranging set of reform proposals in his *Record of Concern for the Under-privileged*. Chong Yag-yong (1762–1836) published half a dozen books on the theme of his central volume, *Design for Good Government*. Other scholars reported new ideas resulting from their travels in China, and some brought back Bibles and Catholic tracts that led to the conversion of some twenty thousand Koreans to Catholicism. In the mid–nineteenth century, these internal stimulants to change were enhanced by the appearance along the coasts of European vessels. News from China told of European invasions. The alarmed regent of Korea adopted the stern measure of proclaiming a policy of such strict isolation as to win for Korea the cognomen of the Hermit Kingdom.[4]

When this isolationism was broken by the treaties with Japan and Western nations, some few Koreans went abroad to Japan and, later, to the United States and Europe for study. Under the leadership of a progressive-minded aristocrat named Kim Ok-kyun and a few associates, the Progressive party was formed, with the avowed intention of adopting reforms modeled on Japan's Meiji Reformation. On 4 December 1884, Kim Ok-kyun led the king to chambers guarded by Japanese troops, ordered the assassination of reactionary senior officials, and announced a series of reforms that included an end to Korea's traditional tributary subservience to China, abolition of class privileges, and reform of taxation and fiscal policies. A key provision of the program was a call for creation of a state council in which policies would be debated and from which programs would be recommended to the king. Chinese and Korean troops quickly subdued the revolt. Kim Ok-kyun escaped to Japan. Thus ended the first move toward modernism.

In reaction to this attempted palace coup, the Chinese sent into Korea a body of troops headed by Yuan Shih-k'ai to control the government. Russia secured special trade rights and also attempted to dominate the Korean king. As a countermeasure, England fortified an island in the Korea Strait. The Korean court sent an envoy to America in 1887 to seek its support. What was most evident was that the affairs of Korea were perilously close to being determined not by its own government or its own people but by foreign power. After the Japanese waged war against China in the winter of 1894–95, in order to eliminate Chinese influence over Korea, Japan attempted to force upon the Korean king—who then adopted the title of emperor to symbolize his claimed equality with the imperial monarchs of China and Japan—a set of reforms that would separate the monarchal functions from the operations of the government, much like the system in Japan. A State Council was established, headed by a prime minister, as were eight other ministries all supported by a bureaucracy. In an effort to strengthen its influence, Japan arranged the assassination of the strong-minded Queen Min, who was the most effective proponent of traditionalism. This led to a surge of anti-Japanese sentiments. But the reform movement continued, leading to establishment of an independent judiciary, adoption of the Western calendar, and the cutting off of the traditional Korean "topknots," along with medical and educational improvements.

In 1896 a new reform movement began under the leadership of Philip Jaisohn (So Chae-p'il), who had taken part in the revolt of 1884 and had afterward gone to America, where he earned an M.D. degree. He returned to establish the Independence Club as a forum in which students could learn parliamentary law and practice reaching decisions through debating and voting. Shortly the club attracted membership from men important in government and broadened its scope to discussion of public policies. A forum was held every Sunday, in which several hundred citizens heard debates on public issues and then participated in general discussions. A newspaper was also founded to carry the ideas of democratic reform to a wider public. Branches of the club were established in other cities. The club organ, the *Independent*, edited by Philip Jaisohn, announced three major objectives: elimination of foreign interference in Korean affairs; promotion of civil rights, including freedom of speech, and promotion of political democracy by converting the Privy Council into an elected parliament; and such "self-strengthening" programs as the establishment of village schools and local factories.

In 1897 the emperor moved to suppress this movement; and Philip Jaisohn returned to America. Among the courageous men who undertook to continue the effort was young Syngman Rhee, who half a century later was to become the founding president of the Republic of Korea. Much was to happen in the intervening decades, to him and to Korea.

Rhee was born on 26 March 1875, into a devout Buddhist family of limited means but respected social standing. In his late teens Rhee enrolled in Pai Jai Academy, a school run by Methodist missionaries. He learned English and commenced to read about the Western nations. When Jaisohn established the Independence Club, Rhee was an enthusiastic member, taking part in the club discussions and proving adept at street-corner agitation. After the departure of Jaisohn, Rhee led a crowd of eight thousand in a sit-down demonstration at the gates of the emperor's palace.[5] He was seized by the police and subjected to six months of brutal torture. After this period of "interrogation" he was sentenced to life imprisonment. In the prison, Rhee helped to organize a school for the prisoners, in which he lectured on European history. He also wrote a book, *The Spirit of Independence,* which was smuggled out of the jail and a few years later was published in Los Angeles. In this book he pleaded the cause of democracy. "In a civilized nation," he wrote, "each subject has his own responsibility. . . . The relationship between you and your nation may seem so remote that you have little reason to love it or to make efforts to save it. Therefore, two enemies must be guarded against: first, the people who try to destroy the nation; and second, those who sit passively by, being without any hope or sense of responsibility."[6]

The Korean emperor made serious and sustained efforts to improve governmental procedures.[7] However, he was caught between conservative officials, who favored return to the protective supervision of China and who also sought to fortify the special privileges of the aristocracy, and liberals whose effectiveness was handicapped by their association with the Japanese. In 1904 the Japanese attacked the Russian fleet at Port Arthur and forced the Korean emperor to allow them to use Korea as their continental base for their war against Russia. The quick and solid successes of the Japanese helped to convince the American and British governments that Japan was the "coming power" in Asia and that stability in the area would depend upon Japanese predominance. Hence, in the peace conference between Japan and Russia, held in Portsmouth, New Hampshire, President Theodore Roosevelt vitiated the "mutual aid" provision of the U.S.-Korea treaty by acceding to Japan's demand for a protectorate over Korea. In 1910 Japan took the next step of annexing the Korean peninsula as a "special province" of Japan.

When the Korean emperor was forced to allow Japanese troops to occupy Korea, he sought to soften Korean opposition by granting amnesty to political prisoners. Syngman Rhee was among those freed from prison. He went to the United States and attempted to persuade the American administration to oppose Japanese seizure of Korea.[8] When this effort failed, he enrolled in George Washington University, where he earned an A.B. He then entered Harvard and obtained his M.A. in European history. After this he studied at Princeton and was awarded his Ph.D. in political science in 1910.

During his two years at Princeton Rhee became a friend of Woodrow Wilson, then president of the university, who often invited him to his home and who recommended Rhee for the speeches on Korea with which he earned small sums of support money. This education and this friendship with Woodrow Wilson proved to be the foundation for Rhee's lifetime career. "He was always to remain grateful for the dual experiences and education which gave him the rare opportunity to bestride the East and the West, and in effect to combine in his own thinking a fusion of the two. This cultural integration was to become one of the great sources of his strength and leadership in the years that lay ahead. His countrymen also were impressed by the fact that he was the first Korean ever to secure a Ph.D. from an American University."[9]

When Woodrow Wilson led the United States into World War I, he announced that his war aims would center on "the right of self-determination of peoples," which principle would lead to the restoration of subject populations to independence. Korean patriots trusted that the mandate applied also to them, since their nation had enjoyed independence for many centuries and had been colonized by Japan for less than two decades. Wilson, however, yielded to the European Allies on this as on many other questions and agreed to the continuance of Japan's sovereignty over the Korean peninsula.

Shocked Korean patriots drew up and publicly proclaimed a declaration of independence and launched a peaceful demonstration against Japan— more than a decade before Gandhi led his "march to the sea" as a nonviolent protest against British rule of India. Thousands of marching demonstrators obeyed their instructions: "Do not throw stones. Do not hit with sticks. Do not strike with your fists. For such are the acts of barbarians." Nevertheless, the Japanese responded to this demonstration with brutal force; and no foreign nation offered Korea support.[10] Despite this failure by Wilson to live up to his declared war aims, Syngman Rhee, as a friend of Wilson's, was presumed to have influence that would later be helpful, and he was selected by three separate Korean groups—in Seoul, in Manchuria, and in Shanghai—as president of the Korean Provisional Republic.

During the years from 1919 until the end of the war between Japan and the United States, the Provisional Republic made sustained efforts to win diplomatic support for the restoration of Korean independence. In Washington, D.C., Rhee maintained an office called the Korean Commission. In China a group of patriots headed by Kim Ku and Kimm Kiusic conducted an anti-Japanese movement, with the encouragement of Chiang Kai-shek's Kuomintang. Kim Ku was a stalwart peasant-type who in his youth assassinated a Japanese official and who persisted in favoring guerilla warfare against Japan. Kimm Kiusic was a gentle intellectual, a graduate of Roanoke College in the United States, and was well versed in French as well as in English. Through their China-based office, the Provisional Republic leaders became embroiled with Communists, much as had Chiang Kai-shek, with the result that the leaders split into leftist and rightist factions. As Professor Chong-Sik Lee summed up the circumstances in his classic study of the exiled nationalist movement:

The Korean nationalist movement between 1931 and 1936 can be sumamrized as follows: Kim Ku's terrorist activities won initial recognition of the nationalists by the Chinese; the Chinese government began to provide the Koreans the financial and spiritual support they needed; then most of the nationalists were divided into two camps, with the majority on the side of the leftists. [11]

This split into rightist-leftist wings marked the entire Korean exile group, in the United States as well as in China. Inside Korea a considerable pro-Communist sentiment developed, because Russia alone among the big powers showed sympathy for the Korean rebels against Japanese authority and helped to supply them with arms, to educate their leaders, and to assist them in creating guerrilla forces in Manchuria.

Japan's rule of Korea was exploitive. Strong efforts were made to obliterate Korean culture. The use of the Korean language was discouraged, and Koreans were virtually required to japanize their names, to use the Japanese language, and to worship at the Shinto shrines. Study of Korean history was restricted and belittled. The Koreans were treated as inferiors and used mostly for common labor. During the war, about a million Koreans were taken to Japan for labor in mines and factories. In Korea the 3 percent of the population that was Japanese received more education and enjoyed far greater privileges than the 97 percent that was Korean. Notwithstanding these injustices, the Japanese insisted that Koreans regard themselves not as a separate people but as a subordinate offshoot of Japan. [12]

This was the situation in Korea when Japan surrendered on 15 August 1945. Exuberant jubilation swept through the peninsula. The people wept, congratulated one another, and cheered. They were to be free again! [13] As they had in the Southeast Asian countries, the Japanese tried to make the best of the circumstances by serving as the agents for transfer of power to a newly independent government. After the dropping of the first atomic bomb, Japanese authorities commenced a search for a Korean leader who would have sufficient prestige to govern and with whom they could deal. On 14 August they reached an agreement with Lyuh Woon Hyung, a Communist-Nationalist whom they had several times imprisoned for his nationalist activities. Lyuh formed a Committee for the Establishment of the Korean State and began to organize a "peace preservation corps" to maintain order until a new government could be established. On 16 August the committee released from prison several thousand nationalists and Communists held as political prisoners. On that same day, the Korean Communist party was reanimated, with leadership assumed by Pak Hun-yong, who claimed authorization from the Russians. On 3 September the

non-Communist members of Lyuh's committee were dismissed, and a
Communist activist named Hu Hun was brought in as vice-chairman. As
one of the members of the committee later explained, "At that time, no
one thought there was anything wrong with their being Communists—we
were all working for independence."[14] Acting quickly, to forestall objec-
tion by the allied victors in the war, the committee on 6 September
proclaimed the People's Democratic Republic of Korea. In order to win
non-Communists into a united front, the committee named the vigorously
anti-Communist Syngman Rhee as president, with the real governing
power to be in the hands of Prime Minister Hu Hun. Lyuh Woon Hyung
was relegated to the ritualistic post of vice-president. These actions were
encouraged and perhaps facilitated and financed by the Soviet Union's
consul in Seoul.[15] Since Japan and Russia were not at war (until August
1945), the Soviets had the only Western diplomatic office in Korea and
were therefore able to guide the establishment of a Communist government.

Divison and Discord

When on 8 September, Lt. Gen. John R. Hodge led American troops
ashore in the harbor of Inchon, the Americans refused to recognize the
People's Republic and set about establishing their own military government in south Korea. Russian troops, who had been fighting the Japanese
only since 6 August, poured into north Korea. In order to prevent a
dangerous clash of these forces, a division of Korea was agreed to by the
Americans and Russians along the 38th parallel, midway in the peninsula.
President Franklin D. Roosevelt had died just a few months earlier. President Harry Truman and Secretary of State Dean Acheson were not fully
informed on what prior decisions Roosevelt had made with the Soviets
concerning Korea. Hastily a conference was convened at Moscow, which
decided that Korea would be subject to trusteeship control, to be managed
jointly by the Soviet Union, the United States, Great Britain, and Nationalist China. It was a grievous mistake, made in haste and with too little
consideration. The Koreans resented and rejected it. And as the presumably temporary line of the 38th parallel hardened into permanence, the
Americans quickly recognized the need for policy revisions.

I had been working as a friend and adviser with Dr. Syngman Rhee
since September 1942, while he was attempting to work out a basis for
reestablishment of Korean independence; and General John H. Hilldring,
assistant secretary of state for occupied countries, sent me a long letter
concerning the mistake that had been made. In it he said:

You and I both know that it wasn't many weeks after the Moscow

Conference before nearly everyone who had had anything to do with the Korean Moscow Declaration deeply and honestly regretted it. But it is one thing to regret a mistake and quite another to come forward and recommend that an international agreement be renounced in order to correct the mistake. The cold war was already on, which further tightened the conviction of most officials, particularly the career diplomats, that any abrogation by us of an agreement with Russia would have disastrous consequences. In any case this was the dilemma of the U.S. Government.[16]

The bungled Korean policies that were a dilemma for the United States were helpful to the Soviet Union, which was enabled to achieve the century-old Russian goal of attaining a foothold on the Korean peninsula. It was a tragedy for Koreans, who found their dream of national independence converted to the nightmare of division of their country under two foreign military regimes that were so hostile toward one another that cooperation between them was impossible. Very soon the 38th parallel in Korea became the tightest iron curtain in the world. Families were divided. The resources of the country were divided. The economic exploitation by Japan, which left Korea impoverished at war's end, was succeeded by the utter disaster of splitting hydroelectric power and the mineral and timber resources of the north away from the populous agricultural south. Compounding the problem, the north was promptly organized into a Communist regime by Russia, which knew what it wanted; whereas in south Korea the lack of an American policy, plus the well-intentioned democratic insistence on free political activity by everyone, including the Moscow-oriented Communists, resulted in turmoil.

The exiled Korean patriot leaders, of whom Syngman Rhee, Kim Ku and Kimm Kiusic were by far the most prominent, returned to Korea in October 1945. Dr. Rhee organized a Society for the Rapid Realization of Independence and demanded elections to establish a genuinely Korean government. Kim Ku insisted upon recognition and establishment of the Provisional Republic of Korea, which had maintained a shadow existence in China ever since 1919. Kimm Kiusic favored close cooperation with the American authorities, with the hope of building a coalition that would be acceptable to both foreign military regimes and could accordingly reunite Korea. Among the three, Dr. Rhee was the most definitely determined against a coalition with the Communists, declaring that "you can't cooperate with cholera."

Among these and all other south Korean claimants to leadership, Syngman Rhee was by far the most effective communicator. He spoke to the Korean people by radio every week during the winter of 1945–46, and in 1946 he made a campaign tour of south Korea, delivering his anti-Communist message with fervent conviction to crowds of many thousands. As students of communism in Korea have found, Communist sentiment was widespread throughout the whole peninsula for the reason cited earlier—that only the Soviet Union (along with Nationalist China after its war began with Japan in 1937) had supported Korea's goal of independence.[17] Rhee's speeches were effective in convincing the populace that "cooperation" with the Communists simply meant "surrender" to them. As Scalapino and Lee viewed the turnaround of opinion that Rhee's leadership accomplished, they noted that he "was emerging as the purest, most strident nationalist."[18]

Meanwhile, "the Communists turned a full-scale attack on Rhee, using their publicity resources which were at the time the most widely circulated in the South."[19] Rhee's speeches were regarded unfavorably by the American authorities, who charged him with blocking an agreement with Russia to bring the trusteeship plan into effect. When I arrived in south Korea in June 1946, General Hodge told me that "Syngman Rhee is so much the greatest Korean statesman that he may be said to be the only one, but unless he ceases his persistent attacks upon Russia he never can have a part in any government which the United States may sponsor in Korea."[20] The reason was that American policy was to implement the trusteeship plan, which Russia strongly favored and which Rhee and other Korean nationalists were effectively blocking.

Several US-USSR joint meetings were held in an effort to reach agreement on a trusteeship program that Koreans could be induced or required to accept. When these talks foundered because of Soviet insistence on provisions that would have turned all Korea over to Communist control, the United States presented the "Korean problem" to the United Nations. In February 1948, the "Little Assembly" of the UN (a special all-members committee that remained in session to supervise the Korean problem) voted to hold elections "in all parts of Korea that were accessible." As all understood, this meant that elections would be held only in south Korea, since the Soviet Union adamantly refused to allow the UN to supervise elections north of the 38th parallel. On 10 May the elections were held for a National Assembly, which proceeded promptly to adopt a constitution, to elect Syngman Rhee as president of the Republic of Korea, and to inaugurate the new administration on 15 August. In December the United Nations General Assembly, meeting in Paris, voted recognition of the Republic as "the lawful government of Korea and the only such government in Korea." This was a clear judgment that the pseudo-regime that the Soviet Union had set up in north Korea was illegitimate. Nevertheless, the two parts of divided Korea continued to have separate governments, with such hostility between them that in 1950–53, after a surprise invasion of the south by north Korea, they waged a bitter war, in which the United Nations fought to help defeat the invaders.

The two leaders who had decisive roles in establishing nationalism in both halves of the peninsula were Syngman Rhee in the Republic of Korea and Kim Il-sung as president of the People's Democratic Republic of Korea in the north. How they gained power and what their leadership has meant is a vital chapter in the history not only of Korea but of the last half century of global politics.

Kim Il-sung's North Korea

The primary question concerning Kim Il-sung's North Korean regime is: To what extent has it truly represented the Korean people and to what degree has it been the creature of Russian and Chinese communism? Since Kim Il-sung has been the central and dominating leader during the entire lifetime of the People's Democratic Republic of Korea, this question in large part revolves around whether or not he gained office through popular support and holds it on behalf of Korea or at the behest of foreign powers. A secondary and no less important issue is the quality of his leadership. What have been its effects?

Leadership—its roots, its nature, and its effects—is the crucial factor for nations as for other organizations. And as Dae-Sook Suh found in his decades of studying Korean communism, it was precisely leadership that was lacking in the period between the time of the Old Communists (who founded and developed the party in Korea) and the New Communists (who came to power after the close of World War II). The reasons he found included a tendency to factional divisiveness among the Korean Communists and strict control over them by the Japanese police:

Many sets of leaders from various groups appeared only to be arrested by the police, and those who escaped arrest, in general, retired abroad. There was no single leader with whom the movement could be identified through [this] span. Because of intensive police surveillance and frequent arrest, the leadership ultimately rested in the hands of audacious and sometimes inadvertent young men who appeared intermittently. Often their lack of proper orientation to the revolutionary cause prompted them to renounce communism under adverse conditions, and those who fled abroad ultimately emigrated without really attempting to revive the cause of communism in Korea.[21]

The New Communists who came to power in north Korea in the years after 1945 were led by a thirty-three-year-old guerrilla chief who assumed the name of Kim Il-sung. He and his lieutenants came to north Korea with the Russian troops. His name was Kim Song-ju before he adopted the name of Kim Il-sung, who was a legendary heroic guerrilla fighter of the prior generation. Kim Song-ju was born on 15 April 1912 into a peasant family in a small village near the north Korean metropolis of Pyongyang, which became the capital of the People's Democratic Republic. After the 1919 demonstrations were suppressed by the Japanese, the Kim family moved to Manchuria, where young Song-ju attended school, (but not long enough to graduate from middle school), and at the age of fifteen joined the Chinese Communist party.[22] Subsequently he engaged in guerrilla fighting against the Japanese.

At this time in his life there was nothing observably remarkable about him. As Scalapino and Lee view him, Kim Il-sung "was by no means alone among Communists as being talented and dedicated. It would be possible to describe in such a fashion at least a hundred Koreans of this period who at one point or another committed themselves to Communism."[23] As they add, Kim was lucky in that he entered north Korea with the Russians just when they were looking for a capable young leader who had ability, ruthlessness, and a willingness to serve their ends. His ultimate triumph over rivals came not from his own popular appeal: "the central reason was simply Soviet support."[24] Dae-Sook Suh agrees that Kim Il-sung was "the choice of the Russians" and concludes that this choice was dictated not so much by his abilities as by the failures of the Old Communists. Suh also gives credit to Kim for "effective manipulations and efficient maneuvers," since "opportunity for the old Communists existed" and "Kim had to undertake difficult political maneuvers to be assured of his position."[25]

Lim Un, in his biography of Kim Il-sung, selected 14 October 1945 (two months after the Russian army entered north Korea) as the critical date that led to Kim's endorsement by the Soviets. A mammoth reception was held in Pyongyang to welcome the Russian "Army of Liberation" and the most prominent of the Korean Christian independence-advocates, the elderly Cho Mansik, was assigned the honorific function of giving the speech of welcome. Afterward a Russian general made a formal reply, in the course of which he mentioned the presence in the crowd of Kim Il-sung. The crowd applauded, apparently believing they were going to see the legendary old chieftain, and the Russians "observed that Kim Il-sung was unexpectedly popular among the Korean people."[26] Kim then was summoned to the podium to make a speech in which he called for unity "to construct a democratic and independent country." The crowd showed its disappointment when it became evident that the speaker was not the legendary figure they had expected. The speech was awkwardly phrased and Lim Un explains that the reason was that it had been drafted and then "translated poorly into Korean" by the political department of the Russian army.[27]

According to Lim Un (who was in a position to know), the Chinese Communists' choice for leader of north Korea was a Korean General named Mu-jong, who had participated in Mao Tse-tung's "Long March" and was the artillery commander in the Chinese Eighth Route Army. After the defeat of the Japanese, "Mu-jong made an energetic lecture tour of North Korea, during which he outlined the course Korea should take in the future. In his speeches, he declared his political principles and so it was like a 'canvassing tour.' He won popularity as he was an eloquent speaker of great resources."[28] However, he was the Chinese, not the Soviet, candidate—and it was the Soviets who occupied north Korea.

Cho Mansik, long known as a nationalist who recognized the value of Communist support for the cause, was a natural choice by the Russians to become their puppet through which to govern north Korea. He was well known throughout the entire peninsula and would have strong appeal to the people in the south as well as in the north. The Russians named Cho Mansik chairman of a People's Political Committee that contained thirty-two members, half communist, half non-communist, representing a "united front," to serve as their instrument for governing the country. At the first meeting of the committee the Russian commander ordered it to take directions from the Communist party concerning government of the provinces. Cho angrily refused and offered to resign, whereupon the order was changed to "cooperate with the Communist Party." In order to ensure that this "cooperation" would actually be subservience, the Soviet commander appointed Kim Il-sung to be Cho's assistant.[29]

In this post Kim Il-sung had power with which to undermine other Communist leaders, including Pak Hun-yong, who had organized Communist units throughout the north. When the Northern Bureau of the Korean Communist Party was organized, the Russians named Kim Il-sung to the critical post of secretary. When the Moscow Declaration to establish trusteeship over Korea was announced on 24 December, Cho Mansik protested against it and resigned from the Political Committee. He was placed under house arrest and disappeared, not to be heard of again. Kim Il-sung took his place.

On 8 February 1946 an "Enlarged Conference" was held in Pyongyang with representatives of all of north Korea's political parties, social organizations, and political committees—all, that is, that were permitted to operate. Kim Il-sung was chairman, and in his speech he ended all pretense of a united front with "patriotic capitalists" and "petty bourgeois nationalists." "We cannot construct a democratic new Korea while we have traitors and renegades in positions of sovereign power," he said.[30]

Kim Il-sung had little appeal for the Korean people., He was unknown when he arrived in Korea with the Russians, and he did not make a good impression. He was short (only a trifle over five feet four inches in height), inclined to stockiness, and wore an ill-fitting blue suit. "His complexion was slightly dark and he had a haircut like a Chinese waiter. His hair at the forehead was about an inch long, reminding one of a lightweight boxing champion." When he stepped to the microphone to make the speech in which he was introduced to the Korean public, on 14 October, "all of the people gathered upon the athletic field felt an electrifying sense of distrust, disappointment, discontent, and anger." He in no way resembled the old guerrilla leader Kim Il-sung whom he pretended to be. This account of his speech, by a former secretary of Cho Mansik, who knew Kim well, continues:

> Oblivious to the sudden change in mass psychology Kim Il-sung continued in his monotonous, plain and ducklike voice to praise the heroic struggles of the Red Army, those allies who had liberated the 30 million Korean people who had suffered such agonies under the oppressive forces of Japanese imperialism. He particularly praised and offered the most extravagant words of gratitude and glory to the Soviet Union and Marshal Stalin, that close friend of the oppressed peoples of the world. The people at this point had completely lost their respect and hope for General Kim Il-sung. There was the problem of age, but there was also the content of the speech, which was so much like that of the other Communists whose monotonous repetitions had worn the people out.[31]

The Russians, however, were confident that Kim would serve their purposes and made him chairman of the North Korean Provisional People's Committee, through which the north Koreans were to be governed. On 23 March 1946, Kim Il-sung made a speech in which he announced a twenty-one-point program for the regime. "The people" were to be protected from "the enemies," who were landlords, reactionaries, and everyone else who opposed the rule of the Communist party. All the people—except such enemies—were to be assured of freedom of speech, assembly, publication, and worship. All farmers and laborers would be organized, and all the people would become members of committees that would meet in discussion groups every week, or more often, to make sure that all were observing the laws. All large enterprises, transport facilities, banks, mines, and forests were to be nationalized. In another speech, on 20 June, Kim launched a violent attack against American "exploitation" of the south Koreans, who, he said, had no hope for the future except that of joining the north under his regime. This was his promise of what his leadership would mean.

Despite his orthodox communism and fawning upon Russia, as the Russian troops were reduced and then withdrawn during the years 1947–48, Kim sought popularity by depicting himself as a sturdy nationalist, "holding to the principle of solving for oneself all the problems of the revolution and construction in conformity with the actual conditions at home, and mainly by one's own efforts. . . . This is an independent, self-reliant policy of solving one's own affairs by oneself under all circumstances."[32] This, he said, was his hope for the future: a Communist Korea that would be free to shape its own destiny, with pride in its own past—which, in his view, meant that the loyalty and obedience formerly given to an absolute monarch was to become loyal subservience to the new proletarian dictator.

As he said in a speech on 22 June, 1946: "In order for us to construct a new and democratic Korea, we must become one family. We must unite the entire North Korean people and the entire Korean people around the Democratic National United Front."[33] In order to communicate effectively with the Korean people, Kim had to teach them a wholly new vocabulary—one in which "unity" meant submission, "freedom" meant totalitarianism, "democracy" meant dictatorship, and "national front" meant communism. In order to accomplish this reeducation, Kim utilized the same methods that had been successful in the Soviet Union and in Mao Tse-tung's China. He combined ruthless force to eliminate or ruin landlords, capitalists, and all other "enemies of the state" and an elaborate propaganda system that included prohibition of news from abroad, strict censorship of speech and the press, and constant reiteration of the official interpretations of history and events over the state-run radio and television and in the schools, culminating in weekly and semiweekly meetings that all (children, farmers, laborers, women, writers, government employees, and everyone else) were required to attend and during which they were expected to listen and to speak in vehement and full agreement. In further enforcement of this communication pattern, elections for officially selected candidates were held at frequent intervals, with no opposition parties and no choice except to vote under close scrutiny either "yes" or "no." By such means north Korea was "unified," except for the one or two million of its inhabitants who "voted with their feet" by leaving their properties, homes, jobs, and ancestral graves in order to slip past police surveillance and somehow get across the border into the south.

Even more than in Stalinist Russia, more than in any other Communist country (except in China for a decade or so before the Cultural Revolution), Kim Il-sung nurtured the "cult of personality." He virtually became the state. A young man with considerable ability and with seemingly endless energy, he concentrated all authority in his own hands. He delivered frequent speeches that dealt with manifold aspects of domestic and foreign policies in exhaustive detail. He went several times to Moscow to explain and justify his version of Koreanized communism and to entreat for more material aid. And all through the years 1945–50, while he was constructing the apparatus of controls and building military power with Russian guidance and armaments, he emphasized repeatedly the unbreakable bond that tied north Korea to the Soviet Union.

Kim Il-sung's government "was the product of Soviet power, not of public popularity,"[34] and the step-by-step evolution of that government from The People's Political Committee to the Korean People's Democratic Republic in August 1948 was closely monitored by Russian advisers. Only long afterward—after the failure to conquer South Korea in the 1950–53 war, and after the entry of China into that war gave Kim the leverage he needed to play off the two Communist giants against one another—was Kim Il-sung able, in January 1972, to affirm boldly that his regime in North Korea had achieved independence. In a conference with Japanese news reporters, he said:

> Establishing *chuch'e* [independence] means, in a nutshell, being the master of revolution and reconstruction in one's own country. This means holding fast to an independent position, rejecting dependence on others, using one's own brains, believing in one's own strength, displaying the revolutionary spirit of self-reliance, and thus solving one's own problems for oneself on one's own responsibility under all circumstances. And it means adhering to the creative position of opposing dogmatism and applying the universal principles of Marxism-Leninism and the experience of other countries to suit the historical conditions and national peculiarities of one's own country.[35]

Independent nationalism for North Koreans meant an enforced acceptance of a foreign ideology, communism, under leadership imposed upon the people without regard for their free choice.

Syngman Rhee's Legacy in South Korea

How much did the development of the independent Korean government in South Korea differ from that in the north? The differences are impressive, despite some significant similarities. Both sides of the 38th parallel were occupied by foreign armies—by Russians in the north, by Americans in the south. In neither half of the peninsula did the people have a truly free choice concerning the nature of the government they were to have; in the north it was imposed communism and in the south, democracy—both alien to Korean traditions. The whole population is unusually homogeneous—in race, language, and culture. In both north and south there were similar yearnings for the reunification of the ancient homeland, for independent self-rule, and for the rapid attainment of modern, Western-style standards of health, education, social equality, economic well-being, and freedom for individual self-expression and development. North and south Koreans alike looked forward to the benefits of sovereign nationalism: the resumption of their own language, their own identity, and their own culture, and an equal status for their country in the world community of nations.

The reality brought to the people of both north and south bitter disappointments. The independence that was proclaimed in the inauguration of their separate governments was at best partial, at least in the immediate period. The two governments were both denied membership in the United Nations, and each was recognized only by the respective Communist and democratic bloc. In both areas social and economic benefits were slow in developing, and in neither segment of the peninsula did the people have reason to rejoice in the government that was established. The benefits they had hoped would come with independence when Japan surrendered proved to be far short of their expectations.

The differences between North and South Korea, however, were deep and significant. Syngman Rhee was not selected by the Americans and imposed upon the south, as Kim Il-sung was selected and placed in power by the Russians in the north. In the south far greater freedom of speech, of political activity, and of individual liberty was attained. The constitution adopted by the Republic of Korea provided for free elections contested by competitive political parties, in contrast with the single-party system in the Communist north. Freedom of speech and of the press within the borders, and free exchange of news with the outside world, were by far greater in the south than in the north. The system of local committees and mandatory discussion meetings that assured surveillance and tight central control in the north was absent from the south. Whereas in North Korea the press, the school system, and public meetings were devoted to the glorification of the Great Leader Kim Il-sung, in South Korea an activist press and vital opposition parties subjected President Syngman Rhee and his government to the acidulous criticism that is endemic in democracies.

Syngman Rhee, far from being the American choice for the presidency of the Republic of Korea, came into that office after sustained efforts by the American military government to prevent his choice.[36] In the elections held on 10 May 1948, under the observation of the American military government and also of a United Nations commission, some 86 percent of all eligible voters in South Korea (men and women over twenty-one) were registered, and 92.5 percent of them voted. The UN commission reported that it found the election to be "a valid expression of the free will of the electorate." The two hundred National Assembly members who were elected cast 180 votes for Dr. Rhee and 16 for Kim Ku. In December the General Assembly of the United Nations voted 43 to 0 that the newly inaugurated Republic of Korea was the "only legal government" in the Korean peninsula. General John R. Hodge, in turning over the governing of south Korea to the Republic, stated the American view:

We all regret exceedingly that the free election could not be held in Korea north of the 38th parallel at the same time as in South Korea. The

United States and the United Nations hope that this can be done and that representatives from North Korea can join those in South Korea in the establishment of a truly National Korean Government joining North and South Korea together in one nation. It is my hope . . . that the newly elected representatives will do everything in their power to form a truly democratic government and to unite Korea."[37]

The view held by the Korean people was stated earlier by Dr. Rhee in his address of welcome to the United Nations delegates upon their arrival to supervise the South Korean election. After greeting them with "profound gratitude and renewed hopefulness," he reminded them of the wrong that must be rectified:

Forty years ago our nation was sacrificed to the ambition of one of the Great Powers, while the other nations of the world stood aside. During the past 28 months our long-suffering people have once again been the victims of circumstances wholly beyond our own control. We have seen justice delayed, pledges postponed, and the hopes of honest men frustrated. It has seeemed through many dark months that a new blight had fallen across our land, even worse than that we were forced to endure while our country, however harshly ruled, was still united.

In those dark months we touched the depths of bitterness, but we refused to despair. We clung then—just as Koreans will always cling, so long as they may live—to the fierce determination that our country must once again be united and must once again be free.

We hail your arrival as a solemn event, not only in our own history, but in the history of the world. No longer do the Korean people stand alone. The free nations of the world have heard our voice and have answered it.[38]

Dr. Rhee was then seventy-three years of age, and from his teens had been engaged unceasingly in the struggle to help make his people free. In this long campaign he alienated some of his own countrymen, who resisted his leadership, and he also aroused the animosity of the United States Department of State, which pursued policies contrary to Korean independence. [39] During all those long decades he was without official status, influential friends, or financial resources. His principal resource was his own personality: his unswerving determination, his depth of devotion to his people, his well-educated and insightful intelligence, and his power of eloquent persuasiveness. As I have elsewhere written of him, reflecting a long and close personal relationship and participation in his crusade:

Dr. Rhee speaks easily, fluently and frequently. He is unrestrainedly articulate. On many occasions he speaks extemporaneously, generally with a simple theme developed with a prolific body of applications and specific illustrations. When he reads a prepared speech . . . he presents it with a skillful utilization of emotional and intellectual emphasis on the main points to be unfolded. His voice is resonant, full-bodied and responsive to a wide variety of meaningful overtones. Even in his latest years he commands a dramatic expressiveness which might be envied by a professional actor. As a natural speaker, with his powers enhanced by long practice and thoughtful consideration of communicative requirements, he responds whole-heartedly to the stimulation of an audience and often shows a fine appreciation for the special requirements of particular situations.[40]

The source of Dr. Rhee's strength, and also of his vulnerability, lay in his combination of Korean and American characteristics, a combination that during his entire career not only fueled his effectiveness but also led Koreans to consider him too "pro-American," and sometimes puzzled Western critics who expected this Harvard-and-Princeton-educated man to be more westernized than he was. As is generally true of strong characters, their weaknesses and their strengths are simply obverse reflections of their most basic traits. So was it with Syngman Rhee:

While the life of Syngman Rhee is complex (like all lives) and unique in its essence and achievements (so that his equal is not likely to appear in Korea soon, if ever again), the general pattern of his development adheres to a simple and vital formula. He is an archtype of the new man who has begun to appear in our century: an integration of the cultures of the East and the West. One of his greatest values and perhaps the chief foundation of his effective leadership is that he successfully synthesized his excellent education in the ancient culture of the Orient with his advanced studies in American and European history and philosophy. At a time when the two disparate hemispheres have been united in a common destiny, he has stood in the center, able with equal ease to see the central meanings of both. One of the keys to the nature of the man is that he speaks with equal facility in Korean and English, but with different styles and emphases in the two languages. He knows how to talk with his own people as well as to ours. And he does not make the mistake of thinking that the two audiences have as yet become one. The synthesis which he exemplifies is one the peoples of the Orient and the Occident are just now beginning to approach.[41]

Like Kim Il-sung in the north, Syngman Rhee found that the independence of the government he headed was limited by the essential help that he had to have from the power that had for three years maintained a military government over the country. Also like Kim Il-sung, Rhee's most basic policy was to do all that was possible toward restoring the unification of the Korean people. But whereas Russia moved surely and steadily to build a strong military force in North Korea, the United States with equal tenacity persisted in refusing to assist or even to permit the creation of a coutervailing force in the South.

On 24 June 1949, just a few days before the scheduled withdrawal of the last American troops from South Korea, Dr. Rhee gloomily reviewed the resources he had for restraining the attack that was threatened from North Korea:

> The American forces in Korea will be out of Korea by the end of this month. What do we have for our defense? Most of our Army men are without rifles, and so is our police and navy. Our defense minister reports that we have munitions which last for only three days of actual fighting . . .
> We are going to ask the U.N. to investigate and make public the reports on how many weapons we have and how much America has given us. It would be highly important [also] for a Congressional investigation committee to come and check it. . . . From our own point of view at present, sufficient supplies of adequate weapons of war for our own defense seems more urgent than economic recovery. We can rebuild our economy and everything else; but if the security is gone, what good is our having anything at all?[42]

On 25 June 1950 an overwhelming force of North Korean troops, tanks, and aircraft launched a surprise invasion of South Korea. President Truman ordered American resistance and persuaded the United Nations to help in repelling the attack.[43] After three years of war a truce was signed that reestablished the division of Korea, virtually along the 38th parallel. In a last effort to rally support for worldwide resistance to Communist aggression, President Rhee on 29 July 1954 addressed a joint session of the United States Congress, to present his own interpretation of global affairs:

> The way to survival for the free peoples of the world—the only way that we Koreans see—is not the way of wishfully hoping for peace when there is no peace; not by trusting that somehow the Soviet Government may be persuaded to abandon its monstrous effort to conquer the world; not by cringing and appeasing the forces of evil; but by swinging the world balance of power so strongly against the Communists that, even when they possess the weapons of annihilation, they will not dare use them.[43]

It was a plea the American Congress did not heed. And shortly after the war that was launched upon South Korea was ended, the attention of the American people and of the world was diverted from Korea by the gradually expanding war in Vietnam. President Rhee was successively reelected to his second, third, and fourth four-year terms as president. By 1960, he was eighty-five years of age and his power to govern was diminished by age and by the continuance of desperately difficult economic conditions. The last election, held that year, was marked by gross miscounting of the ballots by the head of the dominant Liberal party, Lee Ki-boung, on his own behalf as a candidate for the vice-presidency. As a result, Lee and his wife were slain by their only son, who then committed suicide. Syngman Rhee was forced to resign, to spend his remaining five years in Hawaii.

Conclusion

During the succeeding years, South Korea has vastly outstripped the north in economic development. There is also vastly more freedom and respect for human rights in the south than in the north. But in neither segment of the peninsula has a genuinely free or full democracy been attained. The reunification of the nation remains a goal without immediate realistic prospects of success. But it is the principal preoccupation of the leadership in both parts of the divided peninsula. In view of the long history of the homogeneous Korean people, it will not be abandoned short of eventual success.

The struggle of the Korean people for their own independence makes a fitting climax for the general history of the Asian peoples' efforts to attain modernism and nationalism in the brief time span of a mere two or three generations. What they have achieved is tremendous, and what remains to be accomplished in the development of social rights, political freedom, and economic well-being (in many parts of Asia) is a challenge for new generations.

As is always true of any history, the past does not culminate in the present but points onward to a yet-evolving future. The one certainty is that the peoples of Asia have acted with great courage, under the leadership of men who eloquently stimulated and led their advance, to bring their destiny under their own control. The old civilization that was maintained for centuries has largely collapsed, with some values lost and many more gained. The interregnum period of Europeanized colonialism has been surmounted. Much of Asia has not yet created free societies, but the people have grasped the ideal and are working toward it in their own ways. This is what makes the last century as important globally as was the sixteenth century's exploration of the New World.

Epilogue
The Dynamism of Asian Society

This book has depicted two continuing and complex types of confrontation in Asia, both of which have considerable historical consequence. The first was the confrontation between leaders with a new vision and the old traditionalism, in the course of which modernism was attained. The second confrontation has been between these leaders (with their Asian rhetorical viewpoint) and the power of the West, in the course of which national independence was won. Both processes were accomplished relatively rapidly, in historic terms, covering roughly about a hundred years. The fifteen nations reviewed in this book were all different, with different problems, different traditions, and, consequently, different kinds of leadership. Yet there is also an overarching pattern of similarity.

In Asia, as in every other part of the world—wherever people live together in large or small communities—persuasive communication is the lifeblood of the society. Interaction is what makes social organization possible. Goals are set to give direction for cooperative activity. Individuals must be induced to participate in their several ways to make coordinated progress toward the accepted goals. All of this requires leadership, and leadership requires persuasively effective communication.

What this book has sought to do is to depict and to interpret the roles of the leaders who presented to their people the ideal of independent nationality and inspired support for it, and who devised the programs and the policies through which widespread cooperative campaigns were conducted.

Skeptics have asserted that it is impossible to learn anything from history. True believers, on the other hand, seek support for their own convictions by a careful selection from history of particular events and circumstances that fit their own preferences. Somewhere in between these extremes is the objective search for patterns of meaning that are sufficiently coherent to be trends. As Sun Yat-sen put it in one of his speeches, cited in chapter 2, the course of events may be pushed or pulled in one direction or the other but in a planned society (and no society is possible without some plan) the general trend will prevail.

Any meaningful interpretation of history has to depict the main trends of events. There was, as Gibbon noted, a rise and then a fall of the Roman Empire. Without interpretations of this kind, history would be meaningless. The particular pattern of events with which this book deals is clear. It is the advent of modernism and of nationalism in the Far East. The ideal of stability was displaced by the new ideal of progress. A sense of national unity, fired by patriotism, was nurtured. "Family-ism" and "clanism," as Sun Yat-sen was fond of repeating to his followers, had to be replaced with a new concept of "nationalism."

It is because this is the pattern that is examined in this book that the account ends roughly around 1950, when across the broad spectrum of Asia independent nationalism was achieved. Of course there is no ending of the story—not in 1950 or at any other date. It is always rather futile to try to narrate history "up to the present," for the present is always fading into the past. But there is a very special reason why this account relates the coming of independence and stops there.

The reason has already been stated in the Preface and merits restatement. The attaining of independence constituted a special period that was marked by a forward-looking surge of optimistic expectations. The theme represented by the leadership was: "Things are bad now, but when we bring our own affairs under our own control, they will be better." Sacrifices were freely requested on the ground that the anticipated rewards would be well worth their cost. People were heartened by this hope for betterment and by the confidence of their leadership that their combined efforts would succeed. Sacrifice, striving, and optimism were the hallmarks of this period of revolutionary transformation.

The generalized message of the leadership was that the people had been exploited by their foreign colonizers—or, in Japan and in China, by their entrenched aristocracies. With the coming of self-rule, a new day would dawn. Justice would prevail. There would be opportunities, even plenty, for all. The people would have the right to think their own thoughts, to speak freely their own opinions, to pursue their own best interests in their own way. In different parts of Asia the emphasis was adjusted to local conditions. But everywhere this was the essence of the general persuasive appeal that generated popular support.

Not surprisingly, the attainment of independent sovereignty did not and could not bring about fulfillment of such expectations. A new stability had to be sought. Orderliness had to be imposed. Taxes had to be collected. Economic conditions (in the short term) generally became worse, as the long-established management was displaced. New international relationships had to be developed. New ways had to be found for securing an inflow of raw materials, for creating industries, for regulating commerce, for balancing all manner of competing needs.

The leadership that accomplished independence was confronted by entirely different needs and had to discover or invent new ways of dealing with them. In some instances the old leadership persisted into the new and different era. In South Korea, for example, Dr. Syungman Rhee, the lifelong advocate of Korean independence, became the first president of the new Republic, charged with the duty of creating an adequate administrative organization and of dealing with the multiple and varied new demands. In this he did not succeed very well, and he himself clearly understood why. As he said, "I have been an agitator all my life and I can't change now." Agitation, or persuasive advocacy, is one thing—orderly administration is something else. Many of the leaders of newly independent nations (whether old leaders enacting the new role or new leaders confronting the new tasks) could have said what Ramon Magsaysay confessed to his friends, "I do not know what to do."

Historically, one period—one trend—ended and another began. The current period, commencing when independence was proclaimed, is markedly different in different parts of Asia. Japan, South Korea, and Singapore have achieved impressive economic success. India has been successful beyond reasonable expectation in attaining political democracy and has come nearer to solving its serious economic problems than in 1950 appeared possible. China has attained a higher standard of living and somewhat freer civil rights than had seemed probable. Despite such success, in much of Asia both democracy and prosperity are more beckoning goals than attained realities. The assessment of what has been—and what has not been—achieved, demands such careful examination as would necessitate another volume. It goes beyond the purpose of this book.

A major common factor among all fifteen of the new nations in Asia is that they were forced to deal with Western powers across the great gulf of cultural differences. Since the West had more wealth and much more power, the contest was greatly unequal. Consequently, the leaders of the various Asian peoples had urgent need for unusual persuasive ability. It is as though they were playing an international game of poker while holding only two deuces against opponents with three aces or a full house. The Asian leaders had no recourse except to become masters of bluster and of bluff. For such reasons they often were belittled, even ridiculed, and generally misunderstood by Western public opinion and by Western diplomats. It is easy to disparage spokesmen who have to make demands that they lack power to enforce. Nevertheless, what the historical record shows is that by and large it was these disparaged Eastern leaders who prevailed. In any fair assessment, they merit high praise for both courage and skill. Since they were inferior in strength, they had to be superior in sophistication and in artifice.

Not only did these leaders face the formidable opposition of far greater Western power, but they also had to overcome an equally formidable kind of opposition from their own people. Through scores of centuries, the East had maintained confidence that its traditional value systems had proved to have high survival value. It was a major accomplishment of the leaders to persuade their own people to forswear traditional ways and attitudes and, instead, to take all the risks and make all the uncomfortable adjustments of entering into a struggle that required them to deal with Western nations under Western rules.

The confrontation of the East and the West has consisted of many strands: military, economic, social, political, cultural, psychological. The struggles that ensued are far too dynamic and complex to be contained within any single perspective. What portions of the history are examined, and what appear to have special significance, depends on the chosen perspective. The relationships between Asia and the Western nations during the years since the mid-nineteenth century have been analyzed, evaluated, and narrated many times, in many ways. Every selective approach has its own values and its own limitations.

The subject matter of this book, clearly and simply, is the rhetorical leadership that guided and inspired the transition of the East from traditionalism to modernity and, concurrently, from dependence to independence. These two strands are too completely interwoven to permit separation. The leaders who depended upon persuasive communication in pursuit of their goals were well aware of the relationship. What they had to say, and how they said it, are worthy of close attention, for what dependence and independence mean in our modern world is of urgently vital concern.

It is notable that the twentieth century has been marked by the contrary claims of global unity and of segmental national entities. The actual number of nation-states has tripled in the latter part of this century. The need for internationalism has been energized and emphasized by the growth in communication, the threat of massively destructive warfare, and the manifest interconnections of the world's economy. The problem for all peoples has become what it was for the leaders of emerging Asian nations: how to attain and safeguard the right of self-determination while also attaining and maintaining the equally indispensable cooperative global relationships. It is a commonplace that war anywhere threatens peace everywhere; and that poverty anywhere threatens prosperity everywhere. It is also a commonplace that cultural differences constitute barriers that are mutually rejective and in some degree hostile to one another. How are such differences to be reconciled?

The leaders whose careers are examined in this book dealt with virtually these same kinds of contradictory demands. How they did so is worthy of conisderation and of respect. For the past century the East has been challenged to learn from the West. Has the time not come when with equal urgency we all should be learning from one another?

Notes

Introduction

1. For further elaborations of this theme, see. R. T. Oliver, "Sacred Cows, Asian and American: The Language of Social Behavior," *Vital Speeches of the Day* 35 (15 August 1969): 668–72, and idem, "The Varied Rhetorics of International Relations," *Western Journal of Speech Communication* 25 (Fall 1961): 213–21.

2. William S. Howell, Foreword to *Ethical Perspectives and Critical Issues in Intercultural Communication,* ed. Nobleza C. Asuncion-Landé (Falls Church, Va.: Speech Communication Association, 1979), p. x.

3. George Wilhelm Friederich Hegel, *The Philosophy of Right,* trans. T. M. Knox (Oxford: Clarendon Press, 1952), p. 295.

4. E. H. Carr, *What Is History?* (New York: Knopf, 1962), p. 142.

5. See R. T. Oliver, *Communication and Culture in Ancient India and China* (Syracuse, N.Y.: Syracuse University Press, 1971), esp. chaps. 1, 2, 6, 14. See also Pyo Wook Han, "A Sense of Values: The Basis for Liberty and Equality in the Far East," *Vital Speeches of the Day* 24 (15 December 1957): 137–39.

6. Sharif Al Mujahid, *Quaid-I-Azam Jinnah: Studies in Interpretation* (Karachi: Quaid-I-Azam Academy, 1981), p. xix.

7. Sidney Hook, *The Hero in History: A Study in Limitation and Possibility* (Boston: Beacon Press, 1956), p. 154.

8. Ibid., p. 157.

Chapter 1. Meiji Japan

1. See Harold Bolitho, Thomas M. Huber, and Conrad Totman, "The Meiji Restoration: Product of Gradual Decay, Abrupt Crisis, or Creative Will?" in *Japan Examined: Perspectives on Modern Japanese History,* ed. Harry Wray and Hilary Conroy (Honolulu: University of Hawaii Press, 1983), pp. 56–78.

2. W. G. Beasley, *The Meiji Restoration* (Stanford, Calif.: Stanford University Press, 1972), pp. 98–116.

3. Note the claim by Okakura Tenshin, written in 1904, that "our individuality has been preserved from submersion beneath the mighty flood of Western ideas by the same national characteristics which ever enabled us to remain true to ourselves in spite of repeated influxes of foreign thought" (Okakura Kakuzō, *The Awakening of Japan* [New York: Century Co., 1905], p. 187).

4. Quoted in Peter Duus, *The Rise of Modern Japan* (Boston: Houghton Mifflin, 1976), p. 24.

5. Ibid., p. 37.

6. See ibid., chaps. 2, 3; Beasley, *The Meiji Restoration,* chap. 2; and Hilary Conroy, Sandra T. W. Davis, and Wayne Patterson, eds., *Japan in Transition: Thought and Action in the Meiji Era, 1868–1912* (Rutherford, N.J.: Fairleigh Dickinson University Press, 1984).

7. W. G. Beasley, *Select Documents on Japanese Foreign Policy, 1853–1868* (New York: Oxford University Press, 1955), p. 104.

8. R. Tsunoda et al., comps., *Sources of Japanese Tradition* (New York: Columbia University Press, 1965), p. 602.

9. Quoted in Beasley, *Meiji Restoration,* p. 92.

10. Quoted in Duus, *Rise of Modern Japan,* p. 59.

11. Quoted in Joseph Pittau, *Political Thought in Early Meiji Japan, 1868–1889* (Cambridge: Harvard University Press, 1967), p. 33.

12. Joyce C. Lebra, *Ōkuma Shigenobu: Statesman of Meiji Japan* (Canberra: Australian National Press, 1973), p. 5.

13. The text of the Charter Oath is in Tsunoda, *Sources of Japanese Tradition,* pp. 643–45.

14. Duus, *Rise of Modern Japan,* p. 75.

15. Marius B. Jansen, *Sakamoto Ryōma and the Meiji Restoration* (Princeton: Princeton University Press, 1961), p. ix.

16. Mazakazu Iwata, *Ōkubo Toshimichi: The Bismarck of Japan* (Berkeley and Los Angeles: University of California Press, 1964), p. 116.

17. Junsei Ijichi, *The Life of Marquis Shigenobu Ōkuma: A Biographical Study in the Rise of Democratic Japan* (Tokyo: Hokuseido Press, 1956), p. 178.

18. Sandra T. W. Davis, *Intellectual Change and Political Development in Early Modern Japan* (Rutherford, N.J.: Fairleigh Dickinson Press,), p. 14.

19. Ibid., p. 15. See also Richard T. Chand, *Historians and Meiji Statesmen* (Gainesville: University of Florida Press, 1970), in which the author reports that he polled ninety-seven Japanese historians to have them rank in order the forty greatest Japanese political leaders. On page 42 he gives his results: Ōkubo Toshimichi is ranked second and Ōkuma Shigenobu, fourth among all leaders in modern Japan.

20. Kenneth B. Pyle, *The Making of Modern Japan* (Lexington, Mass.: D. C. Heath, 1978), pp. 69–70.

21. Ibid., p. 68.

22. Jansen, *Sakamoto Ryōma,* p. 107.

23. Ōkubo well exemplified Yoshida Shoin's classic statement on leadership: "What is important in a leader is a resolute will and determination. A man may be versatile and learned, but if he lacks resoluteness and determination, of what use will he be?" (quoted in Tsunoda, *Sources of Japanese Tradition,* p. 618).

24. Ibid., p. 657.

25. G. B. Sansom, *The Western World and Japan: A Study in the Interaction of European and Asiatic Cultures* (New York: Knopf, 1962), p. 321.

26. Pyle, *Making of Modern Japan,* p. 91.

27. Iwata, *Ōkubo Toshimichi,* pp. 21–39.

28. Ibid., p. 31.

29. Ibid., p. 32.

30. Ibid., p. 39.

31. Ibid., pp. 43–44.

32. Ibid., p. 49.

33. Ibid., p. 53.

34. Ibid., pp. 107–10.

35. Ibid., p. 115.

36. Ibid., p. 116.

37. Ibid., p. 132.

38. The virtually complete text of this memorandum is in Tsunoda, *Sources of Japanese Tradition*, pp. 658–62.

39. Iwata, *Ōkubo Toshimichi*, p. 252.

40. Ibid., pp. 253–54.

41. Ibid., p. 151.

42. Ijichi, *Life of Marquis Shigenobu Ōkuma*, pp. 42–43.

43. Ibid., pp. 54–55.

44. Ibid., p. 72.

45. Ibid., p. 84.

46. Ibid., pp. 96–100.

47. Ibid., p. 123.

48. Sansom, *The Western World and Japan*, p. 344.

49. Ibid., p. 345.

50. Ijichi, *Life of Marquis Shigenobu Ōkuma*, p. 160.

51. Ibid., p. 189.

52. Ibid., p. 195.

53. Ibid., p. 217.

54. For the history of political party organization in Japan, see Hugh Borton, *Japan's Modern Century* (New York: Ronald Press, 1955), and Robert A. Scalapino, *Democracy and the Party Movement in Prewar Japan* (Berkeley and Los Angeles: University of California Press, 1953).

55. Lebra, *Okuma Shigenobu*, pp. 145–147 and the whole of chap. 8.

56. Ijichi, *Life of Marquis Shigenobu Ōkuma*, p. 254.

57. Ibid., pp. 291–92 for both quotations.

58. Ibid., p. 380.

59. Ibid., p. 398.

60. Yoshitaka Oka, *Five Political Leaders of Modern Japan*, trans. Andrew Fraser and Patricia Murray (Tokyo: University of Tokyo Press, 1968), p. 62.

61. Tsunoda, *Sources of Japanese Tradition*, p. 680.

62. Carmen Blacker, *The Japanese Enlightenment: A Study of the Writings of Fukuzawa Yukichi* (Cambridge: Cambridge University Press, 1969), p. xii. For a full account of Fukuzawa's influence, see Roichi Okabe, "Yukichi Fukuzawa: A Promulgator of Western Rhetoric in Japan," *Quarterly Journal of Speech,* 59 (April, 1973): 186–195.

63. W. G. Beasley, *The Modern History of Japan* (New York: Praeger, 1963), p. 152.

64. Tsunoda, *Sources of Japanese Tradition*, p. 623.

65. Sandra T. W. Davis, *Intellectual Change*, pp. 298–99.

66. For a fuller discussion of Fukuzawa's feminist views, see Mikiso Hane, "Fukuzawa Yukichi and Women's Rights," in Conroy, Davis, and Patterson, *Japan in Transition*, pp. 96–112.

67. Quoted in Masaki Kosaka, ed., *Japanese Thought in the Meiji Era*, trans. David Abosch (Tokyo: The Toyo Bunko, 1958), p. 64.

68. *The Autobiography of Fukuzawa Yukichi*, rev. trans. by Eiichi Kiyooka (New York: Columbia University Press, 1966), p. 381.

69. Ibid., p. 247.

70. Blacker, *The Japanese Enlightenment*, pp. 5–10.

71. Ibid., p. 10.

72. Wayne H. Oxford has made a valuable listing of all of Fukuzawa's known speeches and of his published books. He has also edited the extant texts of

Fukuzawa's speeches, in *The Speeches of Fukuzawa: A Translation and Critical Study* (Tokyo: Hokuseido Press, 1973), pp. 267–281.

73. *Autobiography of Fukuzawa Yukichi,* pp. 334–36.

74. Oxford, *Speeches of Fukuzawa,* p. 22.

Chapter 2. China's Advance

1. Earl Albert Selle, *Donald of China* (New York: Harpers, 1948), pp. 6–7. Partly fictionalized and written as a racy narrative, this book nevertheless is a vivid and generally accurate narrative of the whole course of the process that led China from Manchu absolutism through republicanism and Kuomintang dictatorship to communism, related from the point of view of the remarkable Australian who remained near the center of affairs.

2. E. H. Hughes, *The Invasion of China by the Western World* (New York: Barnes and Noble, 1973), p. 112.

3. Ibid., p. 113.

4. Roger Pelissier, *The Awakening of China, 1793–1949,* trans. Martin Kiefer (London: Secker and Warburg, 1967), p. 207.

5. Ibid., pp. 208–10.

6. Ibid., pp. 210–11.

7. Lyman P. Van Slyke, Introduction to *Sun Yat-sen: His Life and Its Meaning, a Critical Biography,* by Lyon Sharman (Stanford, Calif.: Stanford University Press, 1934), p. v.

8. Ibid., pp. xvi, xii.

9. Nathaniel Peffer, "One of Asia's Three Great Moderns: The Enigma of Sun Yat-sen, Maker of the Chinese Republic, without Honor Save in History," *Asia,* August 1924, pp. 591–94, 657–58.

10. C. Martin Wilbur, *Sun Yat-sen: Frustrated Patriot* (New York: Columbia University Press, 1976), p. 4.

11. Sterling Seagrave, *The Soong Dynasty* (New York: Harper and Row, 1985), p. 70.

12. Ibid., p. 15. Sun's book, *Kidnapped in London,* was published in London by Simpkin, Marshall, Hamilton, and Kent in 1897.

13. Harold Z. Schiffrin, "The Enigma of Dr. Sun Yat-sen," in *China in Revolution: The First Phase, 1900–1913,* ed. M. C. Wright (New Haven: Yale University Press, 1968), pp. 469–70.

14. George Lynch, "Two Westernized Orientals" [the other being Okuma Shigenobu], *The Outlook* 67 (25 March, 1901), p. 671.

15. Hollington K. Tong, *Chiang Kai-shek* (Taiwan: China Publishing Co., 1953), p. 407n.

16. Wilbur, *Sun Yat-sen,* p. 23.

17. Arnulf K. Esterer and Louise A. Esterer, *Sun Yat-sen: China's Great Champion* (New York: Julian Messner, 1970), pp. 132–33. They quote this description from the *Missionary Herald* (Boston), August 1912.

18. Emily Hahn, *The Soong Sisters* (Garden City, N.Y.: Doubleday, Doran, 1943), pp. 120–21.

19. Ibid., p. 122.

20. Quoted in Shao Chuan Leng and Norman D. Palmer, *Sun Yat-sen and Communism* (New York: Praeger, 1960), p. 85.

21. Sun Yat-sen, *San Min Chi I, The Three Principles of the People,* trans.

Frank W. Price (Taipei: China Publishing Co., n.d.). The book contains two supplementary chapters by Chiang Kai-shek and is frequently reprinted.

22. Ibid., lecture 1, 27 January 1924, pp. 1–2.

23. Lyon Sharman, "The Sun Yat-sen Cult," *Asia* 34 (July 1934): 394–95.

24. Saggitarius [pseud.], *The Strange Apotheosis of Sun Yat-sen* (London: Heath Cranton, 1939), p. 10.

25. *Dr. Sun Yat-Sen: Commemorative Articles and Speeches* (Peking: Foreign Language Press, 1957), p. 11.

26. T'ang Liang-Li, *The Foundation of Modern China* (London: Noel Douglas, 1928), p. 117.

27. W. Irwin, "Sinking Sun of China," *Independent,* 17 October 1915, p. 439.

28. Gustav Amman, *The Legacy of Sun Yat-sen* (New York and Montreal: Louis Carrier and Co., 1929), p. 142.

29. James E. Sheridan, *China in Disintegration: The Republican Era in Chinese History, 1912–1929* (New York: Free Press, 1975), p. 58.

30. O. Edmund Clubb, *Twentieth Century China,* 3d ed. (New York: Columbia University Press, 1978), p. 123.

31. Ibid., p. 122.

32. Ibid., p. 425.

33. Sun Yat-sen, *San Min Chu I,* p. 137–38.

34. Harry Paxton Howard, *America's Role in Asia* (New York: Howell, Soskin, 1943), pp. 351–53.

35. H. H. Chang, *Chiang Kai-shek: Asia's Man of Destiny* (Garden City, N.Y.: Doubleday, Doran, 1944). In sharpest contrast is the view of Chiang as weak, deceptive, egotistic, incapable, and utterly undependable, that is presented in Barbara Tuchman, *Stillwell and the American Experience in China, 1911–1945* (New York: Macmillan, 1970–71).

36. Tong, *Chiang Kai-shek,* p. 43.

37. Quoted in Howard, *America's role in Asia,* p. 359.

38. Chang, *Chiang Kai-shek,* p. 182.

39. Quoted in Hahn, *The Soong Sisters,* p. 95.

40. *Wellesley Magazine,* February 1938.

41. Tong, *Chiang Kai-shek,* p. 102.

42. David Nelson Rowe, *Modern China* (Princeton, N.J.: Van Nostrand, Anchor, 1959), p. 47. John King Fairbank, in his book, *The Great Chinese Revolution, 1800–1985,* New York: Harper & Row, 1986, pp. 217–225, presented a brilliant but inconclusive summary of the period, finding it "hard to delineate," but concluding that Chiang tried hard to unify the country and to control the warlords but was handicapped by the necessity of building military strength to counteract Japanese aggression.

43. Hahn, *The Soong Sisters,* p. 105.

44. Seagrave, *The Soong Dynasty,* p. 288.

45. Hahn, *The Soong Sisters,* pp. 269–70.

46. Ibid., pp. 324–26.

47. Paul A. Linebarger, *The China of Chiang Kai-shek* (Boston: World Peace Foundation, 1943), pp. 150–51.

48. Although the cultural differences between America and China are considerable, it is noteworthy that in 1986, while the United States was suffering economically from very large budget and trade deficits and while negotiations to lessen the danger of atomic war were stalled, President and Mrs. Reagan undertook to

increase national unity and raise morale by launching a campaign against drug usage and general moral laxity. *Plus ça change, plus c'est la même chose.*

49. Robert Payne, *Chiang Kai-shek* (New York: Weybright and Talley, 1969), p. 237.

50. Quoted in Rowe, *Modern China,* pp. 136–37.

51. Brian Crozier, with Eric Chou, *The Man Who Lost China: The First Full Biography of Chiang Kai-shek* (New York: Charles Scribner's Sons, 1976), p. 392.

52. Eric Chou, *Mao Tse-tung: The Man and the Myth* (New York: Stein and Day, 1980), p. 7.

53. Stuart Schram, ed., *Chairman Mao Talks to the People: Talks and Letters, 1956–1971,* trans. John Chinnery and Tieyun (New York: Pantheon Books, 1974), pp. 11–12.

54. Chou, *Mao Tse-tung,* p. 77.

55. Eleutherius Winance, *The Communist Persuasion: A Personal Experience of Brain Washing,* trans. Emeric A. Lawrence (New York: P. J. Kenedy, 1959).

56. John H. Kautsky, *Communism and the Politics of Development: Persistent Myths and Changing Behavior* (New York: John Wiley, 1968), p. 165.

57. Studies of these factors were brought together by Robert A. Scalapino, ed., *Elites in the People's Republic of China* (Seattle: University of Washington Press, 1972). Despite the overwhelming virtual deification of Mao, with his statues, his pictures, and his utterances everywhere and constantly dominating attention, Mao ostentatiously repudiated the personality cult in 1949 by forbidding the public celebration of the birthday of any leader or the naming of streets, buildings, or towns after living men. See Dick (Richard Garratt) Wilson, *Anatomy of China: An Introduction to One Quarter of Mankind,* rev. ed. (New York: Weybright and Talley, 1968), p. 119. The extent of the Mao personality cult is accurately indicated in an editorial in the *People's Daily,* 26 March 1964, which asserted that "the moon without the sun gives no light; young rice plants with no rain water will wither; without the study of the thoughts of Mao Tse-tung, even with your eyes open you will miss the direction."

58. Lucian W. Pye, "Mass participation in Communist China: Its Limitations and the Continuity of Culture," in *China: Management of a Revolutionary Society,* John M. H. Lindbeck, ed. University of Washington Press, 1971), p. 3.

59. Michel C. Oksenberg, "Policy Making under Mao, 1949–68: An Overview," in Lindbeck, *China,* p. 101.

60. Mao Tse-tung, *Selected Works* (New York: International Publishers, 1955), 5:411–23.

61. Mao Tse-tung, "Autobiography," in Edgar Snow, *Red Star over China* (New York: Random House, 1938), p. 132. See also Brantly Womach, *The Foundations of Mao Zedong's Political Thought, 1917–1935* (Honolulu: University of Hawaii Press, 1982).

62. Siao-Yu (Hsiao Yu), *Mao Tze-tung and I were Beggars* (London: Hutchinson, 1961), pp. 193–94.

63. Stuart R. Schram, *The Political Thought of Mao Tse-tung* (New York: Praeger, 1963), p. 32.

64. H. R. Lieberman, "Great Question Mark in Asia—Mao," *New York Times Magazine,* 29 October 1950, p. 13.

65. Schram, *Political Thought of Mao Tse-tung,* p. 110.

66. Wilson, *Anatomy of China,* p. 116.

67. Quoted in Schram, *Political Thought of Mao Tse-tung,* p. 81.

68. Along with this quotation, Roderick MacFarquar provides an interpreta-

tion of the broad context in his *The Hundred Flowers Campaign and the Chinese Intellectuals* (New York: Praeger, 1960), pp. 10–11.

69. Fox Butterfield, *New York Times,* dispatch from Hong Kong, 8 January 1977.

70. James Bertram, *North China Front* (London: Macmillan, 1939), pp. 239–40.

71. John McCook Roots, *Chou: An Informal Biography of China's Legendary Chou En-lai* (Garden City, N.Y.: Doubleday, 1978), pp. 2–3.

72. Ibid., p. 18.

73. Ibid., p. 20.

74. Hsu Kai-yu, *Chou Enlai: China's Gray Eminence* (New York: Doubleday, 1968), pp. 42–43.

75. R. S. Chavan, *Chinese Foreign Policy: The Chou En-Lai Era* (New York: Sterling Publishers, 1979), p. 7.

76. Quoted in *Time,* 10 May 1954, p. 29.

77. James Bertram, "Open Door to China," *Nation,* 23 June 1956, pp. 529–31.

78. Freda Utley, *Last Chance in China* (Indianapolis, Ind.: Bobbs-Merrill, 1947), p. 81.

79. Ping-Chia Kuo, *China: New Age and New Outlook* (New York: Knopf, 1956), p. 123.

80. Utley, *Last Chance in China,* pp. 116–17.

81. *New China Advances to Socialism: A Selection of Speeches Delivered at the Third Session of the First National People's Congress* (Peking: Foreign Language Press, 1956), pp. 9–38.

82. Madame Sun Yat-sen, quoted in Chiang Ling Soong, *The Struggle for New China* (Peking: Foreign Language Press, 1953), p. 260.

83. Mu Fu-sheng, *The Wilting of the Hundred Flowers* (New York: Praeger, 1962), p. 216.

84. Mao Tse-tung, *On the correct Handling of Contradictions among the People* (Peking: Foreign Language Press, 1957), p. 16.

85. *Time,* 19 January 1976.

86. Mu Fu-sheng, *Wilting of the Hundred Flowers,* p. 21. This judgment is confirmed by Fairbank, *Great Chinese Revolution,* pp. 5–6.

87. Robert T. Oliver, *Communication and Culture in Ancient India and China* (Syracuse, N.Y.: Syracuse University Press, 1971), pp. 89–90.

Chapter 3. India

1. See Arabinda Poddar, ed., *Language and Society in India: The Proceedings of a Seminar* (Simla: Indian Institute of Advanced Study, 1969), or, for a concise summary, see Hugh Tinker, *India and Pakistan: A Political Analysis* (New York: Praeger, 1967), pp. 124–30.

2. Henry Vincent Hodson, *The Great Divide: Britain—India—Pakistan* (London: Hutchinson, 1969), p. 22. The following quotation is on page 24. See also chap. 3, "The Problem of the States."

3. Indian customs that outraged Westerners are described by Katherine Mayo, *Mother India* (New York: Harcourt, Brace, 1927). For scholarly studies of Indian culture see Sarvepalli Radharkrishnan et al., eds., *The Cultural Heritage of India,* 3 vols. (Calcutta: The Ramakrishna Mission, 1937). (The work was enlarged to five volumes in the 1958 edition.)

4. This problem is vividly portrayed by E. M. Forster in his novel *A Passage to India* (New York: Harcourt, Brace, 1924). It is analysed by Indian and European

scholars in L. S. S. O'Malley, ed., *Modern India and the West: A Study of the Interactions of Their Civilizations* (London: Oxford University Press, 1941) An account that stresses contributions made by English administrators in India is Ralph Trevelyan, *The Golden Oriole* (New York: Viking, 1987).

5. For a discussion of the traditional roots of Indian rhetoric and its oral tradition, see Robert T. Oliver, *Communication and Culture in Ancient India and China* (Syracuse, N.Y.: Syracuse University Press, 1971), pp. 12–83. For a psycholinguistic analysis see Wimal Dissanayake, "The Phenomenology of Verbal Communication: A Classical Indian View" (Paper presented at the seminar on "Communication Theory from Easter and Western perspectives," at the East-West Center, Honolulu, Hawaii, 15–23 December 1980).

6. Tinker, *India and Pakistan,* p. 139.

7. P. C. Roy Chaudhury, *Gandhi and His Contemporaries* (New Delhi: Sterling Publishers, 1972).

8. B. Pattabhi Sitaramayya, *History of the Indian National Congress,* 2 vols. (Delhi: S. Chand, Padma Publication, 1947), 1:5.

9. Ibid., p. 19.

10. Ibid., p. 60.

11. Ibid., p. 61.

12. Ibid., p. 42.

13. William Theodore de Bary et al., *Sources of Indian Tradition* (New York: Columbia University Press, 1958), pp. 720–21.

14. Ibid., pp. 726–28.

15. Aurobindo Ghose, *Speeches* (Calcutta: Arya Publishing House, 1948), pp. 7–9.

16. For an incisive exploration of the centrality of religion in Indian culture, see A. Abid Husain, *The National Culture of India* rev. ed. (New Delhi: National Book Trust, 1978). On page 41 Husain identifies the two basic questions that are considered in the Upanishads: "What is the abiding reality behind the changing world of appearance which I see or feel every day in or outside myself? What is the real purpose of my life which I should make the final criterion of my conduct?" On page 167 Husain gives a modern interpretation of how these questions should be dealt with: "When man tries to apprehend Absolute Reality through his limited intellectual faculties he cannot go beyond the conception of a personal God whom he regards as a being separate from himself. But when he rises above the intellectual level to that of religious intuition, he is conscious of the perfect identity of God, man and the universe."

17. M. K. Gandhi, *An Autobiography, or the Story of My Experiments with Truth,* trans. Mahaved Desai (Ahmedabad-14: Navajivan Publishing House, 1927): 1963, p. 12.

18. Ibid., pp. 37–38.

19. Ibid., p. 51.

20. Ibid., p. 21.

21. Ibid., pp. 287–88.

22. C. F. Andrews, *Mahatma Gandhi's Ideas* (New York: Macmillan, 1930), p. 299.

23. Ibid., p. 116.

24. Quoted in Joan V. Bondurant, *Conquest of Violence: The Gandhian Philosophy of Conflict* (Princeton: Princeton University Press, 1968), p. ix.

25. Frederick B. Fisher, *Strange Little Brown Man: Gandhi* (New York: Ray Long and Richard B. Smith, 1932), p. 4.

26. Andrews, *Mahatma Gandhi's Ideas,* p. 61.

27. Jawaharlal Nehru, *The Discovery of India* (London: Meridian Books, 1956), p. 361.

28. Andrews, *Mahatma Gandhi's Ideas,* p. 250.

29. D. G. Tendulkar, *Mahatma: Life of Mohandas Karamchand Gandhi,* 8 vols. (New Delhi: Government of India, Ministry of Information and Broadcasting, 1960–63), 3:214–15.

30. Ibid. 7:266–85.

31. Dorothy Norman, ed., *Nehru: The First Sixty Years,* 2 vols. (Bombay: Asia Publishing House, 1965), 2:364.

32. Quoted in Homer A. Jack, ed., *The Gandhi Reader* (Bloomington: Indiana University Press, 1956), p. viii.

33. Cf. Tendulkar, *Mahatma* 2:7, 58, 73.

34. Jack, *Gandhi Reader,* p. viii.

35. Tendulkar, *Mahatma* 2:51.

36. Nehru, *Discovery of India,* p. 454.

37. Tendulkar, *Mahatma* 2:44.

38. Andrews, *Mahatma Gandhi's Ideas,* pp. 94, 101, 142; *Tendulkar* 2:45, 4:63.

39. Jag Parvesh Chandler, ed., *Teachings of Mahatma Gandhi* (Lahore: Indian Printing Works, 1945), pp. 405–406.

40. Andrews, *Mahatma Gandhi's Ideas,* p. 307.

41. M. K. Gandhi, *Non-Violence in Peace and War,* 2 vols. (Ahmedabad-14: Navajivan Publishing House, 1942), 1:9.

42. B. R. Nanda, *Mahatma Gandhi: A Biography* (London: Unwin Books, 1958), p. 125.

43. Ibid., p. 232.

44. Tendulkar, *Mahatma* 1:61.

45. Gandhi, *Non-Violence in Peace and War* 1:266. Gandhi's "strength" was composed in large part of self-assurance. Nehru wrote of him that "behind all his courteous interest, one has the impression that one is addressing a closed door" (Frank Moraes, *Jawaharlal Nehru* [New York: Macmillan, 1958], p. 8).

46. Gandhi, *An Autobiography,* p. 38.

47. Tendulkar, *Mahatma,* 2:8.

48. Ibid., pp. 7–8.

49. Ibid., p. 10.

50. "To communicate, the West talks or moves. The East contemplates, sits, suffers" (Louis Fischer, *Gandhi: His Life and Message for the World* [New York: New American Library, 1954]; p. 75). Fischer's aphorism is no more than half-true. But Gandhi utilized the portion of truth that was in it. He spoke with his life as well as with his voice.

51. Michael Brecher, *Nehru: A Political Biography* (London: Oxford University Press, 1959), p. 225.

52. First published in *The Modern Review* (Calcutta), November 1937, pp. 546–47, it was reprinted as appendix E in Nehru's autobiography, *Toward Freedom* (New York: John Day, 1941), pp. 436–37.

53. Nehru, *Toward Freedom,* p. 76.

54. Brecher, *Nehru,* p. 69.

55. C. D. Narasimhaiah, *Jawaharlal Nehru: A Study of His Writings and Speeches* (Mysore: Rao and Raghavan, 1960), p. 141.

56. Nehru, *Toward Freedom,* p. 353.

57. Ibid., pp. 56–57.

58. Ibid., p. 60.

59. Chester Bowles, *Ambassador's Report* (New York: Harper and Row, 1954), p. 102.

60. Vincent Sheean, "Prime Minister Nehru," *New Republic,* 10 October 1949, p. 12.

61. Narasimhaiah, *Jawaharlal Nehru,* p. 167.

62. Dorothy Norman, ed., *Nehru: The First Sixty Years* (Bombay: Asia Publishing House, 1965), 1:477.

63. Robert Trumbull, "Portrait of a Symbol Named Nehru," *New York Times Magazine,* 12 December 1954, p. 67.

64. Hallem Tennyson, *India's Walking Saint: Vinoba Bhave* (Garden City, N.Y.: Doubleday, 1955), p. 137.

65. M. N. Das, *The Political Philosophy of Jawaharlal Nehru* (London: George Allen and Unwin, 1961), p. 21.

66. Nehru, *Discovery of India,* p. 9.

67. Ibid., p. 14. In personal correspondence in 1926 and 1927 he wrote: "Religion as practiced in India has become the old man of the sea for us, and it has not only broken our backs but stultified and almost killed all originality of thought and mind. . . . I have no patience left with the legitimate and illegitimate offspring of religion." Quoted by Brecher, *Nehru,* p. 99.

68. Quoted by M. N. Das, *Political Philosophy of Jawaharlal Nehru,* p. 33.

69. Nehru, *Discovery of India,* p. 19.

70. Nehru, *Toward Freedom,* p. 126.

71. Nehru, *Discovery of India,* p. 15.

72. Ibid.

73. Jawaharlal Nehru, *Soviet Russia* (Bombay, 1929), p. 19.

74. Brecher, *Nehru,* p. 119.

75. Ibid., p. 120.

76. Nehru, *Toward Freedom,* p. 393.

77. Ibid., p. 373.

78. Frank Moraes, *Jawaharlal Nehru: A Biography* (New York: Macmillan, 1958), pp. 214–15.

79. Nehru, *Toward Freedom,* p. 126.

80. Ibid., p. 368.

81. Nehru, *Discovery of India,* p. 17.

82. Krishna Nehru Hutheesing, "Nehru and Madame Pandit," *Ladies Home Journal,* January 1955, p. 83. For an incisive review of the Nehru family, see Irene Khin Khin Jensen, "The Men Behind the Woman: A Case Study of the Political Career of Madame Vijaya Lakshimi Pandit," *Contributions to Asian Studies* 10 (1977): 76–93.

83. This is the judgment of Agnes Doody in "Words and Deeds: An Analysis of Jawaharlal Nehru's Non-Alignment Policy in the Cold War, 1947–1953," (Ph.D. diss., The Pennsylvania State University, 1961).

84. Brecher, *Nehru,* pp. 87–88.

85. Norman, *Nehru* 1:446.

86. Tendulkar, *Mahatma* 4:86, 3:318.

87. Nehru, in *Discovery of India,* said: "I am convinced that the rapid industrialization of India is essential" (p. 412). In contrast, Nehru summarized Gandhi's economic views as follows: "He looked back with yearning to the days of the old

autonomous and more-or-less self-contained village community" (idem, *Discovery of India,* p. 411.)

88. "I am very conscious of the fact that the modern transport is based on internationalism. No country or people can isolate themselves" (Nehru, 2 June 1937, quoted in M. N. Das, *Political Philosophy of Jawaharlal Nehru,* [London: George Allen and Unwin, 1962], p. 198.)

89. Norman, *Nehru* 1:434.

90. Ibid. 4:450.

91. Ibid. 4:451.

92. In 1942 Gandhi said: "Jawaharlal will be my successor. He says he does not understand my language, and that he speaks a language foreign to me. This may or may not be true. But language is no bar to a union of hearts. And I know this, that when I am gone he will speak my language" (quoted in Brecher, *Nehru,* p. 275).

93. Quoted in Sankar Ghose, *Political Ideas and Movements in India* (Bombay: Allied Publishers, 1975), pp. 131–32.

94. J. S. Bright, ed., *Important Speeches and Writings of Subhas Bose* (Lahore: Indian Printing Works, 1947), pp. 57–58.

95. Ghose, *Political Ideas and Movements in India,* p. 131.

96. S. A. Ayer, ed., *Selected Speeches of Subhas Chandra Bose* (Lahore: Indian Printing Works, 1962), p. 204.

97. Ghose, *Political Ideas and Movements in India,* p. 137.

98. M. N. Roy, *India's Message: Fragments of a Prisoner's Diary,* 2 vols. (Calcutta: Renaissance Publishers, 1950), 2:190–218.

99. M. N. Roy, *New Humanism: A Manifesto* (Calcutta: Renaissance Publishers, 1947), p. 36.

100. M. N. Roy, *Radical Humanism* (Calcutta: Renaissance Publishers, 1952), p. 21.

101. Ghose, *Political Ideas and Movements in India,* p. 433.

102. Roy, *New Humanism,* pp. 34–47.

Chapter 4. Quaid-I-Azam of Pakistan

1. Stanley Wolpert, *Jinnah of Pakistan* (New York: Oxford University Press, 1984), p. 4.

2. H. V. Hodson, *The Great Divide—Britain—India—Pakistan* (London: Hutchinson, 1969), p. 37.

3. Sharif Al Mujahid, *Quaid-I-Azam Jinnah: Studies in Interpretation* (Karachi: Quaid-I-Azam Academy, 1981), pp. xxvii–xxviii.

4. Waheed-Uz-Zaman, *Quaid-I-Azam Mohammed Ali Jinnah: Myth and Reality* (Karachi: National Book Foundation, 1976), p. viii.

5. Hodson, *The Great Divide,* p. 38.

6. Quoted in Wolpert, *Jinnah of Pakistan,* p. 8.

7. Mujahid, *Quaid-I-Azam Jinnah,* p. 46.

8. Larry Collins and Dominique Lapierre, *Freedom at Midnight* (New York: Simon and Schuster, 1975), p. 102.

9. Sylvia G. Haim, "The Abolition of the Caliphate and its Aftermath," in Thomas W. Arnold, *The Caliphate* (Karachi: Oxford University Press, 1966), p. 223.

10. Mohammed Ali Jinnah, *Speeches* (Karachi: Pakistan Publications, [1962]), p. 156.

11. Waheed-Uz-Zaman, *Quaid-I-Azam Mohammed Ali Jinnah,* viii.

12. Hodson, *The Great Divide,* pp. 38–39.

13. See Robert T. Oliver. *The Influence of Rhetoric in the Shaping of Great Britain* (Newark, Del.: University of Delaware Press, 1986), pp. 224–26.

14. Matlubul Hasan Saiyid, *Muhammad Ali Jinnah: A Political Study* (Lahore: Sh. Muhammad Ashraf, 1945), pp. 264–65.

15. Quoted in Durga Das, *India: From Curzon to Nehru and After* (London: Collins, 1969), p. 76.

16. Mujahid, *Quaid-I-Azam Jinnah,* p. 231.

17. Joachim Alva, *Leader of India* (Bombay: Thacker and Co., 1945), p. 66.

18. Nilakan Perumal, "Jinnah and His Triumph," *India* (Madras), 15 August 1947, p. 39.

19. Hector Bolitho, *Jinnah: Creator of Pakistan* (London: John Murray, 1954), p. 13.

20. Ibid.

21. Mujahid, *Quaid-I-Azam Jinnah,* pp. 40–41.

22. Syed Sharifuddin Pirzade, ed., *Foundations of Pakistan: All-India Muslim League Documents: 1906–1947,* 2 vols. (Karachi: National Publishing House, [1970]), 1:284–89.

23. Ibid. 1:362–70.

24. Ibid. 1:370–77.

25. Ibid. 1:435.

26. Ibid. 2:290–96.

27. Mujahid, *Quaid-I-Azam Jinnah,* p. 113.

28. Ibid., p. 114.

29. Pirzade, *Foundations of Pakistan* 2:307.

30. Jamil-ud-Din Ahmad, ed., *Speeches and Writings of Mr. Jinnah,* 2 vols., 6th ed. (Lahore: Sh. Muhammad Ashraf, 1964), 1:237–38.

31. Mujahid, *Quaid-I-Azam Jinnah,* p. 116.

32. Keith Callard, *Pakistan: A Political Study* (London: George Allen and Unwin, 1957), pp. 19–20.

33. Saiyid, *Muhammad Ali Jinnah: A Political Study,* p. 296.

34. A. A. Ravoof, *Meet Mr. Jinnah* (Madras: Deccan Times Press, 1944), p. 167.

35. Ahmad, *Speeches and Writings of Mr. Jinnah,* 2:299.

36. Pirzade, *Foundations of Pakistan* 2:327–39.

37. Hodson, *The Great Divide,* pp. 216–18. The whole book, and particularly chapters 13 and 14, deals with the problems of the British withdrawal and the division of the subcontinent.

38. Wolpert, *Jinnah of Pakistan,* p. 319.

39. Quoted in Muhajid, *Quaid-I-Azam Jinnah,* p. 52.

40. Ibid.

41. *Bombay Chronicle,* 21 February 1921.

42. Pirzade, *Foundations of Pakistan* 2:388.

43. Ibid. 2:407.

44. Ibid. 2:425.

45. Ibid. 2:509.

46. Ibid. 2:572.

47. Ibid. 2:571.

48. Wolpert, *Jinnah of Pakistan,* pp. 362–64.

49. Waheed-Uz-Zaman, *Quaid-I-Azam Mohammed Ali Jinnah,* pp. 131–32.

50. Hodson, *The Great Divide,* p. 38.

51. Mujahid, *Quaid-I-Azam Jinnah,* p. 408.
52. Ahmad, *Speeches and Writings of Mr. Jinnah* 2:568.

Chapter 5. Emergence of Indonesian Independence

1. Louis Fischer, *The Story of Indonesia* (New York: Harper and Brothers, 1959), p. 3.
2. Leslie Palmier, *Indonesia* (New York: Walker and Co., 1965), p. 10.
3. J. S. Furnival, *Colonial Policy and Practice: A Comparative Study of Burma and Netherlands India* (Cambridge: Cambridge University Press, 1948); New York: New York University Press, 1956.
4. John Crawfurd, *History of the Indian Archipelago* (3 vols. Edinburgh, 1820).
5. Fischer, *Story of Indonesia,* p. 20.
6. Ibid., p. 44.
7. Ibid., p. 55.
8. S. Tas, *Indonesia: The Underdeveloped Freedom* (Indianapolis, Ind.: Bobbs-Merrill, Pegasus, 1974), p. 110.
9. Fischer, *Story of Indonesia,* p. 55.
10. Tas, *Indonesia,* pp. 110–11.
11. Ibid., pp. 111–139, and Fischer, *Story of Indonesia,* pp. 55–59.
12. Tas, *Indonesia,* pp. 198–99.
13. Charles Wolf, Jr., *The Indonesian Story: The Birth, Growth, and Structure of the Indonesian Republic* (New York: John Day and the American Institute of Pacific Relations, 1948), p. 95.
14. Bruce Grant, *Indonesia* (Melbourne: Melbourne University Press, 1964), p. 17.
15. G. H. Bousquet, *A French View of the Netherlands Indies,* trans. P. E. Lilienthal (New York: Oxford University Press, 1940), pp. 88–89.
16. George McTurnan Kahin, *Nationalism and Revolution in Indonesia* (Ithaca: Cornell University Press, 1952), p. 45.
17. Chr. L. M. Penders, *Indonesia: Selected Documents on Colonialism and Nationalism, 1830–1942* (St. Lucia, Australia: Queensland University Press, 1977), pp. 220, 2222.
18. Roger K. Paget, *Indonesia Accuses: Sockarno's Defense Oration in the Political Trial of 1930* (Kuala Lumpur: Oxford University Press, 1975). See also Grant, *Indonesia,* p. 22.
19. Ibid., p. 21.
20. Sutan Sjahrir, *Out of Exile,* trans. Charles Wolf, Jr. (New York: John Day, 1949), pp. 218–19.
21. Penders, *Indonesia: Selected Documents,* pp. 309–10.
22. Ibid., p. 326.
23. Ibid., pp. 327–28.
24. Tas, *Indonesia,* pp. 161–62.
25. Ibid., p. 168.
26. The disorderly succession of ineffectual administrations during the whole period of Sukarno's presidency is well portrayed by Tas, *Indonesia;* Kahin, *Nationalism and Revolution in Indonesia;* and Herbert Feith, *The Decline of Constitutional Democracy in Indonesia* (Ithaca: Cornell University Press), 1962.
27. Tas, *Indonesia,* p. 350.
28. Grant, *Indonesia,* pp. 36–56.

29. Ibid., p. 41.
30. Ibid.
31. Fischer, *Story of Indonesia,* p. 296.
32. Ibid., p. 297.
33. Grant, *Indonesia,* p. 39.
34. Ibid., p. 40.
35. Fischer, *Story of Indonesia,* p. 298.
36. Grant, *Indonesia,* pp. 41–42.
37. Penders, *Indonesia: Selected Documents,* p. 309.
38. Feith, *Decline of Constitutional Democracy in Indonesia,* p. 38.
39. Ibid., p. 39.
40. Ibid., p. 327.
41. Ibid., p. 515.
42. Ibid., p. 39.
43. Grant, *Indonesia,* p. 39.
44. Feith, *Decline of Constitutional Democracy in Indonesia,* pp. 517–18.
45. Grant, *Indonesia,* p. 53.
46. These four basic cultural variations are specified by G. Hofstede, *Culture's Consequences: International Differences in Work-related Values* (Beverly Hills, Calif.: Sage, 1980).

Chapter 6. The Philippines

1. Quoted in Teodoreo A. Agoncillo, *The Revolt of the Masses: The Story of Bonifacio and the Katipunan* (Quezon City: University of the Philippines, 1956), p. 9.
2. Ibid., p. 28.
3. Quoted in Leon Ma. Guerrero, *The First Filipino: A Biography of Jose Rizal* (Quezon City: National Heroes Commission, 1963), p. xiii.
4. Ibid., pp. xv–xvi.
5. Agoncillo, *Revolt of the Masses,* p. 2.
6. Guerrero, *The First Filipino,* p. 7.
7. Ibid., p. 20.
8. Bernard Reines, *A People's Hero: Rizal of The Philippines* (New York: Praeger, 1971), p. 60.
9. Agoncillo, *Revolt of the Masses,* p. 37.
10. Ibid., p. 45.
11. Ibid., p. 58.
12. Ibid., p. 104. The two preceding passages are quoted by Agoncillo to reinforce his point that wealthy Filipinos sided with the Spaniards because they would suffer from any disturbance of the status quo.
13. The text from which this is quoted is reprinted in ibid., pp. 91–93.
14. Ibid., p. 106.
15. Graciano Lopez Jaena, *Speeches, Articles, and Letters,* trans. Encarnation Alzona, ed. Teodoro A. Agoncillo (Manila: National Historical Commission, 1974), pp. 1, 11. See also Gregorio F. Zaide, *The Philippine Revolution* (Manila: Modern Book Co., 1968), pp. 55–58 for biographical details.
16. David Howard Bain, *Sitting in Darkness: Americans in the Philippines* (Boston: Houghton, Mifflin, 1984), p. 154.
17. Ibid., p. 155.
18. Ibid., p. 164.

19. Agoncillo, *Revolt of the Masses,* p. 180.

20. Ibid., pp. 181–84, contains the full text of both manifestos.

21. Ibid., p. 170.

22. Bain, *Sitting in Darkness,* pp. 177–78.

23. Ibid., pp. 179–185.

24. Alfredo B. Saulo, *Emilio Aguinaldo: Generalissimo and President of the First Philippine Republic—First Republic in Asia* (Quezon City: Phoenix Publishing House, 1983), p. 221. This book, although its organization is hard to follow, is based upon a careful review of documents newly open to scholarly study and offers the fullest available account of the Filipino revolutions.

25. James Henderson Blount, *The American Occupation of the Philippines, 1898–1912* (New York: Putnam's, 1912), p. 104.

26. Saulo, *Emilio Aguinaldo,* p. 423.

27. Ibid., pp. 427–28.

28. Peter W. Stanley, *A Nation in the Making: The Philippines and the United States, 1899–1921* (Cambridge: Harvard University Press, 1974), p. 55.

29. Ibid., p. 56.

30. Ibid., p. 60. Root's judgment was probably influenced by reading a memorandum sent to President McKinley by a member of the Philippines Commission, which said, "The cold practical question remains: Will the possession of these islands benefit us as a nation? If they will not, set them free tomorrow and let their peoples, if they please, cut each other's throats" (Emily Hahn, *The Islands: America's Imperial Adventure in the Philippines* [New York: Coward, McCann, and Geoghegan, 1981], p. 72).

31. Ibid., p. 66.

32. Ibid., p. 72.

33. Ibid., p. 73.

34. Carlos Quirino, *Quezon: Paladin of Philippine Freedom* (Manila: Community Publishers, 1971), p. 79.

35. Quirino, *Quezon,* p. 88.

36. Stanley, *A Nation in the Making,* pp. 140–42.

37. Quirino, *Quezon,* includes the entire text of Recto's speech as an appendix, pp. 391–403,.

38. Ibid., pp. 371–72.

39. Theodore Friend, *Between Two Empires: The Ordeal of the Philippines, 1929–1946* (New Haven: Yale University Press, 1965), p. 49.

40. Quirino, *Quezon,* p. 206.

41. *Philippines Free Press,* 4 November 1933, p. 38.

42. Friend, *Between Two Empires,* p. 151.

43. Manuel Roxas, *Important Speeches, Messages, and Other Pronouncements* (Manila: Bureau of Printing, 1947), pp. 29–44.

44. Ibid., p. 370.

45. Jose V. Abueva, *Roman Magsaysay: A Political Biography* (Manila: Solidaridad Publishing House, 1971), p. 176.

46. Hernando J. Abaya, *The Untold Philippine Story* (Quezon City: Malaya Books, 1967), p. 158.

47. Abueva, *Ramon Magsaysay,* p. 271.

48. Ibid., p. 303.

Chapter 7. Reshaping Southeast Asia

1. Robert L. Schrag, in *Critical Studies in Mass Communication* 2 (December 1985):433, stated his belief that this characterizes the new world of rapid global communication.

2. Minister S. Rajaratnam, quoted in the *Bangkok Post,* 20 October 1968.

3. Rupert Emerson, *From Empire to Nation: The Rise to Self-Assertion of Asian and African Peoples* (Cambridge: Harvard University Press, 1960), p. 94.

4. Ibid. This is the central theme of Emerson's book.

5. Willard A. Hanna, *Eight Nation-Makers: Southeast Asia's Charismatic Statesmen* (New York: St. Martin's Press, 1964), Introduction.

6. For a fuller discussion with finer distinctions see John Bastin and Harry J. Benda, *A History of Modern Southeast Asia: Colonialism: Nationalism, and Decolonization* (Englewood Cliffs, N.J.: Prentice-Hall, 1968), esp. pp. 1–14.

7. The complexity of Buddhism defies brief summation. In another book, *Communication and Culture in Ancient India and China* (Syracuse, N.Y.: Syracuse University Press, 1971), I sought to explain it, especially in chapters 2, 4, and 5. An excellent summation in terms of Southeast Asian peoples is presented in several essays in John T. McAlister, Jr., ed., *Southeast Asia: The Politics of National Integration,* (New York: Random House, 1973), notably A. Thomas Kirsh, "The Thai Buddhist Quest for Merit," pp. 188–201.

8. McAlister, *Southeast Asia,* pp. 3–14.

9. Rupert Emerson, "South and South-East Asia as a Political Region," in Saul Rose, ed., *Politics in Southern Asia* (New York: St. Martin's Press, 1963), p. 2.

10. Ibid., p. 8.

11. Steve Warshaw, *Southeast Asia Emerges* (San Francisco: Canfield Press, rev. ed., 1975), p. 65.

12. John F. Embree, "Thailand—a Loosely Structured Social System," *American Anthropologist* 52 (1950): 181–93.

13. K. Landon, *Siam in Transition* (Chicago: University of Chicago Press, 1939), p. 148.

14. Nicholas Tarling, *A Concise History of Southeast Asia* (New York: Praeger, 1966), p. 269.

15. Ibid., p. 209.

16. Kyaw Thet, "Burma: The Political Integration of Linguistic and Religious Minority Groups," in B. Thayer, ed., *Nationalism and Progress in Free Asia* (Baltimore: Johns Hopkins University Press, 1956), p. 157.

17. J. S. Furnival, *The Governance of Modern Burma* (New York: Institute of Pacific Relations, 1958), p. iv.

18. Lea E. Williams, *Southeast Asia: A History* (New York: Oxford University Press, 1976), p. 242.

19. Quoted in Dick Wilson, *Asia Awakes: A Continent in Transition* (New York: Weybright and Talley, 1970), p. 162.

20. Ibid., p. 264.

21. Hanna, *Eight Nation-Makers,* p. 240.

22. Ba Maw, *Breakthrough in Burma: Memoirs of a Revolution, 1939–1946* (New Haven: Yale University Press, 1968), pp. xxi–xxii.

23. Quoted in Hanna, *Eight Nation-Makers,* p. 200.

24. Ibid., pp. 217–18.

25. Stuart Simmonds, "Independence and Political Rivalry in Laos,

1945–1961," in Saul Rose, ed., *Politics in Southern Asia* (New York: St. Martin's Press, 1963), pp. 196, 199.

26. W. H. H. Wiggins, *Ceylon, Dilemma of a New Nation* (Princeton: Princeton University Press, 1960), p. 391.

27. Ivor Jennings, *Nationalism and Political Development in Ceylon* (New York: Institute of Pacific Relations, 1950), p. 15. See also K. M. de Silva, "D. S. Senanayake and the Passage to Dominion Status, 1942–1947," *Sri Lanka Journal of Social Sciences* 3, no. 2.

28. B. H. Farmer, "Politics in Ceylon," in Rose, *Politics in Southern Asia,* pp. 57–58.

29. Ibid., pp. 66–68.

30. Bryce Ryan, "The Ceylanese Villager and the New Value System," *Rural Sociology* 17 (1962): 9–28.

31. F. Spencer Chapman, *The Jungle Is Neutral* (New York: W. W. Norton, 1949), is a vivid personal account of that jungle warfare and of the means by which the Communist guerrillas strengthened and spread their influence during the war.

32. Harry Miller, *The Story of Malaysia* (London: Faber and Faber, 1965), p. 197.

33. R. S. Chavan, *Nationalism in Asia* (New Delhi: Sterling Publishers, 1973), pp. 245–46.

34. Wesley R. Fischel, ed., *Vietnam: Anatomy of a Conflict* (Itasca, Ill.: F. E. Peacock, 1968), p. 7n.

35. Donald Lancaster, *The Emancipation of French IndoChina* (London: Oxford University Press, 1961), pp. 313–17, presents a lucid account of this transfer of authority.

36. Fischel, *Vietnam: Anatomy of a Conflict,* pp. 231, 230.

37. Theodore H. White, "Indo-China—the Long Trail of Error," in Fischel, *Vietnam: Anatomy of a Conflict,* p. 15.

38. Quoted in Ralph K. White, *Nobody Wanted War* (Garden City, N.Y.: Doubleday, 1968), p. 54.

39. Chapman, *The Jungle Is Neutral,* pp. 164–65.

Chapter 8. The Korean Dilemma

1. Quoted in Yi Kyu-tae, *Modern Transformation of Korea,* trans. Sung Tong-mahn and others (Seoul: Sejong Publishing Co., 1970), p. 272. In forty vivid chapters full of specific incidents, Yi, a journalist, depicts how modernism intruded into Korea and how sturdily the people resisted it.

2. Ibid., p. 42.

3. George Kennan, *Outlook,* 7 October 1905.

4. The development of new ideas in Korea from ancient root sources is discussed in Hong Yi-Sup, *Korea's Self-Identity* (Seoul: Yonsei University Press, 1973). The international rivalries are delineated by C. I. Eugene Kim and Han-Kyo Kim in *Korea and the Politics of Imperialism, 1876–1910* (Berkeley and Los Angeles: University of California Press, 1967). For a full discussion of the Independence Club movement, see Clarence N. Weems, Jr., *The Korean Reform and Independence Movement (1881–1898)* (Ann Arbor, Mich.: University Microfilms, 1954). For Rhee's role see pp. 164–166.

5. Joungwon Alexander Kim, *Divided Korea: The Politics of Development, 1945–1971* (Cambridge: Harvard University, East Asian Research Center, 1975), p. 35.

6. For an account of Rhee's life see Robert T. Oliver, *Syngman Rhee: The*

Man Beyond the Myth (New York: Dodd, Mead, 1955). The quotation is from page 59.

7. Yur-Bok Lee, "Korean-American Diplomatic Relations, 1882–1905," in Yur-Bok Lee and Wayne Patterson, eds., *One Hundred Years of Korean American Relations, 1882–1982* (University: University of Alabama Press, 1986), pp. 12–45. See also Lee's "Great Power Imperialism in Late Yi Korea and Paul Georg Möllendorff," to be published in 1989 by the University of Hawaii Press.

8. Oliver, *Syngman Rhee,* pp. 69–97.

9. Ibid., p. 114.

10. Among the many studies of this "March First Movement," the most detailed and comprehensive is the doctoral dissertation by Frank Prentiss Baldwin, Jr., *The March First Movement: Korean Challenge and Japanese Response* (Ann Arbor, Mich.: University Microfilms, 1975).

11. Chong-Sik Lee, *The Politics of Korean Nationalism* (Berkeley and Los Angeles: University of California Press, 1963), p. 199.

12. See Robert T. Oliver, *Korea: Forgotten Nation* (Washington, D.C.: Public Affairs Press, 1944).

13. For a vivid presentation of Korean feelings at the time, see Pyun Yung-tae, *Korea, My Country* (Washington, D.C.: Korean Pacific Press, 1952).

14. Joungwon Kim, *Divided Korea,* pp. 48–50.

15. Ibid., pp. 51–52.

16. For a complete text of the letter see Robert T. Oliver, *Syngman Rhee and American Involvement in Korea, 1942–1960: A Personal Narrative* (Seoul: Panmun Books, 1978), pp. 95–98.

17. Dae-Sook Suh, in his classic study of Korean communism, summed up the effects of the Korean Communist leaders during the first decade of the party's activities: "They succeeded in wresting control of the Korean revolution from the Nationalists; they planted a deep core of Communist influence among the Korean people, particularly the students, youth groups, laborers, and peasants. Their fortitude and, at times, obstinate determination to succeed had a profound influence on Korean intellectuals and writers" (*The Korean Communist Movement, 1918–1948* [Princeton: Princeton University Press, 1967], p. 132).

18. Robert A. Scalapino and Chong-Sik Lee, *Communism in Korea,* 2 vols. (Berkeley and Los Angeles: University of California Press, 1972), 1:275.

19. Joungwon Kim, *Divided Korea,* p. 59.

20. Oliver, *Syngman Rhee,* p. 219.

21. Dae-Sook Suh, "Some Implications of the History of the Korean Communist Movement for North Korean Development," in Andrew C. Nahm, ed., *Studies in the Developmental Aspects of Korea* (Kalamazoo, Mich.: School of Graduate Studies and Institute of International Area Studies, Western Michigan University, 1969), p. 129.

22. Scalapino and Lee, *Communism in Korea,* pp. 202–30. An adulatory biography sponsored by the Great Leader (as he is called in North Korea) is Bong Baik, *Kim Il-sung: A Political Biography,* 3 vols. (New York: Guardian Books, 1970). A hostile account by a Korean Communist is Lim Un [pseud.], *The Founding of a Dynasty in North Korea: An Authentic Biography of Kim Il-song,* trans. anonymous (Tokyo: Jiyu-sha, 1982).

23. Scalapino and Lee, *Communism in Korea,* p. 229.

24. Ibid.

25. Dae-Sook Suh, *The Korean Communist Movement,* pp. 313–14.

26. Lim Un, *Founding of a Dynasty,* p. 149.

27. Ibid.

28. Ibid., p. 154.

29. One reason for the choice was that Kim was a Presbyterian and presumably would therefore be acceptable to Cho Mansik. See Yong-ho Choe, "Christian Background in the Early Life of Kim Il-Song," *Asian Survey* 26 (October 1986): 1082–91.

30. Scalapino and Lee, *Communism in Korea,* p. 341; see pp. 323–81 for a detailed account of Kim's rise to power under Soviet tutelage.

31. Quoted in ibid., pp. 324–25.

32. Tai Sung An, *North Korea in Transition: From Dictatorship to Dynasty* (Westport, Conn.: Greenwood Press, 1983), p. 36.

33. The complete text of this speech is in Kim Il-Sung, *Collected Works,* 6 vols. (Pyongyang: Foreign Languages Publishing House, 1972), vol. 1.

34. Scalapino and Lee, *Communism in Korea,* p. 349.

35. *Yomiuri Shimbun* (Tokyo), 10 January 1972, translated in An, *North Korea in Transition,* p. 21.

36. For details see Oliver, *Syngman Rhee,* esp. chap. 12, and Oliver, *Syngman Rhee and American Involvement,* chapts. 1–7.

37. Oliver, *Syngman Rhee,* p. 262.

38. Ibid., pp. 244–45.

39. For a full discussion of Dr. Rhee's often antagonistic relations with the U.S. Department of State, see Oliver, *Syngman Rhee and American Involvement,* esp. chaps. 3–4, 14–20.

40. Oliver, *Syngman Rhee,* p. 244. See also Robert T. Oliver, "Syngman Rhee: A Case Study in Transnational Oratory," *Quarterly Journal of Speech* 48 (April 1962): 115–27.

41. Ibid., p. viii.

42. Oliver, *Syngman Rhee and American Involvement,* pp. 248–49.

43. Hongkee Karl, ed., *President Syngman Rhee's Journey to America* (Seoul: Office of Public Information, Republic of Korea, 1955), p. 19.

Selected Readings

Books

Abaya, Hernando J. *The Untold Philippine Story.* Quezon City: Malaya Books, 1967.

Abueva, Jose V. *Ramon Magsaysay: A Political Biography.* Manila: Solidaridad Publishing House, 1971.

Adams, Cindy. *Soekarno: An Autobiography.* New York: Bobbs-Merrill, 1965.

Ali, Chaudhri Muhammad. *The Emergence of Pakistan.* New York: Columbia University Press, 1967.

Alians, Gulan Ali. *Quaid-e-Azam Jinnah: The Story of a Nation.* Lahore: Feroxsons, 1967.

Alinsky, Saul D. *Rules for Radicals: A Practical Primer for Realistic Radicals.* New York: Vintage, 1972.

Allana, Gulam. *Quaid-e-Azam Jinnah: The Story of a Nation.* Lahore: Feroxsons, 1967.

Alperovitz, Gar. *Atomic Diplomacy: Hiroshima and Potsdam.* New York: Vintage Books, 1967.

An, Tai Sung. *North Korea in Transition: From Dictatorship to Dynasty.* Westport, Conn.: Greenwood Press, 1983.

Anand, Balwant Singh. *Cruel Interlude.* Delhi: Asia Publishing House, 1961.

Anwar, Muhammad. *Jinnah, Quaid-e-Azam: A Selected Biography.* Karachi: National Publishing House, 1970.

Armstrong, John P. *Sihanouk Speaks.* New York: Walker, 1964.

Ashe, Geoffrey, *Gandhi—a Study in Revolution.* Bombay: Asia Publishing House, 1968.

Azad, M. A. K. *India Wins Freedom.* New York: Longmans, Green, 1960.

Baig, M. R. A. *Muslim Dilemma in India.* Delhi: Vikas Publishing House, 1974.

Baik, Bong. *Kim Il Sung: A Political Biography.* 3 vols. New York: Guardian Books, 1970.

Ball, W. MacMahon. *Nationalism and Communism in East Asia.* Carlton, Victoria: Melbourne University Press, 1952.

Barnds, William J., ed. *The Two Koreas in East Asian Affairs.* New York: New York University Press, 1976.

Barnett, A. D. *Communist Strategy in Asia.* London: Praeger, 1963.

Bartz, Patricia M. *South Korea.* London: Oxford University Press, 1972.

Beasley, William G. *The Modern History of Japan.* New York: Praeger, 1963.

Bolitho, Hector. *Jinnah: Creator of Pakistan.* London: John Murray, 1954.

Boorstin, Daniel. *The Image: A Guide to Pseudo-Events in America.* New York: Atheneum, 1973.

Bosmajian, Haig A., ed. *Dissent: Symbolic Behavior and Rhetorical Strategies.* Boston: Allyn and Bacon, 1972.

Bourke-White, Margaret. *Halfway to Freedom.* New York: Simon and Schuster, 1949.

Bowers, John W., and Donovan J. Ochs. *The Rhetoric of Agitation and Control.* Reading, Mass.: Addison-Wesley, 1971.

Boyle, John Hunter. *China and Japan at War, 1937–1945: The Politics of Collaboration,* Stanford, Calif.: Stanford University Press, 1972.

Brandes, Paul D. *The Rhetoric of Revolt.* Englewood-Cliffs, N.J.: Prentice-Hall, 1971.

Braunthal, Julius. *The Paradox of Nationalism.* London: Botolph Publishing Co., 1946.

Brecher, Michael. *Nehru—a Political Biography.* Boston: Beacon Press, 1970.

Brinton, Crane. *The Anatomy of Revolution.* New York: Prentice-Hall, 1952.

Brown, Delmer M. *Nationalism in Japan: An Introductory Analysis.* Berkeley and Los Angeles: University of California Press, 1955.

Brun, Ellen, and Jacques Hersh. *Socialist Korea.* New York: Monthly Review Press, 1976.

Burns, James MacGregor. *Leadership.* New York: Harper and Row, 1978.

Buttinger, Joseph. *Vietnam: A Dragon Embattled.* 2 vols. New York: Praeger, 1967.

Cady, John F. *Southeast Asia: Its Historical Development.* New York: McGraw-Hill, 1964.

Callahan, Raymond. *Burma, 1942–1945: The Politics and Strategy of the Second World War.* Newark: University of Delaware Press, 1980.

Cameron, Meribeth, Thomas Mahoney, and George McReynolds. *China, Japan, and the Powers: A History of the Modern Far East.* 2d ed. New York: Ronald Press, 1960.

Carr, E. H. *What is History?* London: Penguin Books, 1961, 1984.

Carroll, John J. *Changing Patterns of Social Structure in the Philippines, 1896–1963.* Manila: Atenio de Manila, 1968.

Champassak, Sisouk Na. *Storm Over Laos: A Contemporary History.* New York: Praeger, 1961.

Chandiwallah, Brickshen. *At the Feet of Bapu.* Ahmedabad: Navajivan Publishing House, 1954.

Chavan, R. S. *Nationalism in Asia.* New Delhi: Sterling Publishers, 1973.

Chi, Hoang Van. *From Colonialism to Communism: A Case History of North Vietnam.* New York: Praeger, 1964.

Cho, Soon Sung. *Korea in World Politics, 1940–1950.* Berkeley and Los Angeles: University of California Press, 1967.

Choe, Ching Young. *The Role of the Taewon'Gun, 1864–1873.* Cambridge: Harvard East Asian Research Center, 1972.

Chu, Godwin C. *Radical Change through Communication in Mao's China.* Honolulu: University of Hawaii Press, 1977.

————. *Revolutionary Language and Chinese Cognitive Processes.* Papers of the East-West Communication Institute. Honolulu, 1978.

Chung, Henry. *The Case of Korea.* New York: Fleming H. Revell, 1921.

————, ed. *Treaties and Conventions between Corea and Other Powers.* New York: H. S. Nichols, 1919.

Chung, Chong-Shik and Jae-Bong Ro, eds., *Nationalism in Korea,* Seoul: Research Center for Peace and Unification, 1979.

Collins, J. Lawton. *War in Peacetime: The History and Lessons of Korea.* Boston: Houghton Mifflin, 1969.

Collins, Larry and Dominique Lapierre. *Freedom at Midnight.* New York: Simon and Schuster, 1975.

Conroy, Hillary. *The Japanese Seizure of Korea, 1868–1910: A Study of Realism and Idealism in International Relations.* Philadelphia: University of Pennsylvania Press, 1960.

Coolidge, Olivia. *Gandhi.* Boston: Houghton Mifflin, 1971.

Crocker, Walter. *Nehru—A Contemporary's Estimate.* New York: Oxford University Press, 1966.

Cushner, Nicholas. *Spain in the Philippines.* Rutland, Vt.: Charles E. Tuttle, 1972.

Dahm, Bernhard. *Sukarno and the Struggle for Indonesian Independence.* Ithaca: Cornell University Press, 1969.

Das, Durga. *India: From Curzon to Nehru and After.* London: Collins, 1969.

Deuchler, Martina. *Confucian Gentlemen and Barbarian Envoys: The Opening of Korea, 1875–1885.* Seattle: University of Washington Press, 1977.

Deutch, Karl W. *Nationalism and Social Communications: An Inquiry into the Foundations of Nationality.* New York: John Wiley; Cambridge: Technology Press of the Massachusetts Institute of Technology, 1953.

Dhawan, Gopinath. *The Political Philosophy of Mahatma Gandhi.* Ahmedabad: Navjivan Publishing House, 1951.

Donmen, Arthur I. *Conflict in Laos: The Politics of Neutralization.* Rev. ed. New York: Praeger, 1971.

Doob, Leonard W. *Patriotism and Nationalism: Their Psychological Foundations.* New Haven: Yale University Press, 1964.

Dore, Francil. *Les Regimes Politiques en Asia.* Paris: Presses Universitaires de France, 1973.

Dreiberg, Trevor. *Indira Gandhi—a Profile in Courage.* New Delhi: Vikas Publishing House, 1973.

Edwardes, Michael. *The Last Years of British India.* London: Cassel, 1963.

Emerson, Rupert. *From Empire to Nation: The Rise to Self-Assertion of Asian and African Peoples.* Cambridge: Harvard University Press, 1960.

Erikson, Erik H. *Gandhi's Truth—on the Origins of Militant Non-Violence.* New York: W. W. Norton, 1969.

Fairbank, John King. *The Great Chinese Revolution, 1800-1985.* (New York: Harper and Row, 1987).

Fall, Bernard B. *The Two Vietnams.* Rev. ed. New York: Praeger, 1964.

————. *The Viet-Minh Regime: Government and Administration in the Democratic Republic of Vietnam.* Ithaca, N.Y.: Institute of Pacific Relations, 1956.

Farrell, Barry, ed. *Approaches to Comparative and International Politics*. Evanston, Ill.: Northwestern University Press, 1966.

Fieldhouse, D. K. *The Colonial Empires*. New York: Delacorte, 1967.

Fischel, Wesley R., ed. *Vietnam: Anatomy of a Conflict*. Itasca, Ill.: F. E. Peacock, 1968.

Fischer, Louis. *The Life of Mahatma Gandhi*. New York: Harper and Row, 1950.

———. *The Story of Indonesia*. New York: Harper and Row, 1959.

Friend, Theodore. *Between Two Empires: The Ordeal of the Philippines, 1929–1946*. New Haven: Yale University Press, 1965.

Furnival, J. S. *Colonial Policy and Practice: A Comparative Study of Burma and Netherlands India* (Cambridge: Cambridge University Press, 1948; New York: New York University Press, 1956.

Gaddis, John Lewis. *The United States and the Origins of the Cold War, 1941–1947,* New York: Columbia University Press, 1972.

Gandhi, Mohandas Karamchand. *Gandhi—an autobiography—the Story of My Experiments with Truth*. Boston: Beacon Press, 1970.

Gettleman, Marvin E., et al., eds. *Vietnam and America: A Documented History*. New York: Grove Press, 1985.

Geyl, Peter. *Debates with Historians*. New York: Meridian Books, 1958.

Ghosh, Sudhir. *Gandhi's Emissary—a Nonconformist's Inside Story of India's Past Twenty Years*. Boston: Houghton Mifflin, 1967.

Gitovich, A., and B. Bursov. *North of the 38th Parallel*. Shanghai: Epoch Publishing Co., 1948.

Glyn, Alan. *Witness to Vietnam: The Containment of Communism in South East Asia*. London: Johnson, 1968.

Goettel, Elinor. *Eagle of the Philippines: President Manuel Quezon*. New York: Julien Messner, 1970.

Goldman, Eric F. *The Crucial Decade (1945–1955)*. New York: Knopf, 1956.

Golya, Frank H., ed. *The United States and the Philippines*. Englewood Cliffs, N.J.: Prentice-Hall, 1966.

Griffiths, Percival. *The British Impact on India*. London: McDonald, 1952.

Grossholtz, Jean. *Politics in the Philippines,* Boston: Little, Brown, 1964.

Guttman, J. Allen, ed. *Korea: Cold War and Limited War*. Rev. ed. Lexington, Mass.: D. C. Heath, 1972.

Gwekoh, Sol H. *Manuel L. Quezon: His Life and Career*. Manila: University Publishing Co., 1954.

Hahn, Emily. *The Islands: America's Imperial Adventure in the Philippines*. New York: Coward, McCann and Geoghegan, 1981.

Halle, Louis J. *The Cold War as History*. New York: Harper and Row, 1967.

Hammond, Thomas T. *Soviet Foreign Relations and World Communism*. Princeton: Princeton University Press, 1965.

Han, Sungjoo. *The Failure of Democracy in South Korea*. Berkeley and Los Angeles: University of California Press, 1974.

Hanna, Willard A. *Eight Nation-Makers: Southeast Asia's Charismatic Statesmen*. New York: St. Martin's Press, 1964.

Harrington, Fred H. *God, Mammon, and the Japanese.* Madison: University of Wisconsin Press, 1944.

Harrison, Brian. *Southeast Asia: A Short History.* New York: St. Martin's Press, 1954.

Harrison, Frances Burton. *The Cornerstone of Philippine Independence.* New York: Century, 1922.

Henderson, Gregory. *Korea: The Politics of the Vortex.* Cambridge: Harvard University Press, 1968.

Ho Chi Minh. *On Revolution.* New York: Praeger, 1967.

Hodson, H. V. *The Great Divide—Britain—India—Pakistan.* London: Hutchinson, 1969.

Hollnsteiner, Mary R. *The Dynamics of Power in a Philippine Municipality.* Quezon City: University of the Philippines Press, 1963.

Honey, P. J., ed. *North Vietnam Today: Profile of a Communist Satellite.* New York: Praeger, 1962.

Hulbert, Homer. *The Passing of Korea.* New York: Doubleday, Page 1906.

Hwang, In K. *The Neutralized Unification of Korea,* Cambridge, Mass.: Schenkman Publishing Co., 1980.

Hyun, Peter. *Man Sei: The Making of a Korean American.* Honolulu: University of Hawaii Press, 1986.

Jain, J. C. *The Murder of Mahatma Gandhi—Prelude and Aftermath.* Bombay: Chetana, 1961.

Josey, Alex. *Lee Kuan Yew.* Singapore: Donald Moore Press, 1968.

Kahin, George M., ed. *Government and Politics in Southeast Asia.* 2d ed. Ithaca: Cornell University Press, 1964.

Kalaw, Maximo M. *The Development of Philippine Politics, 1872–1920.* Manila: Oriental Commercial Co., 1926.

———. *Self-Government in the Philippines,* New York: Century, 1919.

Kalaw, Teodoro M. *The Philippine Revolution.* Manila: Manila Book Co., 1925.

Kang, Young Hoon, and Yong Soon Yim, eds. *Politics of Korean Reunification,* Seoul: Research Center for Peace and Unification, 1978.

Karanjia, R. K. *The Mind of Mr. Nehru.* London: George Allen and Unwin, 1960.

Kim, Hak-Joon. *The Unification Policy of South and North Korea.* Seoul: Seoul National University Press, 1984; distributed by University of Hawaii Press.

Kim, Joungwan A. *Divided Korea: The Politics of Development, 1945–1972.* Cambridge: Harvard University, East Asian Research Center, 1975.

Kim, Kwan Bong. *The Korea-Japan Treaty Crisis and the Instability of the Korean Political System.* New York: Praeger, 1971.

Kirk, Donald. *Wider War: The Struggle for Cambodia, Thailand, and Laos.* New York: Praeger, 1971.

Kissinger, Henry F. *The Necessity for Choice.* New York: Harper and Row, 1961.

Kolko, Gabriel, and Joyce Loklo. *The Limits of Power.* New York: Harper and Row, 1972.

Koo, Youngnok, and Dae-Sook Suh, eds. *Korea and the United States: A Century of Cooperation.* Honolulu: University of Hawaii Press, 1984.

Kripalani, Krishna. *Gandhi—A Life.* New Delhi: Orient Langmans, 1969.

Lacouture, Jean. *The Demigods: Charismatic Leadership in the Third World.* Translated by Patricia Wolf. New York: Knopf, 1970.

―――. *Viet-Nam: Between Two Truces.* Translated by P. Wolf. New York: Random House, 1966.

Lacy, Creighton. *The Conscience of India.* New York: Holt, Rinehart, and Winston, 1965.

Larkin, John A., and Henry Benda, Jr. *The World of Southeast Asia: Selected Historical Readings.* New York: Harper and Row, 1967.

Lee, Chong-Sik. *Japan and Korea: The Political Dimension.* Stanford, Calif. Hoover Institution Press, 1985.

―――. *The Politics of Korean Nationalism.* Berkeley and Los Angeles: University of California Press, 1963.

Lee, Yur-Bok, and Wayne Patterson, eds. *One Hundred Years of Korean-American Relations, 1882–1982.* University, Ala.: University of Alabama Press, 1986.

Levi, Werner. *Modern China's Foreign Policy.* Minneapolis: University of Minnesota Press, 1953.

Liem, Channing. *America's Finest Gift to Korea: The Life of Philip Jaisohn.* New York: William Frederick Press, 1952.

Lim, Un. [pseud.]. *The Founding of a Dynasty in North Korea: An Authentic Biography of Kim Il-song.* Tokyo: Jiyuisha, 1982.

Liska, George. *Imperial America.* Baltimore: Johns Hopkins University Press, 1967.

Liu, Alan P. L. *Communications and National Integration in Communist China.* Berkeley and Los Angeles: University of California Press, 1971.

McAlister, John T., Jr., ed. *Southeast Asia: The Politics of National Integration.* New York: Random House, 1973.

McCune, George. *Modern Korea.* Cambridge: Harvard University Press, 1950.

McKenzie, F. A. *Korea's Fight for Freedom.* New York: Fleming H. Revell, 1920.

Macrids, Roy C., ed. *Foreign Policy in World Politics.* Englewood Cliffs, N.J.: Prentice-Hall, 1958.

Majumdar, S. K. *Jinnah and Gandhi—Their Role in India's Quest for Freedom.* Calcutta: Firma K. L. Mukhopadhyay, 1966.

Maramba, Felix D. *Daniel Maramba: His Life and Times.* Manila: Community Publishers, 1970.

Meade, E. Grant. *American Military Government in Korea.* New York: Columbia University, King's Crown Press, 1951.

Menon, V. H. *The Transfer of Power in India.* Princeton University Press, 1957.

Merriam, Allen Hayes. *Gandhi and Jinnah: The Debate over the Partition of India.* Calcutta: Minerva Associates, 1980.

Miller, Gerald R., and Herbert W. Simons, eds. *Perspectives on Communication in Social Conflict.* Englewood Cliffs, N.J.: Prentice-Hall, 1974.

Moon, Penderel. *Divide and Quit.* London: Chatto and Windus, 1961.

Morley, James W. *Japan and Korea: America's Allies in the Pacific.* New York: Walker, 1965.

Moseley, George. *China Since 1911.* New York: Harper and Row, 1969.

Muhith, A. M. A. *Bangladesh: Emergence of a Nation*. Dacca: Bangladesh Books International, 1978.

Nakamura, Hajime. *Ways of Thinking of Eastern Peoples*. Honolulu: East-West Center Press, 1964.

Nam, Koon Woo. *The North Korean Communist Leadership, 1945–1965*. University, Ala.: University of Alabama Press, 1974.

Nayar, Kuldip. *Distant Neighbors—a Tale of the Subcontinent*. Delhi: Vikas, 1972.

————. *India—the Critical Years*. Delhi: Vikas; London: Weidenfeld and Nicholson, 1971.

Nayar, Pyarelal. *Mahatma Gandhi—The Early Phase—The Last Phase*. 3 vols. Ahmedabad: Navajivad House, 1965.

Nehru, Jawaharal, *An Autobiography*. London: Bodley Head, 1949.

————. *The Discovery of India*. Calcutta: Signet Press, 1945.

Oh, John Kie-chiang. *Korea: Democracy on Trial*. Ithaca: Cornell University Press, 1968.

Oliver, Robert T. *Communication and Culture in Ancient India and China*. Syracuse, N.Y.: Syracuse University Press, 1971.

————. *Leadership in Twentieth-Century Asia: The Rhetorical Principles and Practices of the Leaders of China, Korea, and India, from Sun Yat-sen to Jawaharlal Nehru*. University Park, Pa.: Center for Continuing Liberal Education, Pennsylvania State University, 1966.

————. *The Psychology of Persuasive Speech*. New York: Longmans, Green, 1942. Rev. ed., 1957. Reprint. New York: David McKay, 1968.

————. *Syngman Rhee and American Involvement in Korea, 1942–1960: A Personal Narrative*. Seoul: Panmun Books, 1978.

————. *Syngman Rhee: The Man Behind the Myth*. New York: Dodd, Mead, 1955.

————. *Verdict in Korea,* State College, Pa.: Bald Eagle Press, 1952.

Oliver, Robert T., and Dominick A. Barbara. *The Healthy Mind in Communion and Communication*. Springfield, Ill.: Charles C. Thomas, 1962.

Pacis, Vicente Albano. *President Sergio Osmena: A Fully Documented Biography*. 2 vols. Quezon City: Philippine Constitution Association and Araneta University Research Foundation, 1971.

Pak, Chi-Young. *Political Opposition in Korea, 1945–1960*. Honolulu: University of Hawaii Press, 1980.

Palais, James B. *Politics and Policy in Traditional Korea*. Cambridge: Harvard University Press, 1968.

Pannikar, Kavalan M. *Asia and Western Dominance*. New York: Collier, 1969.

————. *Asia and Western Dominance: A Survey of the Vasco Da Gama Epoch in Asian History, 1498–1945*. Rev. ed. London: George Allen and Unwin, 1959.

Park, Myung-Seok. *Communication Styles in Two Different Cultures: Korean and American*. Seoul: Han Shin Publishing Co., 1979.

Pike, Douglas. *Viet Cong: The Organization and Techniques of the National Liberation Front of South Vietnam*. Cambridge, Mass.: Press of the Massachusetts Institute of Technology, 1966.

Prizzia; Ross. *Thailand in Transition: The Role of Oppositional Forces*. Honolulu: University of Hawaii Press, 1985.

Pye, Lucian W. *Chinese Commercial Negotiating Style*. Yarmouth, Maine: Intercultural Press, 1986.

———. *Politics, Personality, and Nation-Building: Burma's Search for Identity*. New Haven: Yale University Press, 1962.

Quirino, Carlos. *Quezon: Paladin of Philippine Freedom*. Manila: Community Publishers, 1971.

Ralston, Hayden Joseph. *The Philippines: A Study in National Development*. New York: Macmillan, 1942.

Raskin, Marcus G., and Bernard B. Fall. *The Vietnam Reader: Articles and Documents on American Foreign Policy and the Vietnam Crisis*. New York: Random House, 1965.

Reichauer, Edwin, and John K. Fairbanks. *A History of East Asian Civilization*. 2 vols. Boston: Houghton Mifflin, 1961–64.

Rejai, Mostafa, with Kay Phillips. *Leaders of Revolution*. Beverly Hills, Calif.: Sage, 1979.

Riggs, Robert E. *Politics in the United Nations*. Urbana: University of Illinois Press, 1958.

Roberts, Ron E., and Robert M. Kloss. *Social Movements: Between the Balcony and the Barricade*. St. Louis: Mosby, 1974.

Romein, Jan M. *The Asian Century: A History of Modern Nationalism in Asia*. Translated by R. T. Clark. Berkeley and Los Angeles: University of California Press, 1962.

Rose, Lisle A. *After Yalta*. New York: Scribner, 1973.

Roxas, Manuel. *Important Speeches, Messages, and Other Pronouncements*. Manila: Bureau of Printing, 1947.

Rudolph, Lloyd T., and Susanne H. *The Modernity of Tradition: Political Development in India*. Chicago: University of Chicago Press, 1967.

Sayeed, Khalid B. *Pakistan—The Formative Phase, 1857–1948*. London: Oxford University Press, 1968.

Scalapino, Robert A., ed. *North Korea Today*. New York: Praeger, 1963.

Scalapino, Robert A., and Chong-Sik Lee. *Communism in Korea*. 2 vols. Berkeley and Los Angeles: University of California Press, 1972.

Schnabel, James F. *Policy and Direction: The First Year*. Washington, D.C.: Office of the Chief of Military History, 1972.

Schramm, Wilbur, and Daniel M. Lerner, eds. *Communication and Change: The Last Ten Years—and the Next*. Honolulu: East-West Center, University of Hawaii Press, 1976.

Schulman, Irwin J. *Mao as Prophet, Hero, Magician, and God*. Pittsburgh: University of Pittsburgh Center for International Studies, 1972.

Sharp, Gene. *Gandhi Wields the Weapon of Moral Power*. Ahmedabad: Navajivan, 1960.

Singh, Drushwant. *Train to Pakistan*. London: Chatto and Windus, 1956.

Smith, Ralph Bernard. *Vietnam and the West*. Ithaca: Cornell University Press, 1971.

Smith, Roger M. *Cambodia's Foreign Policy*. Ithaca: Cornell University Press, 1965.

Stanley, Peter W. *A Nation in the Making: The Philippines and the United States, 1899–1921*. Cambridge: Harvard University Press, 1974.

Steinberg, David Joel, ed. *In Search of Southeast Asia: A Modern History.* Honolulu: University of Hawaii Press, 1985.

Stewart, Charles, Craig Smith, and Robert E. Denton, Jr. *Persuasion and Social Movements.* Prospect Heights, Ill: Waveland Press, 1984.

Suh, Dae-Sook. *Documents of Korean Communism, 1918–1948.* Princeton: Princeton University Press, 1967.

————. *The Korean Communist Movement, 1918–1948.* Princeton: Princeton University Press, 1967.

Symonds, Richard. *The Making of Pakistan.* London: Faber and Faber, 1949.

Taylor, George E. *The Philippines and the United States: Problems of Partnership.* New York: Praeger, 1964.

Tendulkar, D. G. *Mahatma: Life of Mohandas Karamchand Gandhi.* 8 vols. New Delhi: Publications Division, Government of India, 1963.

Tewksbury, Donald. *Source Materials on Korean Politics and Ideologies.* New York: Institute of Pacific Relations, 1950.

Tinker, Hugh. *Experiment with Freedom—India and Pakistan 1947.* London: Oxford University Press, 1967.

Touraine, Alain. *The Voice and the Eye: An Analysis of Social Movements.* Translated by Alan Duff. Cambridge: Cambridge University Press, 1981.

Trager, Frank N. *Burma's Independence.* New York: Praeger, 1966.

Trager, Frank N., and William Henderson, eds. *Communist China, 1949–1969: A Twenty-Year Assessment.* New York: New York University Press, 1970.

U.S. Office of Strategic Services. *The Korean Independence Movement.* Washington, D.C., 1945.

U.S. Department of State. *North Korea: A Case Study in the Techniques of Takeover.* Washington, D.C., 1961.

Vandenbosch, Amry, and Richard Butwell. *The Changing Face of Southeast Asia.* Lexington: University of Kentucky Press, 1966.

Vo, Nguyen Giap. *People's War, People's Army.* New York: Praeger, 1962.

Wainwright, Philip, and Mary Doreen. *The Partition of India.* London: George Allen and Unwin, 1970.

Warshaw, Steven. *Southeast Asia Emerges.* Rev. ed. San Francisco: Canfield press, 1975.

Weber, Max. *The Theory of Social and Economic Organization.* Edited by Talcott Parsons. New York: Free Press, 1964.

White, Ralph K. *Nobody Wanted War: Misperception in Vietnam and Other Wars.* Garden City, N.Y.: Doubleday, 1968.

Whiting, Allen S. *China Crosses the Yalu: The Decision to Enter the Korean War.* New York: Macmillan, 1960.

Wilder, William D. *Communication, Social Structure, and Development in Rural Malaysia: A Study of Kuala Kampung Bera.* Atlantic Highlands, N.J.: Humanities Press, 1983.

Williams, Lea E. *Southeast Asia: A History.* New York: Oxford University Press, 1976.

Wilson, Dick. *Asia Awakes: A Continent in Transition.* New York: Weybright and Talley, 1970.

———, ed. *Mao Tze-Tung in the Scales of History.* Cambridge: Cambridge University Press, 1977.

Wood, James L., and Maurice Jackson. *Social Movements: Development, Participation, and Dynamics.* Belmont, Calif.: Wadsworth, 1982.

Young, Marilyn B. *The Rhetoric of Empire: American China Policy, 1895–1901.* Cambridge: Harvard University Press, 1968.

Zaide, Gregorio F. *Philippine Political and Cultural History.* 2 vols. Manila: Philippine Education Co., 1949.

Articles

Abbreviations

CE	*Communication Education*
CJ of CAP	*Communication Journal of Communication Association of the Pacific*
CM	*Communication Monographs*
CQ	*Communication Quarterly*
CRR	*Communication Research Reports*
CSSJ	*Central States Speech Journal*
ETC	*A Journal of General Semantics*
HCR	*Human Communication Research*
IJIR	*International Journal of Intercultural Relations*
JC	*Journal of Communication*
JQ	*Journalism Quarterly*
QJS	*Quarterly Journal of Speech*
RSQ	*Rhetoric Society Quarterly*
SM	*Speech Monographs*
SSCJ	*Southern Speech Communication Journal*
ST	*Speech Teacher*
TS	*Today's Speech*
WC	*World Communication*
WJSC	*Western Journal of Speech Communication*

Beatty, Michael J., Ralph R. Behnke, and Barbara Jane Banks. "Elements of Dialogic Communication in Gandhi's Second Round Table Conference." *SSCJ* 44 (Summer 1979): 386–98.

Becker, Carl. "The Japanese Way of Debate." *NFJ* 1 (Fall 1983): 141–47.

———. "Reasons for Lack of Argumentation and Debate in the Far East." *IJIR* 10 (1986): 75–92.

Casmir, Fred L. "International, Intercultural Communication: Selected Annotated Bibliography." Speech Communication Association, 1987.

Chua, Elizabeth G., and William B. Gudykunst. "Conflict Resolution Styles in Low- and High-Context Cultures." *CRR* 4 (June 1987): 32–37.

Crocker, Lionel. "Carlos P. Romulo, Orator." Parts 1, 2. *Today's Speech* 9 (September, November 1961): 1–3, 14–16.

Dance, Frank E. X. "The Tao of Speech." *CSSJ* 32 (Winter 1981): 207–11.

Dinh, Tran Van. "Ho Chi Minh as a Communicator." *JC* 26 (Autumn 1976): 142–47.

D'Monte, Darryl. "Dynastic Politics, Indian Style." *New Leader,* 13 January 1986, pp. 11–12.

Doi, L. Takso. "The Japanese Patterns of Communication and the Concept of *Amae*." *QJS* 59 (April 1973): 180–85.

Ellingsworth, Huber W. "Anthropology and Rhetoric: Towards a Culture-Related Methodology of Speech Criticism." *SSCJ* 28 (Summer 1963): 307–12.

———. "National Rhetoric and Inter-Cultural Communication." *CQ* 17 (February 1969): 35–38.

Fathi, Asghar. "The Role of the Islamic Pulpit." *JC* 29 (Summer 1979): 103–106.

Fischer, J. L., and Teigo Yoshida. "The Nature of Speech According to Japanese Proverbs." *Journal of American Folkore* 80 (1968): 34–43.

Gudykunst, William B., and Tsukasa Nishida. "Attributional Confidence in Low- and High-Context Cultures." *HCR* 12 (Summer 1986): 525–49.

———. "Individual and Cultural Influences on Uncertainty Reduction." *CM* 51 (March 1984): 23–36.

———. "The Influence of Cultural Variability on Perceptions of Communication Behavior Associated with Relationship Terms." *HCR* 13 (Winter 1986): 147–66.

Haglund, Elaine. "Japan: Cultural Consideration." *IJIR* 8 (1984): 61–76.

Han, Pyo Wook. "A Sense of Values: The Basis for Liberty and Democracy in the Far East." *Vital Speeches of the Day* 24 (15 December 1957): 137–39.

Ishii, Satoshi. "Characteristics of Japanese Nonverbal Communicative Behavior." *CJ of CAP,* Special Issue, 1973.

Jan, George B. "Public Opinion's Growing Influence on Japan's China Policy." *JQ* 48 (Spring 1971): 111–19.

Jensen, J. Vernon. "Rhetoric of East Asia—a Bibliography." *RSQ* 17 (Spring 1987): 213–31.

———. "Communicative Functions of Silence." *ETC* 30 (September 1973): 249–57.

———. "Teaching East Asian Rhetoric." *RSQ* 17 (Spring 1987): 135–49.

Jensen, J. Vernon, and Irene Khin Khin Jensen. "Cross-Cultural Encounters: The Newly Arrived Asian Student." *CSSJ* 17 (Winter 1983): 371–77.

Jensen, Khin Khin. "The Men Behind the Woman: A Case Study of the Political Career of Madame Vijaya Lakshmi Pandit." *Contributions to Asian Studies,* 10 (1977): 76–93.

Kang, Joon Mann. "Reporters and Their Professional and Occupational Commitment in a Developing Country." *Gazette* (Dordrecht, Netherlands), 40 (1987): 3–20.

Kim, Seung-Kuk. "The Formation of Civil Society and the Rise of Regionalism in Korea." *Korea Journal,* 28 (June, 1988): 24–34.

Kitao, K. "Difficulty of Intercultural Communication between Americans and Japanese." *CJ of CAP* 9 (1980): 80–89.

King, Stephen W. Yuko Minami, and Larry Samovar. "A Comparison of Japanese and American Perceptions of Source Credibility." *CRR* 2 (1985): 76–79.

Kuniharo, Masao. "Indigenous Barriers to Communication." *The Japanese Interpreter* 8 (Winter 1973): 96–108.

Lik, Kuen Tong. "The Meaning of Philosophical Silence: Some Reflections on the Use of Language in Chinese Thought." *Journal of Chinese Philosophy* 3 (1976): 169–83.

Lomas, Charles W. "Public Discussion in Japan—Index to Democracy." *QJS* 32 (October 1946): 311–16.

McCroskey, James C., William B. Gudykunst, and Tsukasa Nishida. "Communication Apprehension among Japanese Students in Native and Second Languages." *CRR* 2 (December 1985): 11–15.

Merriam, Allen R. "Charismatic Leadership in Modern Asia: Mao, Gandhi, and Khomeini." *Asian Profile* 19 (October 1981): 389–400.

———. "The Contribution of Jayaprakash Narayan in Preserving Free Expression in India." *Free Speech Yearbook* (Speech Communication Association) 1981, pp. 9–15.

———. Symbolic Action in India: Gandhi's Nonverbal Persuasion." *QJS* 61 (October 1975): 290–306.

Morrison, John L. "The Absence of a Rhetorical Tradition in Japanese Culture." *WJSC* 36 (Spring 1972): 89–102.

Neulien, James W., and Vincent Hazleton, Jr. "A Cross-Cultural Comparison of Japanese and American Persuasive Strategy Selection." *IJIR* 9 (1985): 389–404.

Nishida, Hiroko. "Japanese Intercultural Communication Competence and Cross-Cultural Adjustment." *IJIR* 9 (1985): 247–69.

Nishiyama, Kazuo. "Interpersonal Persuasion in a Vertical Society—the Case of Japan." *SM* 38 (June 1971): 148–54.

Nomura, Naoki, and Dean Barnlund. "Patterns of Interpersonal Criticism in Japan and in the United States." *IJIR* 7 (1983): 1–18.

Nordstrom, Louis. "Zen and the Nonduality of Communication: The Sound of One Hand Clapping." *Communication* 4 (1979): 15–27.

Okabe, Roichi. "Cultural Assumptions of the East and West: Japan and the United States." *Intercultural Communication Theory* (Sage Publications), 1983, 21–44.

———. "*Yuben* in the Early Twentieth Century: A Case Study in the Promulgation of Western Rhetoric in Japan." *Speech Education, Journal of the Communication Association of the Pacific,* 7 (Fall 1979): 1–11.

———. "Yukichi Fukuzawa: A Promulgator of Western Rhetoric in Japan." *QJS* 59 (April 1973): 186–95.

Oliver, Robert T. "Asian Public Address and Comparative Public Address." *ST,* 23 (March 1974): 101–108.

———. "Communication—Community—Communion." *CQ* 15 (November 1967): 7–9.

———. "The Confucian Rhetorical Tradition in Korea during the Yi Dynasty (1392–1910)." QJS 45 (December 1959): 363–73.

———. "Culture and Communication." *Vital Speeches of the Day* 29 (15 September 1963): 721–24.

———. "The Rhetoric of Power in Diplomatic Conferences." *QJS* 41 (October 1954): 288–92.

———. "The Rhetorical Implications of Taoism." *QJS* 47 (February 1961): 27–35.

———. "The Rhetorical Tradition in China: Confucius and Mencius." *TS* 17 (February 1969): 3–8.

———. "Sacred Cows, Asian and American: The Language of Social Behavior." *Vital Speeches of the Day* 35 (15 August 1969): 668–72.

————. "Speech and the Community: Social Disease of Irresponsible and Ineffective Speech." *Vital Speeches of the Day* 29 (15 May 1963): 459–62.

————. "Speech in International Affairs." *QJS* 48 (April 1962): 171–76.

————. "Speech Training around the World." Parts 1–3. *ST* 5 (March, September 1956): 102–108, 179–85; 7 (March 1958): 121–26.

————. "The Varied Rhetorics of International Relations." *WJSC* 25 (Fall 1961): 213–21.

Penner, L. A., and T. Any. "A Comparison of American and Vietnamese Value Systems." *Journal of Social Psychology* 101 (1977): 187–204.

Prosser, Michael. "Communication Problems in the United Nations." *SSCJ* 29 (Winter 1963): 125–32.

————. "Communication and Non-Western Cultures." *TS* 17 (February 1969).

Reynolds, Beatrice. "Lao Tzu: Persuasion through Inaction and Non-speaking." *CQ* 17 (February 1969): 23–25.

————. "Mao Tse-tung: Rhetoric of a Revolutionary." *CSSJ* 27 (Fall 1976): 212–17.

Schneider, Michael J., and W. Jordan. "Perceptions of the Communicative Performance of Americans and Chinese in Intercultural Dyads." *IJIR* 5 (1981): 175–91.

Simonson, Solomon. "The Categories of Proof in Indian Logic." *Philosophy and Phenomenological Research* 6 (September 1945–June 1946): 400–409.

————. "Four Modes of Interpretation." *The Review of Religion* 4 (May 1945): 339–45.

Singh, Kusum J. "Gandhi and Mao as Mass Communicators." *JC* 29 (Summer 1979): 94–101.

Sullivan, John H. "The Press and Politics in Indonesia." *JQ* 44 (Spring 1967): 99–106.

Ting-Toomy, Stella. "Japanese Communication Patterns: Insider Versus the Outsider Perspective." *WC* 25 (Fall 1986): 113–26.

Tinker, Hugh. "U Nu, the Serene Statesman." *Pacific Affairs* 30 (1957): 120–37.

VanDer Kroef, Justus M. "The Press in Indonesia: By-Product of Nationalism." *JQ* 31 (Summer 1954): 337–46.

Walsh, J. F., Jr. "An Approach to Dyadic Communication in Historical Social Movements: Dyadic Communication in Maoist Insurgent Mobilization." *CM* 53 (March 1986): 1–15.

Wang, James C. F. "Values of the Cultural Revolution." *JC* 27 (Summer 1977): 41–46.

Index

Name Index

These are a few of their princely names, these are a few of their great, proud glittering names.

—Thomas Wolfe, *Of Time and the River*

Subject Index

Human history is in essence a history of ideas.
—H. G. Wells, *The Outline of History*